An

Intimate

Portrait

of

South Africa's

Racial

Reckoning

THE
INHERITORS

EVE
FAIRBANKS

Simon & Schuster
New York London Toronto
Sydney New Delhi

Simon & Schuster
1230 Avenue of the Americas
New York, NY 10020

First Simon & Schuster hardcover edition July 2022

Small portions of this book first appeared, in different form,
in *The New Republic*, *The Guardian*, *Moment* magazine,
and publications of the Institute of Current World Affairs.

For information about special discounts for bulk purchases,
please contact Simon & Schuster Special Sales at
1-866-506-1949 or business@simonandschuster.com.

The Simon & Schuster Speakers Bureau can bring authors to your
live event. For more information or to book an event, contact
the Simon & Schuster Speakers Bureau at 1-866-248-3049
or visit our website at www.simonspeakers.com.

Interior design by Lewelin Polanco

Manufactured in the United States of America

1 3 5 7 9 10 8 6 4 2

Library of Congress Cataloging-in-Publication Data is available.

ISBN 978-1-4767-2524-6
ISBN 978-1-4767-2529-1 (ebook)

My inheritance has become for me like a lion in the forest.

—*Jeremiah 12:8*

Contents

CONTENTS

A Note on Usage

MOST SOUTH AFRICANS USE THE lower case for the adjectives "black" and "white," as in "black South African voters" or "a white farmer."

To refer to some South Africans as black was an innovation by Steve Biko and others in the country's 1970s Black Consciousness movement. Though skin color long dictated the way people moved and lived in South Africa, in the nineteenth and early twentieth centuries the more commonly used adjectives were "European," "African," "Bantu," and—a bit later—"non-white."

Biko believed the apartheid government treated South Africans as a mass when it suited them—as in when it denied everyone who was not "European" the full right to vote—and divided them when it suited them, too. It divided people who spoke Bantu languages from South Africans of Indian descent and so-called colored people, or South Africans of mixed racial heritage. And it sought to divide those who spoke Bantu languages further by tribe—into the Zulus, the Sothos, and so on, to whom it apportioned separate territories.

In his writings advocating that his fellow black South Africans embrace the word "black" and become proud of it, Biko mostly used the lower case—as did the African National Congress, South Africa's leading black-liberation movement, and most subsequent

black South African thinkers and writers. When white government leaders began to use "black" and "white," they typically
used the upper case to underscore their contention that "Black"
and "White" people, in South Africa, were cultures as distinct,
long-standing, and defining as the Persian or Chinese peoples—
separate tribes that might have commerce with each other but
could never really become one nation. To capitalize the words
"White" and "Black" was the apartheid government's attempt to
seize back some semantic power.

I thus use "white" and "black" in the pages that follow, unless
a quoted passage deployed a different usage or the person with
whom I spoke wanted me to do otherwise.

THE
INHERITORS

Prologue

SHE SET OUT AT NIGHT. That was how it worked in Soweto: black people woke before dawn because it took hours to get to work on the buses to the formerly white-only city. From as long as she could remember, Malaika would hear men and women rising at 4:00 a.m. to stoke coal fires to make tea. The walls of the shack she lived in with her grandmother, her mother, her aunt—whom she called her sister—and her uncles were made of sheets of corrugated iron and the shacks were so close to each other she could hear the people living three homes away waking up, their grumbling and the clattering of their pots.

She'd always try to go back to sleep. But when she was eleven, she had to start to wake up at that time, too. Her mother enrolled her in a formerly all-white school across the ridge, and the bus ride took two hours. When she got up from the blanket on the floor she used as a bed, the stars had already set, and the haze leaking into the shack from her neighbors' fires made her trip over her grandmother's still hot stove, burning her arms.

But it was worth it, she told herself. In the dark she clipped her hair, packed her backpack, put on her uniform—a black skirt and a bright turquoise sweater with a pink-and-purple crest embroidered on the breast—and waited for one of her uncles to walk her to the bus stop.

1

If she could've had one wish, it would've been to walk with Godfrey, her favorite of her mother's brothers. The other two uncles who lived with her played dice on the streets to earn pocket money and seemed to her, already, to have the manner of grandfathers, grumpy and cynical.

But Godfrey was sober, beautiful, ageless. He never looked, she thought, like a Soweto man. He worked hard, but whenever he'd come home he'd bring a different aura into the shack. He wore new shoes and gorgeous dress shirts with a few buttons left open at the top to expose his velvety chest. And he was kind, getting down onto the floor no matter what he was dressed in to talk and laugh with Malaika. His laugh was like the electric lights they often didn't have; when Godfrey laughed, she could forget the power in the shack only worked some of the time.

Her country, South Africa, only integrated racially in 1994, when she was two years old. There had always been a primary school for black children—who were kept out of white neighborhoods by the most rigid system of racial segregation the modern world has ever known—a fifteen-minute walk away. But her mother implied the point of going to the formerly white school, now that she could, was to be more like Godfrey when she grew up: empowered, loose, and free. Godfrey's job took him to places with amazing things. When he'd come home, he'd bring bags full of food, pretty jewelry, and candies with creamy centers the hawkers in Soweto didn't sell. She knew, because she had tried them all. "Where did you get those?" she would ask him.

"In Never-Never," Godfrey would laugh.

That was where he told her he worked. "Never-Never." He said the furniture was made of chocolate there and the gutters flowed with liquid gold. She wasn't sure whether to believe *that*, but it had to be a wonderful place if it made Godfrey so happy. Being with him made her forget the reason she needed a chaperone in the street. Walking in Soweto wasn't safe, people said. Muggers could crouch behind the thigh-high piles of trash along the way and attack little girls. Her new school actually sent a bus to Soweto that took black students directly to its doorstep, but Tshepiso, her sister, was so ashamed of the family's shack she refused to let the other kids on the school bus see them picked up there.

So Malaika took the city bus. Thinking about Godfrey made her forget, too, how sad that made her. The other riders were much older—housemaids and so-called garden boys, who still had the jobs they'd had before South Africa's racial discrimination ended.

They seemed drained, exhausted, like beggars instead of inheritors, carrying their maids' uniforms or garden tools in the same kinds of bags homeless people lugged along the elevated highway that split the old black from the old white city, along with extra empty sacks to receive their white *madams'* used clothes or leftover food. On the bus, they'd sit and put their heads in their hands, trying to catch a little more sleep as an itinerant preacher roamed the aisles, singing a forlorn apartheid-era hymn:

Morena ke o tshepile.
Onkise qhobosheaneng.

In God I trust.
God, take me to your refuge.

Onthuse ke tshabele teng.
Ha ke le qhobosheaneng le hao ha dina ho mphilela.

Help me to run there.
When I get to your refuge, they won't be able to find me.

Never-Never wouldn't need a preacher like that. There was no *they* who still blocked black people's paths there.

3

The bus wound through north Soweto, between mine dumps and landfills, until it started to climb. At the top of the hill, the world seemed to get both darker and more beautiful. This was where the bus entered the formerly white city. The people who lived there seemed still to be sleeping, but the lights illuminating their gardens—swimming pools and banana trees and purple-flowered jacarandas—stayed on, like heaven, all night. The bus plunged so quickly over the top of the ridge she would almost get dizzy. But looking out the window, with the haze dissipating, she could see to the horizon. The white neighborhoods rippled out to it until the lights got so dense and bright that they mimicked a sunrise. Was that Never-Never? She didn't know, but she thought it would be enough.

Introduction

WHEN I GOT TO SOUTH AFRICA in 2009, it looked, and people acted, like a storm had swept through, the kind that tears petals off flowering trees—the ones too new to fall otherwise—and scatters bright green and pink and gold all over the lawns and sidewalks, leaving the air fresh and the birds twittering in the trees. Cape Town felt like that, fresh after a storm. The city sits at the Cape of Good Hope, near the narrow, bouldered southern tip of Africa, where the Indian and Atlantic Oceans swirl together in a sweep of bird-entangled mist around outcroppings of 600-million-year-old granite. Lording over the city is a peak called Table Mountain, almost perfectly flat on top and veined through the sides with richly jungled vertical chinks and ribbons of purple sandstone.

You can hike to the top in two hours. From the summit, the city's ringed neighborhoods look like nothing more than grit flung up on a beach after high tide: the shimmering skyscrapers are the oyster shells, the houses the pebbles, and the lawns and blue pools the bits of battered glass. Long skirts of ridges billow south from Table Mountain in a swirl around a bay. A few years before I got there, the government built a fancy new highway along the water, cut into the sides of these ridges.

The highway spits you out into a spray of suburbs, each prettier than the last. There are ivory houses roofed with solar panels, boardwalks built out to the sea, and surf shops and wine bars with offerings from the vineyards to the north. People seem to stay in the cafés all day in their wetsuits, even on weekdays, as if the rules of ordinary time had dissolved, as if there were no more Sunday or Monday, no morning or afternoon. Some of them look disoriented, as if a whirlwind had deposited them with their wineglasses in front of the floor-to-ceiling seafront windows and they were still trying to get their minds around the environment that had appeared all around them.

In a sense, a storm had swept through. Fifteen years earlier, politically speaking, South Africa became a different country overnight. Imagine waking up in Paris and discovering that a remote part of China—a place you might only know from news headlines or from the tiny letters printed on the tags of your clothing— was right there, no longer distant but around the corner, just a five-minute walk away. Imagine going to sleep in China and waking up in Paris. Or imagine, if you can, antebellum America as we see it in old photographs: enslaved Americans on plantation fields, General Robert E. Lee on his horse, and Abraham Lincoln in the White House. And then imagine that, one morning, all the people who lived then woke up to a black man on Lee's horse and a black man in the White House.

Something like that happened in South Africa in 1994. In one election, a state fastidiously divided into racial castes— where white people made the laws, wrote the news at the top papers, and taught the history at the tony universities—became the first modern nation wherein long-disenfranchised people of color would make the laws, run the economy, write the news, decide what history to teach, and wield political dominance over a substantial white minority. Unlike in the other postcolonial African countries, white South Africans—about 15 percent of the population—stayed on to be governed by people they had oppressed for centuries.

I grew up in a place and time—America in the '90s—where we were told this *kind* of change had already happened. I was ten years old when the country elected Nelson Mandela its first black president. My American president, Bill Clinton, sent his deputy, Al Gore, to the inauguration. "Thank God Almighty, we are free at last," Mandela said, quoting Martin Luther King Jr. On TV, I watched Gore stand with the United Nations secretary general and clap and smile benignly; they had the mien of proud elders watching a protégé country at a coming-of-age ceremony, one marking a type of transition they'd already accomplished.

My state, Virginia—the old seat of the Confederacy—had finally elected a black governor. Francis Fukuyama, the political scientist, named the '90s "the end of history," beyond which there would likely be no significant political conflict. American children of my generation were supposed to be among the first in history to lead literally sui generis lives—we could be anything we wanted to be, because the agitating sources behind humanity's conflicts, from racism to war, had at least been understood, if not yet totally vanquished.

I remember the crackle of America Online's dial-up tone, a crunch that sounded like millennia collapsing—the end of humanity's physicality, its atavisms, its suffocating family and small-town insularities. That dial-up tone linked my bedroom to other bedrooms all around the world. I played in chat rooms, which were so innocent in the beginning. So innocent: I made a friend in one named Jerry, a fifty-something painter, and my mother let me visit him by myself in Michigan. Jerry turned out to be a total gentleman and gave me a painting he'd done of Mother Teresa.

Online, I chose a new name. Screen names were a glimpse of this new universe where there would be no barriers to self-creation. I made an avatar, red-haired and sexy in a nerdy way. She wasn't real. But at times, she felt more real to me than my own body did. I dyed my real hair red, and it briefly felt as if the persona I had made on the internet could haul my frail, corporeal self along with it, and that the internet, thus, might prove my generation's tool for human redemption.

But that talk of the end of history also cut against what I *saw*. Outside my house, the history we were told we'd left behind was still there. Around the corner, Lee Highway led to J.E.B. Stuart High School, both named for Confederate generals. I became obsessed with the history of the American Civil War, because it was everywhere. I begged my parents to take me to all the nearby battlefields—Manassas, Antietam, Gettysburg. On the way back, sometimes we stopped at a scenic overlook where I could just see the Lincoln Memorial, lit up like a star on the far side of a river.

My elementary school librarian recommended a young adult biography of Thomas "Stonewall" Jackson, another general in the Confederate army. My mother thought I was intrigued by Stonewall because he resembled my father, whom I adored. They both had beards, a devotion to mildly hypochondriac rituals—my Dad kicked off every evening with a pile of pills to help his skin, glands, and lungs; Stonewall ate the same thing every night to aid his digestion—and reputations for eccentricity. (Stonewall's came from his fealty to odd superstitions, like sucking on a lemon in battle; my father's from his obsessively wide-ranging interests, encompassing plant biology, the Koran, and the Merovingian era of French history.)

But honestly, I think I saw a bit of Stonewall in myself. All the celebration of the dawn of a mapless new millennium was also frightening. I worried intensely over whether I would go on to live a meaningful or, in particular, a moral life.

Like my father, I had a wide-roving curiosity, hopping from pioneer history to watercolor crayons to the science of caves to the violin. Sometimes I hated it, because I felt sure it would condemn me to lead a random life, never discerning my life's purpose—which people said was crucial to becoming a success. Deeper was the fear that I would do wrong things without realizing it. I confided to my diary I wanted to become an Orthodox Jew, if only to impose a rigid set of do's and don'ts upon my future.

I think I also had an early, murky apprehension of the personal fallibility of the father I adored, and of the dangers that lay ahead as his traits began to blossom in me. His diverse interests had imperiled his career, and thus our family's security. He was a political science professor, but he struggled to conform to the requirement for niche focus that characterizes modern academia. Ultimately, he abandoned his steady job. My mother was furious.

According to my biography, Stonewall had grappled with similar issues. He grew up poor and nomadic thanks to his own father, whose love of gambling and early death left the family staggering under debt. Nineteenth-century America was supposed to be a classless society, yet his mother was forced to sew richer women's clothes to make money. Humiliated, he resolved he would adopt a set of rules for living that would guarantee he led a blameless life.

As he began to build a military career, he made a project of discerning that life's guiding rules. They began with the Bible, as Jackson was religious. Follow God's precepts. Always keep your promises. Never tell a lie. The discipline extended to small habits, like daily sucking a lemon; these rituals imparted a sense of focus and mission. His friends thought he was peculiar. But he felt certain his rules would assure the truth of the axiom: "You may be whatever you resolve to be."

And, for a time, they did. Over the course of eighteen months fighting in the Civil War, from his call-up to his death by friendly fire in 1863, Jackson's principles helped him grow into a leader of seemingly awesome physical and moral power. He never lost a battle except for one he fought on a Sunday, in contravention of his rules. The soldiers in his brigade came to admire him for his consistency. Southerners revered him as a god. He got his nickname from a triumph of his rules: When, during a battle, the Confederates began to retreat, Jackson held firm. He had made himself a promise not to turn tail, and soon, the battle line was restored. Another general marveled he'd held strong as "a stone wall."

From his depiction in the young adult book, I kind of loved Stonewall. And yet I was fully aware his "life's work"—the kind I wanted to find—had been in service of an ideal that, three years after his death, was confirmed the greatest evil in which America has ever been complicit. Stonewall had applied his rules to the problem of human slavery. He looked in the Bible and found the Israelites took slaves. Case closed. Abraham Lincoln acknowledged that, had he been born in the South instead of the North, he almost certainly would have accepted slavery, too.

And, thus, Stonewall's rules ensured a life well lived in every respect save one—but the greatest one. It disturbed me. But I also felt sorry the book ended with his death. I read the last page over and over, doodling on it, imagining what would have happened if he'd lived. I felt acutely curious how he would have dealt with the transition. What home would he have made in a country where his rules no longer worked?

As a teenager, I read again and again a huge book of interviews with formerly enslaved Americans about the months after the Civil War ended. They revealed arresting complexities that weren't often described in my history classes. Many of the interviewees recalled feeling unsettled and burdened, not only free. "You would just cry" out of apprehension for the future, one woman said, "without letting the [white people] see you." A man, Walter Emerson, wondered what to do about his name. He *liked* the sound of his surname, which was that of a planter. He wanted to keep it. And yet, he wrote, even black Americans' names could feel like an invisible chain they hadn't yet cut: a chain to history, to "veiled and mysterious events" in the past, to "business transactions, violations of faith and loyalty, assaults; yes, and the unrecognized loves."

I wanted to inhabit the war's aftermath, and I started to feel I'd been born in the wrong era. Amused by my turbulent emotions around the Civil War, my high school friends printed a passport-sized mug shot of Abraham Lincoln and instructed me to put it into my wallet next to a faded sweetheart pic of Tom Cruise. It pained me to know I was likelier to get into bed with Top Gun than ever to meet the people I felt held the answers to my deepest questions face to face.

And then I got to South Africa.

After college, I started to work as a journalist in Washington, D.C. But restless in the scrum of reporters striving to wring something interesting out of a handful of hopelessly guarded, well-scripted politicians, I moved to Cape Town. The geography was wilder than anything I could have imagined. In the summer, the sky was deep blue and the wind was fierce; it turned over buses and swept pedestrians off of their feet. Clinging to the lampposts, their bodies near-parallel to the pavement, they made the downtown look topsy-turvy, like a child's snow globe knocked over on its side. In winter, clouds enshrouded the head of Table Mountain and great rivers of rain poured down the cliff face and into the city like the tears of a sorrowing god.

The built environment, however, was jarringly familiar. It reminded me of home—all of home. It was as if the various geographical strata of American society—urban, suburban, country; East, Midwest, mountain West—had gotten compressed into a far smaller area. Fifty miles beyond Cape Town, in the mountains that run up South Africa's west coast, there was cowboy country, with

wide fenced ranches punctuated by townlets with John Deere dealers and boot-and-hat wholesalers. Closer in was a ring of suburbs
with streets named for flowers, three-bedroom houses, and the occasional, gigantic American-style shopping mall. The city itself was
divided between poorer residential areas of hand-built corrugated-iron shacks and a downtown of stately old townhouse-studded
slopes that called to mind certain bourgeois-bohemian neighborhoods of San Francisco. In this hilly downtown, burger-and-milk-
shake joints nestled against fair trade coffee roasters, hipster
haircut salons called Boy Girl and Scar, galleries showcasing graffiti art, and copious artisanal bakeries and raw food bars.

It was so familiar I briefly wondered if it served U.S. expa-
triates. But South African history has unusual parallels with the
American story. The settlers who gave it its contemporary name
first arrived by boat from Europe—mostly Holland—in the late
1600s. After farming on territory governed by the Dutch East
India Company and, then, the British Empire, many struck out
in wagons into the hinterlands, declaring themselves torchbearers
of liberty. They set up republics with constitutions modeled on
America's.

In the twentieth century—their ranks swelled to several
million—their leaders split off from the British Commonwealth
and took South Africa, by then a diamond-shaped territory double the size of Texas, fully independent. This act nurtured feelings
of exceptionalism and pride. By implementing apartheid, which
fastidiously partitioned public space by race and reserved the best
jobs and land for white people, they experienced an apparent ex-
plosion of economic success, producing great quantities of food,
building dams and highways and skyscrapers, and mining the flatlands. They sent soldiers to nearby countries to make war, they
said, against communist "terrorists"; considering them part of the
global Good Fight, the American Central Intelligence Agency sent
agents to help.

Just a decade later it was gone. Weakened by a sustained black liberation fight, in the '90s white predominance crumbled. Under apartheid, white people had not only been the majority in the halls of power. They'd essentially been those halls' *only* occupants. Nearly overnight, the many celebrated heroes of a government that believed it had many enemies became losers who had labored for a collapsed and discredited cause. And people of color took their places in the president's office, in Parliament, on the committees that write the school history books. It's a degree of change many Western societies undergoing much slower demographic shifts have only barely begun to imagine.

I see, now, that I was transfixed by Stonewall as a child not because I wondered how he might have faced one of the most radical challenges human beings can face—navigating an external change that redefines who we are, undoing our carefully constructed selves. I lingered on him because he wouldn't have had to face that even *if* he'd survived the end of the Civil War.

Many leaders and analysts once liked to think America—at least in some broad, moral way—had already gotten past the point South Africa arrived at in the '90s when it began to try to construct a multiracial society undefined by ancient prejudices and historical wounds. It wasn't true, though. In the last twenty years, the gauzy, forced confidence that defined my childhood has yielded to a mood of deep frustration, even dread. It turns out we may just have tried to skip over so much of the struggle and the incredible psychological alteration that coming to terms with a difficult history entails. And, by denying the way the past still works on the present, we may have made its influence more threatening.

So what follows is a story that illuminates what lies ahead of us. A fantasy book, but real. Sometimes I tell people recent South African history, very loosely, collapses two hundred and fifty years of American history into about thirty—from our antebellum era well into our future. The U.S. census bureau only recently began projecting the year in which America will become a so-called "majority-minority" nation. Thanks to their country's demographics and history, South Africans never had the luxury of dawdling at the psychological precipice of great change. In the blink of an eye, in the tallying of a vote, they were in it.

History often borrows its force from the supposed power of characters like Napoleon, or the Zulu king Shaka, or Barack Obama. But preeminence is like a walled compound. The lives celebrities affect remain barely visible to them past the social, physical, and psychological barriers erected by their authority; the noise is muted if people bang at the gate. I've explored South Africa, instead, through people we sometimes call ordinary—though Christo, Dipuo, and Malaika aren't ordinary.

One thing I've learned is that every person in a society undergoing a change like South Africa's feels, and struggles against, utterly unanticipated effects—materially and at the level of the soul. Even the people who wanted it or who could benefit from it struggle. Paradoxically, I saw it might be the people who most needed or wanted change who ended up struggling the hardest with it.

Not long after I arrived in South Africa, I went to visit a farmer named Andre. I'd read about him in a newspaper. Under apartheid, he supported the white regime. But then he changed his mind. After apartheid ended, he started a program to mentor black farmers, who hadn't previously been allowed to own large commercial farms. He got his farmers' union—all old white men—to sign on. Before dawn, they would drive to their black neighbors' houses to put themselves at their service. Andre's neighbor, Moses, who grew up poor in a segregated area, wanted help setting up a digitized accounting system, so Andre helped him.

It was a feel-good story. Andre received me in the farmers'

union building, a shed decorated with a line of framed photographs of the union's presidents over history: a string of grave-looking white faces. "But we're all people," Andre said he had realized. "We sink or swim together, now I see."

After I got into my car to leave, though, I heard a tap at the driver's side window. It was Andre. I rolled the window down.

"Can I ask you a question?" he said, poking his head in. "As a journalist, you travel around. So. Our young people. Do you think they're even more racist than we were?"

"What do you mean?" I asked, taken aback.

"My son," he said. "To be honest, I'm doing this for my son. He's sixteen. I want him to be able to take over our farm. If our black neighbors go down, we all go down."

But Andre was distressed by something he was observing in his son. He said his son lashed out bitterly about the new black-led government, even calling black people by a derogatory term Andre wouldn't have used under apartheid.

This wasn't supposed to be happening. It was supposed to be older white South Africans who might remain stuck in the past. It seemed to Andre, though, that other, queer, frightening changes were occurring. "I'm afraid for my son," he told me through the window. He lowered his voice. "I'm afraid *of* my son."

PART
1

1

Dipuo

WHEN MALAIKA'S MOTHER, DIPUO, WAS ten years old, she began to read books a neighbor brought back from her job as a maid in a white area. The neighbor brought home all kinds. But the books Dipuo loved most were the paperback romances by Danielle Steel, the American author. Her very favorite was *A Perfect Stranger*, in which a beautiful young woman falls in love with the man sitting next to her on a plane. The woman had a fur jacket and her own private porter to handle her luggage, and in the few hours it took her to soar over America from San Francisco to New York, she and her seatmate shared glasses of champagne. When Dipuo's mother took her out of Soweto, the so-called black township south of Johannesburg where they lived, to visit rural relatives—a rare event—she just packed their clothing into plastic bags.

By the late '60s, Johannesburg was a city of a million and a half people. It had a haze over it so deep Dipuo couldn't see the tops of the buildings that surrounded the train station. But nearly half of South Africa was commercial farmland, and after just twenty minutes of motion, out the train window, she could see russet-backed cattle and antelopes and egrets standing solitary in glinting dams. Some of her mother's cousins lived in rural villages with clay-brick huts clustered around a *lekgotla*, a central square where a sub-chief presided over parties and trials. In the winter the air there was very dry, but in the summer thunderstorms strafed the landscape and blew over camel thorn trees, whose roots brought up the fossils of sea animals that had lived there when the whole place was still under an ocean.

After she arrived, Dipuo would help her aunts pick spinach and light the morning fire for tea and hot porridge. Waking up at dawn, just before the pipit birds began their syncopated calls in the bushes, felt a little bit magical, though she knew very well that her relatives' villages lacked resources and she woke at the same time in the city, anyway, to get her mother's stove going. But her aunts had chickens, and some of their husbands had cows that stamped in dusty corrals behind the thorn bushes that divided the homes from the pastureland.

"The general belief of [South Africa's] primitive peoples, it would appear, is that all possess an equal right to the soil, the water, and the light of the sun," one early European visitor to the area wrote contemptuously. Dipuo's mother's community didn't see that as a negative. It was how it was. If somebody's cow got stolen and the thief couldn't be identified, the entire village had to make restitution. When a man slaughtered one of his own cows, he was expected to give parts of it to his extended relatives.

Historians surmise Dipuo's ancestors arrived in southern Africa over the course of a millennium as they slowly left East Africa, which was becoming overcrowded. After passing through the southern Great Rift Valley—the thousands-of-miles-long gorge that divides Africa's forested center from flatlands near the sea—and over the grassy highlands in what is now Zimbabwe, they split, some continuing to the southeastern coast of the continent and others trekking west to the high plains with camel thorn trees.

Dipuo's mother's elders, though, reckoned their community came into being when their first forefather made his way, like Jonah, out of the belly of a fish. That forefather was quick on his feet and canny, and he eluded assassins who pursued him to the edge of a river by transforming himself into a rock. In frustration, one of his pursuers picked up the rock and hurled it over the river, muttering, "I would kill that guy with this if I saw him!" When the stone landed on the other side, it turned back into a man, and he smiled.

In that community, canniness was a prized trait. The way you proved your wit was to speak in metaphors and proverbs. The more elliptically you spoke, the more respected you were. When Dipuo's mother, Matshediso, was born, she would have been called a *ngoana*, or a "little being" not too different from an animal. Only when she began to talk would she become a *mothoana*—a person. People used hundreds of riddles: *Mollo o tswala molora*, men would say. Fire begets ashes. This referred to how overinvolved parents could yield helpless offspring. Mothers tutored their children: *Ntho e senang maoto le mapheo, e lebelo le makatsang e senang ho thibeloa e lilomo ke dinoka, le marako?* What doesn't have legs or wings but moves fast and can't be stopped by walls or rivers?

Ke lentsoe, was the answer. The human voice.

In some ways, little girls and boys were fairly equal. They played together and, if a girl showed a predilection for herding cattle—a boy's job—she might be allowed to do it. But by the time Matshediso was born, missionaries had established schools, and mostly only boys attended them. "The thinking went: a girl will eventually move into her husband's family's compound, so why invest in schooling her?" Dipuo told me.

Women were called *mosadi*, literally "the ones who stay at home." When a girl menstruated, everything changed. Negotiations began over her marriage, and after a man's family paid a bride-price for her, she'd be expected to pick her husband's crops and—if he was a community leader—to build his second or third wives' houses.

But Matshediso had other ideas. She wanted some control

over her own life. And in the '50s, people were returning from a place they made sound so different. *Egoli*, they were calling it. The city of gold. Or *Maboneng*: the place of lights. There were so many nicknames for the city rising to the north where the pasturelands pleated into ridges veined with gold. The people who returned said its gutters looked filled with gold nuggets until you crouched to look and saw they were the dried-up, gilted seed pods from tens of thousands of purple-flowering trees white people had imported from India.

As Johannesburg grew up around gold mines, it came to be considered the world's largest "urban forest." From the ground, though, it was a dense network of concrete overpasses and bypasses, each built over old, too small streets and intersections. I once read about a caterpillar that molts the skin off its face every year. Instead of abandoning the skins, it stacks them atop its head—three, four, five—until its own molted faces become its magnificent, unwieldy crown. Johannesburg was magnificent and unwieldy like that. Pedestrians streamed at all hours along the shoulders of highways and the honking of cars was constant. Some of the on-ramps had been squeezed in so tight they curved too abruptly, and drivers were always crashing into their barriers at low speed, tying up the highways for miles at a time. At night, though, the men who traveled there said the neon billboards atop the twenty-five-story buildings made the whole city look as if it were floating two hundred feet above the ground.

Women couldn't work on the gold mines. So Matshediso set off to work in what people were calling "the kitchens." By that time, South Africa had separate schools for white kids, black kids, kids of Indian descent, and so-called colored children, or kids of mixed racial heritage. Your race was embedded in the digits of a national identification card; it determined what you could do for a living and even every step you could take. In the cities, people of color weren't allowed to leave their townships, treeless reserves set on the outskirts of the city, to walk in white neighborhoods unless they carried a "pass" signed by the white person who employed them.

In Johannesburg, black women were maids. They cooked and cleaned in white families' literal kitchens. By the time Matshediso got to Soweto, the phrase "the kitchens" had shed its specificity and referred to a more symbolic place: the part of white society reserved for black people. "The kitchens" meant a whole world— one where black nannies brought up white kids from birth but weren't present at their high school graduations. Where white families gave black maids free lunch but served it on separate dishware. "White people—they had this tendency to give black people their old food," Dipuo remembered when I met her.

The few times Dipuo accompanied her mother to "the kitchens," she bitterly noted, white *madams* gave her mother leftovers while tearing open fresh bags of kibble for their pets. But then she smiled. "For us, it *was* nice food." She and her friends "looked forward to our mothers coming home from work. There would be nice chicken stew, and leftovers saved from breakfast. Bacon."

The mother of one of Dipuo's friends also worked in a white woman's "kitchen," and the girls would trade what their mothers brought home. Dipuo might get a casserole and her friend, sandwiches. They loved the pearly-pink meat, the white bread, the green lettuce, and the bright yellow mustard, all jewel-like colors they rarely saw in Soweto. The food was leftovers, but it somehow seemed closer to an ideal, resembling the primary colors Dipuo's schoolteachers taught her on the laminated posters they hung up on the cracked chalkboards. Sometimes, Dipuo would save the sandwich her friend gave her for days, as if it would get better the more patiently she waited.

Her best friend Gadifele lived in a yellow house around the corner. Gadifele and her little brother Kgadi were orphaned young; by the time they were teenagers, they were raising their younger siblings alone. Dipuo loved Gadifele, but to be honest, she also loved her house. It had multiple rooms. Dipuo's family—her mother and three of her four brothers—lived in a twelve-by-fifteen-foot corrugated-iron shack in the back of somebody else's yard. In the summer the shack boiled like an oven; in the winter it was like a freezer.

Matshediso hadn't found the life she had imagined for herself in Soweto. After arriving, she gave birth to five children by several different men. So many of the men in Soweto were transient, sleeping in dormitories while working multiweek shifts on the mines and then returning to their villages and to the wives they considered their "real" ones. Early on, she tried to dignify the shack by painting its door a fresh robin's-egg blue. But she quickly became overwhelmed.

As a child, all Dipuo really understood was what she wanted was always too much. "She'd make you feel bad if you wanted Christmas clothes or school shoes," Dipuo told me. "She'd always shout: 'Where do you expect I can get that money? I earn so little. Your fathers have run away, the bastards.'"

Sometimes, when she was in a better mood, she would sit with Dipuo and tell her stories about her father. He'd been handsome, her mother said, and "looked just like Percy Sledge," a distant, dreamy black American soul singer "everyone in Soweto fell in love with" in the '70s.

From the early twentieth century—when the Afrikaner republics and a couple of British colonies amalgamated to become "South Africa"—black teachers, doctors, and thinkers opposed white leaders' efforts to segregate the races. These black leaders founded the African National Congress (ANC), a black-liberation movement; in the '50s, led in part by the young Nelson Mandela, the ANC mounted nationwide work stayaways and bus boycotts.

Mandela started out dedicated to nonviolence. But after the

white regime's police shot to death sixty people protesting the "pass laws," he decided to form an underground military wing of the ANC. Named Umkhonto we Sizwe, or "Spear of the Nation," it set out to sabotage the economy, bombing railroad tracks and oil refineries. The government retaliated. In 1962, it captured Mandela and raided a Johannesburg safe house called Liliesleaf, arresting nineteen top ANC leaders and sentencing many to life in prison.

That deeply demoralized Soweto for a decade. But in the '70s—when Dipuo was born—a new leader emerged. Steve Biko wrote newspaper columns about a philosophy he called Black Consciousness, an appeal to black South Africans to reacquaint themselves with their inherent dignity before asking white people to give it to them. Biko noted the ANC seemed especially proud of its white allies—people like Bram Fischer, the grandson of an Afrikaner political luminary. These were the kinds of people most township residents felt so distant from, and they wondered why such allies hadn't yet improved their conditions, though whiteness was supposed to afford people power.

"Black people need to defeat the one element in politics which is working against them," Biko said—"a psychological feeling of inferiority." You had to liberate yourself from caring what white people thought of you. Sometimes Biko wrote in a sharply intellectual vein, drawing on Frantz Fanon; other times he was cheeky, brazen. He took familiar melodies from hymns black churches used, like *Lizalis' idinga lakho*—"fulfill your promise, God; all races must be saved"—and refashioned their lyrics into insulting political statements like *Amabhulu zizinja*, or "White people are dogs."

Young people in Meadowlands, Dipuo's Soweto neighborhood, passed Biko's columns around. Men started wearing Afros and women played James Brown's "Say It Loud—I'm Black and

I'm Proud" off tapes smuggled in from neighboring Botswana. Nevertheless, Matshediso told Dipuo her father was denying his paternity because Dipuo was "too black."

The other people in his family had freckles and gold streaks in their hair. Their lighter complexion led their neighbors to call them "white." Generations earlier, the story went, a white farmer raped one of the family's matriarchs. The family wasn't proud of this. Yet it seemed there was something they also quietly prized about this heritage, like an heirloom that's not au courant to display but which you keep locked in a safe just in case, someday, it's worth a great deal at auction.

But Matshediso gave birth to "a black daughter," as Dipuo put it. When she was born, Dipuo's skin was darker than her father's. In a year or two, after her baby fat melted to reveal sharp features and what people called a "Caucasian" nose, most of her father's family acknowledged her.

But her father never could. He never admitted Dipuo was his child.

At one point, Matshediso was so poor she didn't have the coins to commute to "the kitchens." She had to pick up more humiliating work: scrubbing the floors of other black women, women to whom she had every ability to be equal. "So I took care of my siblings," Dipuo said.

A little brother, Vina, came when she was six and another, Ali, when she was nine. Ali, she recalled, "was basically my child." In effect, Dipuo became a mother before she was ten. "He cried a lot. He shit a lot. I did all the cleaning, the rinsing. My own childhood ended completely."

Lonely, Dipuo took to reading the Danielle Steel romances. People sometimes acted, in Soweto, like romantic love couldn't— or shouldn't—exist. First, there were the conditions imposed by the white regime, which forced fathers to travel to distant mines and mothers to toil day-in, day-out in other people's houses, neglecting their own domestic spaces and relationships. But also, sometimes older black people said flirting and romance was a kind of betrayal of black people's duty. "We were always told: Freedom first," Dipuo said. She perceived that politically minded elders disliked seeing crushes between young people. Their message was, "How could you prioritize an intimate thing when others are dying?"

"We were involved in a class struggle," Essop Pahad, a leading ANC activist, later told a journalist. "Anything else was soft, diversionary." Members of the ANC called each other "comrade," even their spouses and children. Their commitment to the liberation struggle was more important than any family tie. When Govan Mbeki, an activist imprisoned alongside Mandela, was finally released, a journalist asked him how it felt to see his son again. He just grinned and said, "Not much finer than seeing the others [in the ANC]. Thabo Mbeki is no longer my son. He is my comrade!"

Still, Dipuo loved reading about Raphaella, the heroine of *A Perfect Stranger*. Raphaella had fur coats, silk bedlinens, and a house with stained-glass windows. But Dipuo was most touched by the tenderness the *people* in her life showed her. When she eventually admitted to the man she met on the plane that she was afraid of getting into a serious relationship, he reassured her that he loved her so much he'd wait for her forever. *Next month, next year, I'll be here*. Raphaella had treasures. But the loveliest thing was the way she was considered a treasure by somebody else.

The other respite came once a year when Dipuo's mother took her shopping downtown. Black women were allowed to walk past the white people's department stores. At cheaper shops, her mother would only buy a few things like Tupperware containers. But through the department stores' tall panes of glass, Dipuo could see soft velvet hair bows and bright dresses. She'd gaze at the rows of black-patent-leather Mary Janes, their toes polished so bright that she could see her reflection.

But when she touched the windows, her fingertips came away sticky from cleaning fluid put there by black men who arrived before dawn to clean the windows on precarious ladders. It reminded Dipuo she was still outside on the street. And that any effort to touch white life would somehow end up leaving *her* dirty. The toes of the Mary Janes warped her face, too, broadening her narrow "Caucasian" nose in their convex, mirrored surfaces, as if to remind her: you are still black in our eyes, above everything.

2

Christo

AS A CHILD, CHRISTO'S PREFERRED companions were the native trees on his father's farm. There was the false olive, with leaves so pale they looked dusted with silver; the fever trees with their lime-green bark; and a dozen kinds of acacias, from the gnarled bushes with more thorns than they had leaves to the camel thorn trees, which could grow to fifty feet and whose crowns were wider than they were tall. A camel thorn tree stood a few paces from the front of Christo's farmhouse. When Christo sat under it, he could often hear the tinkle of his sister practicing the piano and the rhythmic clanks of his father working on a pickup truck in the garage. That was disappointing. He wanted to feel alone. But on the weekends, almost nobody drove by the farmhouse, though it abutted a big road. And if he closed his eyes and tuned out the other noises, and then opened them again and squinted at the fields, he'd see no other houses and he could imagine he was unchaperoned in an uninhabited wilderness.

I drove with an acquaintance one summer to Christo's family farm. South African farming country is picture-book beautiful: a quilt of yellow corn and green alfalfa hemmed in with twinkling metal windmills and tall cypress trees. From the middle of the country north to the Botswana border, the roads are so straight they look drawn with a ruler and the earth is so flat the clouds become the mountains: tremendous and billowing, they crack to let through beams of sunlight that pool on the fields like the spotlights on a Broadway stage.

The farther we got from Johannesburg, the more creatures emerged out of the fields: locusts, tortoises, four-foot monitor lizards, and a tiny antelope called a steenbok whose antlers are barely bigger than a human hand. It doesn't take long, leaving South Africa's cities, to feel like a mere diplomat entering a kingdom ruled by nature. One night, I was cruising a highway when something huge hit my windshield and shattered it. I swerved to the shoulder, inspected the splintered glass, and picked out a long, lustrous blue feather: a wild guinea fowl. A different evening, I stopped to look for a place to pee and waved around my cell phone flashlight. I saw what looked like a string of Christmas lights, the kind that adorn bistros in Brooklyn. And then I heard a rustle. The lights were the reflective eyes of some fifty wildebeest, a horned animal that's like a cross between a horse and an ox but dyed a dull sapphire. They were standing so close I could hear them breathing.

By the time we got to our destination—a little town near the Kalahari Desert where Christo's father, Johannes, had asked me to meet him—the sky was black and lightning was cleaving it open. Hurrying me into his pickup, Johannes said he wanted to take the longer way home to his ranch precisely *because* it had started to rain. He loved trucks, he said, and he especially loved piloting them over muddy *dongas*.

A *donga* is an erosion gully that running water carves in South Africa's dusty soil. The word comes from the isiZulu *udonga*. That makes it rare in white South African usage. White people have been in South Africa, now, for four hundred years, but they rarely borrowed words from the country's black languages. Even the terms they used to describe black culture were imported from Europe: *assegais* and *knobkerries*, their words for the weapons black South Africans used, derived from Portuguese and Dutch, though black people had their own words for them. They called the sor-ghum porridge many black people ate *pap*, from Low German. When, in the twentieth century, South Africa's rulers formally seg-regated black from white people, they called rural black areas the *tuislande*, from the Dutch for "homelands."

But a *donga* was a *donga*. Cuisine was one thing. But there were features of the land itself that only black people, in the be-ginning, could teach white people the names for. Johannes pointed us at a *donga* and blasted over it. The truck guttered and canted forty-five degrees to the left, and I felt afraid. But he just roared with laughter.

By the time we got to his farm's gate, the rain had dissipated to a sprinkle, and Johannes told me to wait under the camel thorn tree. He returned with a shoebox of mini-bottles of Baileys Irish Cream friends had brought him as souvenirs from trips abroad. He rarely left the farm, he said, because of how much he loved his cattle. They responded to the sound of his voice. He drove the length of the farm every morning, sticking his head out the win-dow of his truck and calling to them like Saint Francis.

After we drank a toast, Christo's mother, Trudie, brought me indoors and showed me the photographs she'd hung in the house's dark main corridor. She'd hung them so densely they looked like they held up the walls instead of vice versa: framed pictures of her grandchildren crawling all over her as if she was a tree; portraits of Christo on his wedding day; and snapshots of Christo and his brother, Jaco, in their high school rugby uniforms, crouching and holding each other in formation.

The next morning, over coffee in the farmhouse's kitchen, Trudie confessed that it had been a relief to end up with such a "normal" family. Her father, Piet, managed a gas station in a nearby city called Vryburg, a dumpy crossroads for long-haul truckers. As a gas pump operator, Piet seemed to have fallen from grace. His cousins were successful ranchers and the Botha family—his surname—was renowned. Louis Botha, a famous early-twentieth-century general, was a relative.

But Piet was so poor his family had to live in a one-room cottage behind somebody else's house. Trudie's mother tacked a curtain onto the ceiling to separate the "kitchen" from the "bedroom" and the family only ate meat when the gas station's owner deigned to give them offcuts that had started to spoil in his freezer. To make up for that degradation at work, at home Piet was terrifyingly strict. Inside the room's four walls, he became its Old Testament God, its meticulous creator and punisher. Trudie had to jump to her feet when he entered the cottage, and before bed, he'd insist the family place each object—down to every thimble—back in the place he had appointed for it.

"I had a soft heart," Trudie explained. She wanted to be a nurse. In the afternoons, she'd get onto her hands and knees to search beneath the hedges for rabbits. She built a field hospital for injured insects, scooping up wounded butterflies to nestle them in matchboxes she'd outfitted with cotton balls "like little beds for them to sleep in." When they died, Trudie wept. And then her father would taunt her, calling her *Trudie Trane*, or "Trudie Tears."

After Piet died, Trudie discovered a handwritten account of his life he'd penned in middle age and carried everywhere in his briefcase. The Piet that emerged from these pages wasn't a lowly gas station employee but the scion of a breed of huntsmen, wanderers, and conquerors. When his great-great-grandfather first moved to the Kalahari Desert to ranch, wild animals carried off his cattle. And yet he ended up prevailing, building a hundred-cow herd. When an imperious colonial bureaucrat tried to collect a toll from his ancestor at a bridge, Piet wrote, his ancestor harnessed an ox to the tollgate's pillar, whipped it forward, and ripped the tollgate out of its foundations.

That kind of defiant attitude was vital to Piet's forebears. In the mid-1600s, a manager with a spice-trading corporation called

the Dutch East India Company—VOC in its Dutch acronym—
established the first colony at Africa's southern tip. In the beginning, Cape Town only was meant to be a "refreshment station"
for Dutch ships bound for richer spice markets in the East. One of
Christo's other ancestors, Johan Depner, was a soldier the VOC
sent to the Cape to defend the wine and wheat farms the corporation established.

Depner hailed from a village in Prussia outside the Russian city
now called Kaliningrad. He grew up in a farmhouse, which probably made his childhood fairly comfortable. But the Thirty Years'
War had devastated croplands, and Depner abandoned Prussia to
walk or hitch rides a thousand miles across northern Europe to
board a VOC ship.

Even as far away as Prussia, people had heard of the VOC.
Historians have described the Dutch East India Company's reach
in the 1600s as comparable to the entire corporate power of the
twenty-first-century United States. It created the first stock exchange in modern times and put up a fleet of a hundred thousand sailors. Thousands of innkeepers in alleyways branching off
Amsterdam's main square daily recruited new bodies to tend its
colonies. It raised its own armies, minted its own coins, and ran
its own trials. And the distant lands to which it ferried men were
often reported to be Edenic.

That was in keeping with the hopes then. A few decades before Depner got to Amsterdam, a Dutch doctor began publishing
pamphlets describing the miracles in Europe's overseas colonies.
He described them as places men could start again, unburdened
by the millennia-long legacies of their ancestors' mistakes. The
animals were so big, he claimed, a poor man couldn't go hungry
and land was so plentiful it would be pointless for there ever to be
war. Some of the most luscious reports had to do with the colonies
on the continent called America. America was "beyond believing,"
an early settler breathlessly wrote. The deer "come when they are

called" and crabs and oysters "leap into my kettle." The English preacher John Winthrop compared the passengers who joined him on an early ship to America to the disciples who sat at Christ's feet during the Sermon on the Mount, implying they were, in a figurative or literal sense, the agents of the Second Coming.

The idea of a fresh start was important. The seventeenth-century Europe Depner crossed was a peculiar place—animated, first, by the conviction that new boundaries were daily being passed by mankind, boundaries previously only crossed by gods. Andreas Vesalius, a Flemish doctor, overturned the understanding of human anatomy Galen had established a thousand years earlier. The astronomers Johannes Kepler, Galileo Galilei, and Nicolaus Copernicus applied math to demystifying the heavens, neatly forecasting the motions of comets and planets.

And then, in 1687, Sir Isaac Newton published his *Principia*. The *Principia* had an impact on the world as radical as the Bible. It proposed that the universe—previously widely believed to be a mystical gift bestowed by a divine source—was rationally comprehensible by the human mind and driven by the pure premise that "every action has an equal and opposite reaction." Philosophers like John Locke applied the *Principia*'s logic to ethics and human affairs, suggesting it proved man could create more perfect societies since within each person lay the capacity to understand the truth and, by extension, the best course of action. European poets began to compose heroic odes to engineers instead of war heroes. The Dutch dedicated themselves to demystifying their landscape, originating the microscope and a system of dikes to manage the floods that routinely swamped their country. The point was to conquer nature, but in a way that suggested they were nature's allies instead of its adversaries. They called their project to redirect rivers "persuasion," a word lifted directly from Locke's philosophy of reason.

It's often forgotten, but Newton and most of these Enlightenment thinkers were also deeply Christian. They hoped the Enlightenment was confirmation Europeans had learned how to be good enough in God's eyes to become his partners. It's strange, then, how possessed Europe *also* was by self-doubt. Every breakthrough came with a corresponding terror that they were screwing up a once-in-history opportunity or that their new energy wasn't motivated by holy rationales but by greed—that they were no less selfish than their forefathers. As they circumnavigated the earth, VOC sailors performed a ritual of hurling fancy hats overboard. It was a desperate tithe driven by the anxiety they were growing too rich—that what they were pursuing wasn't progress, but greed.

Dutch landscape painters of the seventeenth and eighteenth centuries depicted the typical Dutchman as an austere, virtuous farmer dressed in black surveying a flock of contented sheep. In reality, the Dutch landscape of the time was one of felled trees, violently dredged rivers, and the smell of tar and sulfur from the shipbuilding industry. By the late seventeenth century, Holland's economic growth was driven by trade and industry, not agriculture. Merchants scrambled to buy fine china, spices, and sugars from the East and crocodile skin purses from Africa; this mercantilism began dramatically to deepen economic inequality. The merchants would step out of their houses in Amsterdam, the ones they'd decorated with the optimistic paintings, and stumble over children in tatters begging on their doorsteps.

Wealthy Europeans of this era also loved to design botanical gardens. The most luxurious of these originally tried to mimic the Garden of Eden. But by the seventeenth century they began to take on a strange quality. They started to include hell—and then to become dominated by the vision of it. One aristocrat's botanical garden featured a "thunderstorm" with fake rain and sound effects of screaming sinners. Another's deposited visitors into a dank cavern with a wax Satan who hurled insults voiced by a hidden gardener.

Rich Europeans flocked to these hell-gardens in droves. Scholars warned about portents that, as mankind was striving for his highest potential, he was risking eternal damnation. People whispered that, at the edges of Europe, commoners were spotting comets shaped like coffins or, in the words of one writer, "an arm holding a great sword as if about to strike us down." There were unverified reports of "monstrous births" and verified outbreaks of bubonic plague. "The thick smoke of human sins, rising every day, every hour, every moment" is kindling "the hot and fiery anger of the Supreme Judge," a Lutheran bishop predicted. Newton tallied his sins (like "making a mousetrap" on the Sabbath) to prepare for what he believed would be an imminent divine reckoning.

The promise of a new world somewhere else provided a critical beacon of hope. Locke called the mind at birth a *tabula rasa*, a blank slate. Unfortunately, this slate usually got scribbled on with nonsense and wrong ideas when its owner was a child, condemning the adult to bias, confusion, and sin. Europe felt itself to be that burdened adult. It posited it could create a perfect world. But it was constantly reminded of its failures to do so in the form of enduring war, epidemic disease, economic bubbles, and bad leaders.

Many Europeans conceived of Asia, Africa, and America as last chances. "Whatever we desire in the paradise of Holland is here," a Dutch colonist in America raved. Some travelers beat a path to Africa to pursue a potent story: that of "Prester John," a Christian emperor said to rule a land whose streets were paved with gold and whose piazzas housed the fountain of youth. It was also said Prester John was threatened by "heathens" bent on destroying his kingdom. By going to Africa and rescuing Prester John, Europeans could square a stubborn circle: they could attain staggering wealth, even immortality, *and* confirm their Christian virtue all the while.

Enlightenment theories proposed that anybody might have a chance at greatness, regardless of their parents' situation. Benjamin Franklin particularly praised Holland's burgher system in which "ordinary" elected citizens wielded power over towns, saying it should be the model for American democracy. But in reality, it was very hard to become a burgher. You had to have money.

Most of the Cape's early settlers were people European society rejected. In the beginning, southern Africa wasn't sought by adventurers with the biggest ambitions. It had few natural harbors, meaning voyagers who survived the months-long sea journeys—a trip on which an average of a quarter of passengers died—sometimes lost their lives in sight of landfall as their ships broke apart on the rocks. The VOC sent its first Cape Town governor there as punishment after he disgraced himself in the East by profiteering. Mainly "illiterates, criminals, and rascals" went there, Hermann Giliomee, a historian of the Afrikaners, wrote.

Cape Town became where the VOC charges could make a stand: as people who might be *nobler* and more virtuous than their titled brethren. Soldiers and laborers began to refer to themselves as burghers unprompted, then as *Boers*—"farmers" in Dutch, not subjects—and then as Afrikaners, or "Africans." The first man to use the word *Afrikaner* was a laborer found drunk on the job. Rebuked by a bewigged VOC judge, he spat back, "You can't tell me what to do. I am an Afrikaner"—as opposed to a European and, thus, exceptional.

And handfuls of settlers began to strike out into the interior, often without permission. Twelve years after Johan Depner landed at Cape Town, he quit his job as a soldier, married a farmer's daughter, bought cobbler's tools and a bed, and set out for a range of mountains that, as yet, had no white government.

Before Trudie's ancestors got to the desert, they lived in a richer town on the southern coast. A ridge divided that town, Oudtshoorn, from the sea. The north side of the ridge was dry, ideal for raising ostriches, and in the nineteenth century, demand for ostrich feathers was peaking in industrializing Europe. Oudtshoorn became a boomtown: Trudie's great-great-grandfather told tales of how *his* father, as a boy, ran miles to the coastal train tracks and squeezed his body between the rails, watching as the engines roared just a foot over him, raining ash on their way to Cape Town.

And yet the family left. In the middle of the nineteenth century, much larger groups of Europeans set out inland in ox wagon trains. They came to be known as *voortrekkers*, or "the ones who walk ahead." As they moved inland, news trickled back that nearly every last man in some of these pioneer groups died of malaria. But that only intensified the excitement. These were the kinds of hardships that would prove serfs could be the equals of kings.

As they spread out, the Afrikaners named the places they found. They gave the towns and natural features around Cape Town have aspirational monikers like Eerstehoop, or "first hope." Farther out, they named them for their discoverers, in the way European nobles got to name their estates. What a thrill! that a formerly poor Dutch man named Meurel could have his own mountain called Meurelskasteel, or "Meurel's Castle." Farther out still, the names reflected the wonder and trials of exploration. There was Verkeerdevlei, or "the marsh where we took a wrong turn," and Knersvlakte, or "the flatlands where we gnashed our teeth."

The Kalahari Desert, where Trudie's ancestors eventually settled, was shrouded in the most terrifying legends. The first Europeans who traveled there sent back reports of salt pans so vast and featureless you'd lose your orientation and mistake up for down, east for west; at night, under the moon, you could imagine you were stranded on Scotland's forbidding, snow-clad moors. In the 1870s, an English traveler named Parker Gillmore rode through the Kalahari for weeks. He couldn't find water and his horse almost died of thirst. He could see flocks of birds wheeling overhead and forests of camel thorn trees, but driving a shovel ten feet down by their roots yielded only dust.

Sometimes, local people showed up at his camps selling ostrich eggs filled to the brim with water. Wild ostriches were notoriously aggressive, and Gillmore couldn't understand how the men got close enough to steal their eggs. But tales abounded that the area's native inhabitants could divine underwater streams or track animals for days without drinking. "They possess [faculties we], for the most part, are without," another traveler wrote. "Even a child ten years of age, removed from its parents over a hundred miles, [can] return unerringly." For Gillmore, the Kalahari had both a magical and an unnerving quality. Plants—and people—flourished there in ways that he, a scion of enlightened England, couldn't fathom.

Young European barons started traveling to southern Africa as a kind of spring break adventure. By contrast, they wrote about the white settlers they met with barely veiled contempt. One visiting lord claimed the Afrikaners risked degrading their heritage by "slipping" below the level of black people, lazing about in ramshackle houses while barking at "miserable slaves" like pretender kings. "The mistress of the [Afrikaner] family has little idea of what, in society, constitutes female delicacy," another declared. The men ate "mutton boiled to rags. . . . Most can neither read nor write."

In fact, these travelogues contain more than a whiff of jealousy. Gillmore noted sadly in his journals that, as a child, he dreamed of stalking majestic bears. But by the time he grew up, all the game left in settled England was small. He felt disdain for the anemic lordlings who spent a whole day kitting themselves out like Henry the Fifth in order to shoot a single, terrified partridge.

Still, such descriptions hurt the Afrikaner settlers. To fight back, some dubbed their wagon train venture "the Last Trek," the final, figurative journey Europeans had to make to demonstrate their right to exercise dominion over the earth. One tale circulated that an Afrikaner woman, bidden to stop moving by some imperious colonial authority, shouted, "We are ready to cross the [mountains] on our bare feet and die in liberty!"

They set up a half-dozen independent republics, which international observers noted were some of the first to take root after the American Revolution. And they gave the towns they founded farthest inland the most triumphal names. Not far from what would someday become Johannesburg, they named a village Nylstroom, or "the river Nile," to express their belief they were approaching the literal land of milk and honey. Trudie's hometown, Vryburg, simply means "the city of freedom."

Trudie got a reprieve from Piet's tyranny when he sent her to a girls' boarding school in Vryburg. Some of her roommates had more cosmopolitan parents, and they'd gotten ahold of turntables and American LPs. She fell in love with Elvis Presley.

Her country's government, by then, had imposed a strict, moralistic artistic censorship. It didn't allow television into the country and radio DJs couldn't even play Bob Dylan's "Blowin' in the Wind." But since people didn't see Elvis perform on television, it wasn't clear just how transgressive, how sexual, his body language was. Trudie adored the images of his face she saw on the LP covers: the heavy-lidded eyes, the chiseled nose, the jaunty lick of hair over his forehead. And his *voice*. Its mix of warmth and vulnerability made her shiver.

Sports—track meets, rugby matches, and get-togethers where teenage boys competed in informal games like tug-of-war—were a focal point of farm-town life. The boys' fathers barbecued chops over fires they made in diesel drums while their mothers and sisters served cakes. In secret, Trudie asked her mother to sew her a provocative dress like she'd seen in a friend's American magazine to wear to one of the track meets—a tight, white minidress that ended where her fingertips did when she held her arms straight along her thighs.

Her friends blow-dried her auburn hair into ringlets and tied white bows into the curls; she went barefoot with bows tied around each of her toes, too. At the event, she noticed a boy who looked just like the face she'd seen on the Elvis LPs. He turned out to be a musician: his voice was rich and masculine, "yet almost a little bit fragile," Trudie remembered, like Elvis's. Trudie showed me a couple of pictures of Johannes when he was young. The resemblance was remarkable: he had sideburns; dark, V-shaped brows; and lips that curved dramatically like a Cupid's bow.

The two began to date. Under a full moon, a few months later, Johannes proposed marriage. Waiting outside the church in her wedding dress, Trudie told me she felt like she was going to throw up. Johannes was twenty-one; she was nineteen, and they barely knew each other. But walking down the aisle, she felt a wave of peace come over her. She sensed she was getting what an Afrikaner girl was supposed to get—a marriage to a stable man set to inherit cattle—and something not everybody got. A few of Trudie's older school friends mentioned, in passing, that they rarely spoke to their husbands. But when Trudie moved into Johannes's grandfather's farmhouse, she and her husband played board games and talked late into the night. She felt Johannes was her *pêl*, not just her husband. It's an Afrikaans word without a perfect English analog, but it means something like "intimate friend."

Only one early experience had felt unsettling. It happened

on her honeymoon. She and Johannes planned a road trip in his Toyota pickup truck. The idea was to drive around the country visiting beaches and safari parks. But they set out later than they'd intended, and it started to pour rain. They immediately got lost.

Peering through the streaks of water on the windshield, everything looked unfamiliar. Even the roads felt alien, gravelly and bumpy under their tires. The Toyota's headlights lit up the figures of black men and women running from the rain. Johannes and Trudie had entered a so-called black homeland.

Many European missionaries, and even some early Afrikaner leaders, said they respected the black people they encountered. Gillmore—the English traveler—marveled at a black "king" he met in the Kalahari named Kama. Kama's posture was "upright as if he had been drilled" and his mien "self-possessed," Gillmore wrote, and his scientific knowledge of botany was "perfect. I could not help thinking what a perfect type of aristocrat he was."

But Gillmore also made the unsettling observation that, soon after their encounter with Europeans, some indigenous Africans were daring to try to outstrip them. Kama preferred English-style suits over "native" dress, and Gillmore observed, unhappily, that he looked sharper in them than young Englishmen did.

In 1867, an Afrikaner boy found a diamond in a riverbed. Within a couple of decades, tens of thousands of diggers and speculators flooded into southern Africa to mine diamonds, gold, and platinum. When Gillmore stopped at South Africa's richest diamond field, he witnessed fat white overseers indolently ordering around black laborers. To accomplish their dreams of wealth, Gillmore discovered that many of the black workers walked hundreds of miles back and forth between their family homes and the diggings. "Undaunted, they will persistently walk day after day, from night till morning, endur[ing] heat, thirst, and hunger."

The black diggers seemed stronger to him than the Europeans by European standards—perhaps even more virtuous. The Afrikaners sometimes still called themselves the *Boers*—"farmers"—to express the sense that God had selected them to turn Africa into a new garden of Eden. But black people became the first serious commercial farmers in South Africa's interior in the late nineteenth century, ferrying cornmeal to the mines in their own wagons. One of the first recorded poems composed in South Africa was a nervous ditty revealing fear black people would eventually overtake white people—that they would win at the settlers' own game.

The black man comes first; the white man comes later.
The white man seizes the land; the black man seizes it later.
The white man lives now; the black man lives later.
The white man laughs now. The black man laughs later.

The mine managers came up with the first organized system to curtail competition. Black workers were confined to dormitories on locked compounds and could only travel with a pass signed by a white employer. But trouble began at the same time between the Afrikaners and the British. After precious metal was discovered under the Afrikaner republics' land, the British declared war. In achieving victory in 1902, the British were brutal. They put thirty thousand Afrikaner women and children in concentration camps and destroyed more than half of the men's cattle and farm implements.

At the turn of the twentieth century, the Afrikaners—who comprised a little more than half of the country's white population—became an increasingly visible underclass. Poor white families massed at the edges of Johannesburg in tent encampments, mixing with and competing with black people for work. It wasn't clear what would happen to white people in a colony who "allow[ed] their heritage to slip from their hands and [sink] into the class of unskilled laborers," a school inspector fretted. Nowhere else, yet, in the colonial world had white people so clearly "lost caste."

Observing this, a group of Afrikaner leaders decided to try and reverse it. They developed the Dutch dialect they spoke, Afrikaans, into an academic language and formed mutual-help societies in which Afrikaners invested in each other's businesses. And then, in 1938, they put on a show.

It was supposed to be a couple of ox wagons resembling the kind the *voortrekkers* rode a century earlier; the drivers were kitted out with soft suede shoes crafted from the skins of a curly-horned antelope and shotguns in case of an encounter with hostile tribesmen. The message was: You are not fallen. Your rugged identity ennobles you.

The idea took hold in a way the organizers hadn't even imagined. On the day of the wagon train's departure, tens of thousands of Afrikaners converged on the Cape Town square where the oxen were being harnessed, dressed up in pioneer costumes. Independent groups put up their own processions all around the country. Some were led by torches representing the light of civilization; onto others, onlookers tossed relics like old plow handles. In a city on the southern coast, women turned out in their pajamas at three in the morning to hear the mayor declare, "The Afrikaners will flourish so long as God is on his throne."

The show kicked off a political reawakening that culminated in the Afrikaners taking nationwide political power from English-speaking politicians. They strove to make racial segregation even more explicit, sending emissaries to the American South. Hermann Giliomee, the Afrikaner historian, told me that when the

South Africans saw Alabama's segregated buses and colleges, "they thought to themselves, 'Eureka! Now *here* is the answer.'" And they formalized a "homeland system" that revoked black people's South African citizenship and assigned them to new "countries" purportedly corresponding to their tribal origins.

Politically, this homeland system was always a farce. The homelands had puppet rulers and commanded almost no patriotic loyalty among their "citizens." They were apportioned only 13 percent of South Africa's territory, despite the fact that black people already constituted more than two-thirds of the population. No other nation ever recognized the homelands, and black people couldn't travel overseas on their worthless homeland passports. Many never bothered to get them. "They said I was now a citizen of 'Bophuthatswana' and I must get my passport from Bophuthatswana," one Johannesburg resident bitterly told a reporter. "I didn't even know where Bophuthatswana was."

The government tried to obscure these homelands, as well as the townships, from white citizens. It sculpted the landscape to offer white people the impression South Africa was a "white" country. It located the townships behind mountains or in valleys so white people, from their houses, couldn't easily see them. A white man I knew confessed to me that, growing up near a township in the late 1970s, he truly believed South Africa's demographics were "90 percent white." That was how it looked to him from his farmhouse stoop and from the nearby village's main drag—like he lived in a white country. Only when he climbed the ridge behind his father's farmhouse did he wonder. He could see columns of smoke rising from behind the farthest mountain. Who was generating all that smoke?

The homeland system sought to make real what white leaders proposed in the abstract—that black people were the foreigners, almost like figures of the imagination who only materialized when summoned. But the first night of her honeymoon, Trudie got the powerful impression *she* was the foreigner. That she was the one who didn't know her country. She and her husband had entered a world in which they felt completely lost. Yet they hadn't even driven two hours.

3

Dipuo

IN 1976, THE WHITE REGIME finally allowed television into South Africa. When TVs arrived in Soweto, Dipuo interpreted it as an effort on the part of the white government to show the world it was basically moderate. "But it helped radicalize us." She flashed me a wicked smile, still enjoying the irony. "That effort by the apartheid people to show they were humane."

Many black South Africans saw glimpses of white people's lives while working in their homes or gardens. These glimpses didn't always make white life seem fully enviable. White families could seem sadly isolated. But after television came—a single state-run channel aired soap operas with white actors—black South Africans were able to see the story white South Africans told *themselves* about the way they lived. And that story was dramatic, heroic, richly lit. A black deli worker I knew in Johannesburg told me that, growing up in Soweto in the '80s, she became dead set on marrying a white man.

That desire didn't stem mainly from the conviction a white man would be rich. It arose because the white lovers on the soap operas looked so romantic compared to many of her black friends' parents—whose partnerships, if they had them, were frayed by overwork and poverty and tainted by the political conflict churning all around them. "It is only white people," the girl decided, "who have real love."

She told me she still believed that.

Dipuo, though, was affected by the soap operas in a different way. She looked hard at the *settings* of white people's lives. These were milieus black people weren't allowed to try to create in the townships—tall office buildings and restaurants. Sowetans had to apply to the government to run a business, and virtually the only kind they could get a permit for was to operate a minibus taxi that ferried people to work in the white neighborhoods.

South African political leaders insisted segregation was also for *black* people's benefit. A prime minister named Hendrik Verwoerd, known as "the architect of apartheid," said black people had a different "culture" and the more white and black people "intermingled," the unhappier black people would be. But if the so-called white lifestyle couldn't be natural to black people, Dipuo wondered, then how come the TV executives were making money parading that lifestyle in front of Sowetans? Surely they recognized black people wanted the same things white people did. That only made apartheid seem crueler, the recognition that white people *knew* they were spouting opportunistic lies. Hearing white people say that to live in townships or homelands was what black people really wanted started to make Dipuo very angry.

Dipuo was only five when the largest anti-apartheid protest ever erupted in Soweto. In June 1976, tens of thousands of black students walked out of school to object to "Bantu Education," the cruder curriculum the apartheid regime used in black schools. Out of all the hours black children spent in the classroom, a quarter were dedicated to needlework, cooking, and gardening, because—in the words of South Africa's secretary of education—these children had to be ready to "earn a living in the service of Europeans." History and geography weren't really taught at all because, a black student recalled, a black child was not expected to "know the condition of his country nor the truth about the world." Bantu Education also required black children to take difficult subjects like biology in Afrikaans, which wasn't the language almost any of them spoke at home.

As the Sowetan students marched, the police shot and killed a twelve-year-old protester. Protests spread to other cities, and the following year, hundreds of thousands of black children—a big percentage of the country's whole black schoolgoing population—just refused to show up for the new term. Every year thereafter, the Soweto schools grew emptier. Black students publicly burned their ID cards and spray-painted their former school walls with the name "MANDELA."

At first, Dipuo simply felt afraid. "Lots of schoolchildren," she said, hid in her mother's landlady's house while she cowered in the outhouse and gunshots echoed through the streets. In 1986, though, when she was fourteen, Dipuo also dropped out of school. Her mother fought her over it. "They'll kill you," she would cry when Dipuo prepared to go protest. "These people"— white people—"will always be in power. You don't have guns. *You're* not the police. They will simply shoot you and you'll vanish. Or they'll throw you from the tenth floor of a building and say you committed suicide."

This wasn't paranoid. In 1978, Steve Biko died in police custody. Before that, in 1971, a young teacher and activist named Ahmed Timol fell to his death from the tenth floor of a Johannesburg police building. The police claimed he committed suicide—a laughable idea, since the government's own inquest saw evidence that his injuries were consistent with being savagely beaten. Timol became a byword in black South African households: both a bitter complaint about the injustice of apartheid and a warning about what would happen to you if you tried to disobey.

But Dipuo was beginning to feel her mother had a kind of Stockholm Syndrome. It was a crime to quote ANC leaders or to pass around ANC literature. Famously, a black mechanic was condemned to prison after his boss spotted him drinking out of a mug with an ANC slogan on it. Dipuo's mother refused even to say Nelson Mandela's name.

But Dipuo suspected her fear of white authorities had also become an excuse for doing nothing. To Dipuo, her mother represented a dark irony. Through a decades-long campaign of repression, white people had managed to engineer a black population whose traits seemed to validate their own prejudice: the belief that black people were weak or sheeplike.

As Soweto turned more restive—young people roamed the streets during the day, singing liberation songs—Dipuo's mother withdrew into the shack. She became, Dipuo remembered, "obsessed with God." When Dipuo brought up politics, her mother would always reply, "God will help us. God will make things better. God loves us."

But what kind of God was this? Her mother never explained why a loving God would permit apartheid in the first place. "She did not say there was a different 'God of black people,'" Dipuo told me. "She couldn't put it like that. But she did suggest he would only help us so far, as black people. God helps black people, but only so far."

So Dipuo grew up looking up to "thugs," as she called them. A thug was anybody who made his money illegally. Since legal wealth was basically impossible to come by in Soweto, thugs had the only really nice things. They wore Converse sneakers and Dickies shirts. "If you were seen dating the biggest thug, nobody would touch you," said Dipuo. "Nobody wore beautiful clothes like you."

Since nobody could easily leave the township, the thugs mostly robbed other black people. One gang "adopted a paramilitary style," an academic observed, "raiding schools . . . and parties [and] preying on commuters on trains." Sowetan elders hated them for that. Dipuo's mother said if she ever spotted Dipuo riding in a car with a thug, she would feel she had lost an "ultimate battle."

But the thugs' bad reputation among her elders just made Dipuo feel more affection for them. Thugs broke the rules. And why shouldn't they? What were these rules?

The rules were what kept her mother cripplingly depressed and exhausted, ferrying back and forth like a slave between the township and "the kitchens." The rules were wrong, and they had to be broken. Everything in her world was upside down, and whoever was upending the order of things, however chaotically, was to be commended. When she began staying out late, flouting her mother's orders, Dipuo decided the feeling she'd grown up learning to call "fear" was really joy. To feel "fear" meant you were doing something noble. And what she'd grown up learning to call "bad" was good. To make somebody with authority angry meant you were succeeding.

4

Christo

THREE MONTHS AFTER HER HONEYMOON, Trudie realized she was pregnant. She loved pregnancy. It transformed her husband further: before he came home from the fields at night, he'd stop at a roadside stall and buy her favorite kind of chocolate. She'd be lying in bed waiting for him, and he'd sit down on the edge of the bed, break the bar up, and place the pieces onto her tongue one by one.

After laboring all night in a clinic, she delivered a boy. "He was the most beautiful thing under the sun," she remembered. "I went to the bathroom, and when I came back, they had propped him up on pillows they had packed onto my bed. He was wrapped up tight, like a little sausage. But those round eyes—I will never forget them. Even so small and short"—she laughed—"he was already beautiful."

She wondered, briefly, "what kind of person he would be"— what the world would make of him. Four years earlier, an anticolonialist postman had stabbed Prime Minister Hendrik Verwoerd to death right in South Africa's Parliament building. In 1970, a few months before Christo was born, a prominent minister, Desmond Tutu, started campaigning against apartheid overseas.

And the United Nations passed a resolution demanding other countries stop hosting South African sports teams. The International Olympic Committee expelled South Africa, which was a strangely hard blow. The Afrikaners were always looking for proof they met or exceeded the highest Western standards, and South Africa fielded a disproportionate number of Olympic medalists. Their swimmers, boxers, runners, and cyclists beat Great Britain's medal haul at the 1952 Summer Olympic Games.

Yet Trudie told me she also somehow felt unworried. At the church where she married, she had Christo baptized in the same christening robe her mother-in-law wore for her baptism sixty years earlier. Christo looked perfect, the white robe offsetting his intense, unusually dark blue eyes. At the baptism, the preacher handed Trudie a Bible. "This is all you will need," he reassured her, "to take care of him."

When Trudie brought Christo home, the farmworkers rushed to get a look. One maid named Elsie snatched him out of Trudie's hands and twirled him in the air. Elsie had five children of her own, but a few months earlier, she had lost a baby boy. It seemed to Trudie she adopted Christo as a replacement. Everyone in the family noticed Elsie seemed to develop a special affection for Christo. "There was not one thing I needed," Christo once told me, "for which I couldn't go to Elsie and she would help me."

When Trudie conceived again, her doctor told her the pregnancy was risky and prescribed bed rest. For months, Elsie took over the operations of the house. When Christo was a toddler, Elsie put him to sleep. Elsie woke him in the morning. Elsie decided how to comb his hair and what he would wear. She bathed him and observed the way his blue eyes darkened further as he aged.

When he started to speak, she noted his instinct to look on quietly instead of chatter. The rest of his family described Christo as shy. But Elsie thought differently. She thought of him as *watchful*. She observed his wish to help around the house and the way he insisted on going out into the fields to accompany her husband, who drove one of Johannes's tractors. "He loved pumpkins, potatoes, and rice," Elsie told me when we met, and smiled. "That child was *mine*."

One of Elsie's older sons, Thomas, became Christo's best friend. Over the phone, we arranged to get together at a fast-food restaurant near where he now works on a mine. At a greasy table under a wall-mounted TV blaring soccer, he actually teared up remembering Christo. "He was, from a young age, like an older man," Thomas said. Johannes gave Christo a pickup truck when he was sixteen. After Thomas admired it, Christo offered to sell it to him.

Thomas had felt shocked, then, by what felt like an act of unusual generosity from a white farmer's son. Friends of his complained that their parents' bosses' kids teased them or even beat them. "But when Christo saw I liked the truck, he wanted me to have it," Thomas said.

His smile turned playful when he talked about how he and Christo wandered Johannes's fields together at dusk, aiming their handmade slingshots at birds. On many South African farms, black workers gave their white bosses private nicknames in their languages. Sometimes, these nicknames had a scornful edge. An Afrikaner farmer I knew learned after twenty years that his workers had been calling him "Slojo" behind his back, or "oiled whetstone"—a dig at the way his prematurely bald, pale head sweated in the sun. They called his acquisitive neighbor "Makwanga," which means "*this* is mine and *this* is mine and *this* is mine."

But Thomas came to Christo one day and informed him the black kids on the farm had decided to name him "Thosho." Thomas said it meant "the one who helps the others."

That was a relief for Christo to hear. He'd always felt a little out of place in his own family. Trudie had two children after him, a boy and a girl, and both of them loved music, like their father. When the local farming community gathered for games or dances, Johannes would entertain with his "family band." He played the concertina and sang while Trudie or Christo's sister played an electronic organ. Christo's brother, Jaco, played the guitar.

When I asked Christo what instrument he played, he just winced. "Once, I played the drums," he said. "But after that, my father never asked me to join them again."

He told me he "grew up in the fields." When he wasn't hanging out with Thomas, Christo loved to wander his father's farmland alone. He'd walk its boundaries, which took an hour and a half. It felt like his *and* unknown; the trails through the brush were always a little different every time, thanks to the cattle and wild animals who persistently beat new paths through it. He'd fool around at the perimeter until dark, when the camel thorn trees faded to outlines and the crickets rose into an encompassing chorus. When he could play no longer, he'd fling himself onto his stomach and breathe. It felt like the smell of the soil replenished him, like it could be his food and water.

White South Africans of a certain age, the ones who grew up under white rule, sometimes told me—sheepishly—they felt they had "charmed" childhoods. A friend of mine grew up upper-middle-class in Johannesburg. Nobody questioned his right to take his bike after school and ride out as far as his legs would carry him, past the rings of suburban houses with their topaz swimming pools and past the black reeds that fenced the public parks into the gray hills beyond the city limits. It had all felt like his for the exploration, the private hunting grounds in which he captured fireflies and lizards and brought them home in glass jars.

Another white man told me he had a similarly "Huck Finn" boyhood. Race was almost never formally discussed in his school. Neither was the ANC. The Soweto Uprising wasn't on his 1980s school curriculum, nor was the 1962 arrest of ANC leaders at their Johannesburg safe house, Liliesleaf. I asked him what he'd learned about the history of apartheid. "Nothing," he said. "The government just tried to make it seem normal, like the air we breathed." As an example of colonialism, his curriculum prescribed the American Revolution.

Some nights, he and his mother took a stroll down their block. Only twenty years later did this man learn that they walked right past Liliesleaf. The raid there changed the course of South African history; the property is now a major museum. But when he walked past it, Liliesleaf was locked up and unlabeled. It looked just like any other suburban house, jasmine trailing sweetly off its wrought iron gate.

Christo was only five, though, when he received his first intimation his world might not be what it seemed. It came in the form of several open-backed trucks, the kind farmers used to transport cattle. Only furniture poked out of these trucks: wooden tables, gilded mirrors. The same kind of furniture his parents had in their house.

The trucks were transporting white people fleeing Angola, which liberated itself from Portuguese rule in 1975. The "refugees," as his father called them, stopped at Christo's farm for food and water.

White *refugees*? The idea was alien. When the adults around him *did* mention South African history, they vaguely implied it was a contest between good and evil with an inevitable outcome. "The whites came to South Africa and wanted a piece of land," Jaco, Christo's brother, remembered a school instructor telling the boys. "They were willing to buy it, so they were true to their word. *They* were honorable. The 'native,' however, goes back on his word. And murders people."

The refugees only stayed an hour. But the visit made a vivid impression. "They looked so sad," Christo remembered.

"Uncertain." He felt seized with fear for his own mother and father. Adults weren't supposed to look like that—so lost, so defeated. The thought of his parents heaping their belongings onto a truck and wandering the earth in search of safety gave him strange chills.

Most of the photographs Trudie hung in the farmhouse depict domestic scenes. In almost all of them, Christo looks a little somber and inscrutable—except in one Trudie laminated into her personal recipe book. In that one, he's about five years old, beaming at the camera, his blue eyes crinkled up with joy. And he's wearing a costume: a set of green mock military fatigues with a "USA" badge on the breast.

Christo developed the desire to become a soldier—specifically, a reconnaissance officer—after the refugees came through. It had as much to do with his natural temperament. Reconnaissance officers worked as military scouts, creeping behind enemy lines. He loved the idea his quietness could be an asset, not an awkward quirk. And he loved the thought of going north to protect his country—to nearby Angola, where his country was at war.

As a whole, apartheid was traveling against history. Over the course of the '50s and '60s, as more and more laws were promulgated in South Africa to bolster the white regime, other African countries were shuffling off their colonial yokes. In 1951, the Gold Coast—now Ghana—held Africa's first fully democratic vote and elected a black man its prime minister. Soon after that in South Africa, the government legislated racially segregated bathrooms and declared the ANC "illegal," banning it from recruiting members or meeting publicly. In 1965, the British colony of Bechuanaland won its independence, becoming Botswana. The next year in South Africa, the apartheid government declared a famously cosmopolitan, integrated Cape Town neighborhood a whites-only zone. In 1968, Swaziland, South Africa's neighbor, became free.

Two years later in South Africa, the government stripped black people of their citizenship. And the country geared up militarily, instituting a draft for white men.

Many black South Africans who had any resources left. Some went to Europe, but others headed for black-run Botswana, Zimbabwe, Mozambique, Zambia, and Angola, where the Umkhonto we Sizwe, the ANC's military wing, was setting up camps. The South African military pursued them to some of these places—and it did more than that in Angola.

The ANC got some money and military assistance from the Soviets; it regularly flew the Umkhonto we Sizwe leaders to Moscow to receive training. The idea that South African black liberation leaders would be backed by Moscow alarmed the apartheid regime. But it was also convenient. Even as South Africa seemed to resist a twentieth-century flow of progress toward freedom, its leaders could burnish their credentials as Western allies by stressing the "red peril" that threatened to make the African continent a communist outpost.

After its liberation, Angola had become embroiled in a civil war between pro-communist and pro-Western factions. The South African government never officially revealed it sent tens of thousands of troops to intervene in Angola, fighting for the anti-communist side. But the American Central Intelligence Agency funneled agents and funding to do so. South African politicians described both foreign black communist-aligned fighters *and* black South African liberation fighters as "terrorists."

The state-run TV channel ran an "honor roll" every Sunday night that listed the white soldiers who'd been killed in the "border war," as South Africans were calling the string of conflicts over their northern borders. At school, Christo and Jaco learned to march in formation in the fields and to clean and assemble R1 assault rifles. Sometimes, slithering on his belly through his father's farmland, Christo would imagine he was sneaking up on somebody important—on some covert meeting related to the border war. Or a mystery which, once he pieced its clues together, would save his family or his town.

This isn't an uncommon kind of boyhood fantasy. But when he was eight, a friend of his father's suggested there might be frightening things happening in his family's fields already.

The man was an army reservist. He came to dinner and sat next to Christo. Christo was incredibly excited. He confided how he liked to play soldier at the edges of the farm.

But then the man leaned down and whispered, "If you had the information *I* have, you wouldn't play like that in the fields anymore."

He went on to say terrorists had set up camp just fifty miles away in Botswana. From that base, he said, they were smuggling weapons into South Africa and planting land mines on farms like Christo's.

It was an unverified rumor. But Christo never did play in the fields quite the same way again. An impression began to take shape in his mind that what *looked* like reality—the weekend barbecues, the peaceful, misty mornings cut through by the lowing of cattle—wasn't reality. It was a sham, a flimsy screen through which the bayonet of a harsher truth—that he and his family and friends had powerful enemies—could poke at any time. Instead of wandering the fields alone, he started playing a new game with his father's workers' sons. He divided them into "the army" and "the terrorists."

He'd tell the boys to crouch on the opposing sides of a fence and pretend to shoot at each other. Because of the numbers, some of the black kids played white South African soldiers. But "what I know," Christo said, "is that *I* was never a 'terrorist.'"

5

Christo

THE IDEA OF HONOR INCREASINGLY played on Christo's mind. He always wondered how he could emulate his father, a man who brought joy to the community with his music. In school, Christo began to take on self-sacrificial roles. He was proud of his nickname—"Thosho," the one who helps the others—and he prided himself on keeping other kids' secrets. Often he refused to tattle on boys who orchestrated pranks. A teacher once caned him so hard for his secrecy the skin on his thigh tore open. His mother only found out when she came to tuck him in that night and saw he'd bled through his duvet.

In rugby, which virtually every white boy played in school, Christo sought a position called the hooker. The hooker stood in the middle of the scrum, or the pile-on formation that restarted the game after a foul. It wasn't a role mothers loved to see their sons play because, when the referee blew the whistle, a dozen meaty boys crushed in on the hooker and drove his body into the dust. But it was a crucial, martyr-ish job, which mitigated Christo's shyness. In living up to his nickname, he felt there was a destiny he had been born for.

Christo couldn't get enough of war movies and TV shows. There was *Boetie Gaan Border Toe* (*Little Brother Goes to the Border*), in which a lazy teen learns maturity through his military service, and *Grensbasies 13* (*Border Base 13*), a thriller in which a soldier, ordered to liberate a South African prisoner of war, falls in love with the prisoner's sister. Christo might have watched *Grensbasies 13* hundreds of times. Making war on terrorists began to seem necessary to activate all the most beautiful possibilities of life: the hope to be virtuous, the chance to be a hero, even the dream of love.

In August 1986, a green envelope arrived in his family's postbox. The envelope contained Christo's draft letter, assigning him to a February 1989 intake at a military base. "It's started now," he thought. The knowledge his dream was on the way to coming true made him flourish. He blossomed academically; a girl named Nicolene was the only one who could beat him in history exams.

When Christo got his letter, he had to send it back with information like his height, weight, and any illnesses. And there was a box you could check if you'd like to be considered for the Special Forces, which included the reconnaissance units. A year earlier, Angolan soldiers had captured a South African Special Forces officer, whom they were torturing in solitary confinement; his story appeared constantly in the Afrikaans-language newspapers. Being in the Special Forces was considered so dicey a conscript's father had to sign the request. Christo fought with Johannes over it; it was one of the only arguments the two men ever had.

Johannes told me he got a chill when Christo said he wanted to be considered. It felt like a premonition: that if he let him, something terrible would happen, something that would culminate with his son's name on the Sunday night honor roll. But Christo followed Johannes around the farm, begging. When Johannes relented, he told Christo grimly, "I'm signing your death sentence."

Everyone in the family remembered the February day Christo left. The night before, his father barbecued lamb chops and Trudie cooked his favorite dishes—potato salad and a liquid custard poured over cake. Christo couldn't sleep; at 4:30, he finally got out of bed, and at six the family drove to Vryburg, where a military bus awaited.

As the bus pulled off, Johannes fought a powerful urge to cry. Afrikaner men weren't supposed to cry. Whenever Johannes wept, even as a toddler, his father would shout, "Be a man!"

"When I got home, I couldn't walk, I couldn't talk," he recalled to me. "I was like a paralyzed person." The only thing that broke the spell was working on cars. "Someone brought a gearbox for me to fix, and I felt the heaviness lift."

Christo's little brother Jaco felt afraid, too. But he also felt a strange thrill, one he kept to himself. When he rode in the car with his mother, he occasionally spotted a young man in fatigues holding a thumb out on the side of the road. Trudie always made a point to stop to give such soldiers a lift. She told Jaco they'd put their young lives on hold—pawning, for a time, all the things teenage boys want, like to have fun or date girls—for the sake of protecting *her*, someone else's mother. "We always pick them up," Trudie said. It was a credo. "You stand for your land. You protect your land."

The fact that Christo went enthusiastically to military training bestowed honor on the family. Every white male had to go to boot camp, and the military chased down draft dodgers. But Jaco knew some managed to escape the draft anyway, fleeing to Europe or undertaking endless educational programs to string out academic exemptions. Catch-all terms for men like these were *verraaiers*—traitors—or *slapgatte*, literally "floppy asses." A *slapgat* was a hedonist or layabout who didn't care enough about honor.

Jaco sometimes worried he had a bit of the *slapgat* in him. He hated marching in formation at school. He only joined Christo's war games in the fields if he could spend time in the kitchen with his mother preparing the snack boxes. But at least the family had minted one unqualified non-*slapgat*. One sparkling son who lived up to the ideal of the Afrikaner. As he watched Christo's bus pull away, Jaco told me he thought: *We don't shy away from our duty*.

"But what," he added, "if your duty takes you to the wrong place? We didn't think of that."

6

Dipuo

Soon after Dipuo left school, she helped create something called a "People's Committee." People's Committees were independent groups, often run by young people, that enforced local laws behind the white-supported township councilors' backs. They adjudicated ordinary things like whether somebody's washing line was intruding on another person's yard. But they also organized political protests. By the '80s, the apartheid government had imprisoned enough ANC luminaries or forced them into exile that the ANC lacked a strong presence on the ground.

To Dipuo and her friend Gadifele, the ANC had started to seem like a group of ancient gods—prayed to, but no longer expected to show up in real life. Gadifele did get handcuffed at a protest next to the girlfriend of an imprisoned ANC leader. It was exciting. She felt like she was getting arrested alongside Mary Magdalene, someone who'd had a direct experience with divinity.

Yet on the streets, other young black people began to raise the questions atheists raise about God. Why don't the miracles the Bible describes, like resurrections or the feeding of hundreds of people with two loaves of bread, happen in real life? Can angels exist if they never seem to intervene in our problems on earth?

Because there were no adults in it, the house Gadifele shared with her brother Kgadi became one of two "People's Houses" in

Meadowlands, their Soweto neighborhood. These were headquarters for People's Committees. Dipuo took me there one day. Dusk was falling, and she wanted to get home. But just being asked to recall the late '80s enlivened her, Gadifele, and their friend Jacobetta, who'd worked with them as an activist.

The women began to act out the meetings. In the '80s, there was often a curfew in Soweto. Cops, peering in through a lit window and seeing a group of teenagers, could grow suspicious, so before the meetings started Gadifele hung heavy rugs on a curtain rail to block the light. To mimic that, Dipuo rose from the couch and pulled Gadifele's curtain shut. Then Gadifele lit a single candle on her coffee table.

That's what they did then—huddled around a single flame. The curfew disrupted their lives and abrogated their rights. Activists argued against it. But having to work around it also made them feel secretive, larger than life. Gadifele demonstrated how the candle had magnified the teens' shadows on the walls, turning the boys into men and the young women's Afros into two-foot crowns.

Kgadi, Gadifele's brother, had gotten hold of a fancy radio that picked up international frequencies. The teens tuned it to an illegal station, Radio Freedom, which aired for an hour five times a week out of black-run Zambia seven hundred miles north. Sometimes Oliver Tambo—then the head of the ANC and in exile—would speak. Other times, a DJ would play South African songs by exiled musicians—like "Mayibuye," or "Return," a song by Miriam Makeba, the South African jazz singer.

Sihlupheka phantsi kwamabhulu,
Lifikil'ixesha ngoku lenkululeko.

We have long suffered under their rule.
The time for liberation has come.

"Were you ever arrested?" I asked Dipuo.

"No, not really," she said breezily.

That wasn't true. Dipuo was arrested during protests numerous times. "But it was just the ordinary fourteen-day thing," she explained.

That's what she called getting thrown in jail: "the fourteen-day thing." Fourteen days was the length of time the apartheid government could incarcerate you without bringing a charge.

The police put protesters in jail for fourteen days as often as they could. But as much as anti-apartheid rhetoric stressed the indignities of apartheid, it was important for Dipuo and her friends to project power, and the way they could do this was to give others— and themselves—the impression the fourteen-day thing barely touched them. That to be held without charge for two weeks in a dirty, bare cell was not really a big deal. Without state-issued guns, without tanks, without the law on their side, a part of the women's power rested in defiant stoicism. If you suffered, victory lay in smiling while you endured it.

That reminded me of a small grocer I knew in Johannesburg, a sixty-five-year-old black man named Nelson. Nelson loved to talk about the past. And his stories of life under apartheid often had a strange lightness, even a sense of play. What were you going to do, be bitter all the time? There had to be a way, he told me, to make some fun out of apartheid, though he acknowledged that instinct sounded perverse.

Nelson always dreamed of being his own boss. But under apartheid, it was extremely difficult for a black man to do business. Black people weren't allowed to own most kinds of companies in the cities unless they had permits. If you hadn't been born in a certain township, you couldn't even linger there unless you carried your pass from a white employer.

That didn't stop Nelson from trying. He began to work as

an informal trader, ferrying goods between Johannesburg and the homeland where he was born. When the police stopped to ask for his "pass," he'd defiantly say he didn't have one. And then they'd arrest him and, sometimes, try to "sell" him to a farmer.

The police could do that. Farmers could request convict labor from jails, paying the wardens. The police thought black captives would fear this deal, since farmers could exploit prisoners more than ordinary laborers. So they'd dangle it as a threat—and then offer a way out: tattle on family members who worked for the ANC.

Nelson loved to see the surprise on the wardens' faces when he rejected their deal. It revealed they didn't know him, he said. They didn't know his weaknesses, and that was a kind of power he had over them. Sometimes, when he wasn't in jail, Nelson would walk in all-white parks at night. This, too, was illegal, and extremely dangerous. But testing the political system's limits thrilled him. It was the way he charted the limits of his own bravery and character.

One night, stopping to urinate in a public bathroom, he heard voices close by speaking Afrikaans. The police—and they were about to come in. Frantically, he searched for a ventilation hole to crawl out of and escape, but there wasn't one. Then he remembered he had on a hat worn by the elders in his church.

It happened to resemble the military-style brimmed felt cap some black security guards wore. No black person would ever mistake the two. His church was popular, and its vestments were well known among black people. But he thought the Afrikaners might, so he walked straight out of the bathroom door, tipped his cap to the white policemen, and walked on.

This was one of Nelson's favorite stories. He told it all the time—to his customers, to his grandsons. The joy of discovering *just what white people still didn't know about him* lifted his spirits so much he began to sing to himself in the dark.

Mayibuye!

Despite the women's precautions, policemen came to the People's House at night. Dipuo and her friends began to act out a typical scene, talking in the present tense. "They'd knock," Jacobetta said. She was frail, but she sat up straight in her chair and bellowed, like the policeman might have. "Open the door!"

"They do not always knock," Gadifele disagreed. She rose from the couch. "Sometimes, they just kick it in." She crouched down, as if hiding from a sight line, while Jacobetta flopped back against her chair and snored loudly. Then Jacobetta opened her eyes.

"They wake you up," Jacobetta said, mock-rubbing her eyes in bleary confusion.

Dipuo had been sitting next to me on a sofa. She got up, stood by the front door, and clenched her fists to play the part of the white policeman. It had felt terrifying at the time, but now Gadifele giggled as Dipuo widened her legs and squatted to mock the white policemen's stance. Dipuo strode into the living room, swiveling her hips this way and that and snatching a cushion out from under Jacobetta's bottom with a gleeful cackle. Then she raised her fist and put it into an "O" in front of one eye like a pretend flashlight.

Gadifele said the policemen would often whip pictures out of their uniform pockets. "And they ask you: Do you know this guy?"

"You have to think fast," Jacobetta whispered. She clapped a hand over her mouth. It was important not to say what came to your mind. Even if you recognized the face in the picture, "you have to act as if you have never seen him."

Or the police stormed the house, looking for weapons. If they didn't find something, they might leave something: a bug, a hidden bomb. Once, the police mailed a black lawyer—a young father—a cassette player. When he took it out of the package and pressed "play," the device exploded, killing him instantly.

Dipuo sat back down on the couch and the women became more somber. Gadifele pointed to a small framed picture of a grinning toddler in a glass display case: Mandla, her youngest brother. "That one," she murmured. During a police search, "they"—police officers—"stabbed him and he died."

After Mandla's death, Gadifele watched her brother Kgadi grow angrier. Kgadi was around when I visited the People's House. He had watched the women's conversation silently from the doorway leading to the kitchen. When Gadifele got up to make coffee, he let her slip past him, caught my eye, and gestured for me to follow him out the front door.

In the twilight, a boy on a tricycle was riding in wobbly circles in the front yard. As we watched him, Kgadi made a quiet confession. "I wanted to be like them," he said.

Strangely, the more he came to see the white policemen as enemies, he also perceived them as role models. He remembered them so well—the young white men with hard looks in their eyes and ammunition slung around their necks. Looking into their eyes, he came to believe the only thing that separated him from them—that made him a less effective defender of his people— was their weaponry. He could match their anger and their resolve. What he didn't have was the gear and the training.

Kgadi began to believe the way to battle them was to wear their clothes, to step into their identities. To carry their kinds of guns. He told Gadifele he was going to a training camp Umkhonto we Sizwe was operating in Angola. One May morning, Gadifele awoke and he was gone.

7

Christo

FIRST, THE MILITARY BUS TOOK Christo to boot camp. When he got his vaccines and his short haircut on a parade ground, he felt "the most happy," he told me, he'd felt in his whole life. Then another bus ferried him to Oudtshoorn—the village where his ancestors farmed ostriches. In the twentieth century, Oudtshoorn became home to a training base for commanding officers. Christo's boot camp performance was good enough to qualify him for officer training.

The training in Oudtshoorn was punishing. Every day his platoon marched endlessly around the base's dusty limits while pursued by giant horseflies. Christo's platoon was supposed to get a twenty-minute break between marches. But his platoon sergeant, whom he called a "sadist," sometimes didn't let his platoon break at all. The trainees slept in stiflingly hot barracks near an administrative building they nicknamed "the Kremlin." They called it that because communists were supposed to be pathologically cruel people, and so, it seemed, were their officers. The trainees called the base's top officers "the Politburo."

Seven minutes after reveille sounded at 5 a.m. each morning, the platoon sergeants would rush into the barracks to inspect each trainee's bed, on which he'd laid out his belongings in a specific order: razor, shaving cream, toothpaste, toothbrush, soap bar,

Bible. If he got it wrong, his whole platoon had to do push-ups. If a trainee lagged during a drill, an officer would make him run around cradling rocks in his arms for three hours until he collapsed. Outdshoorn was hot for much of the year, and these disciplinary sessions could be so intense an ambulance was on call in case of heatstroke.

"I don't even know the correct word" for the punishment, Christo said grimly. "You got fucked up. They did stuff to break you. They were playing with your mind."

And yet Christo also loved Oudtshoorn. He loved the austerity of it. The reality Christo saw around him growing up—the apparent peace, the relative prosperity—seemed unsettlingly distant from the Afrikaner origin myth. Africa was supposed to be tough, a proving ground. Christo felt he was being purified in Oudtshoorn, distilled to some essence through choking down the horrible food and enduring the humiliation and physical pain. He was being permitted to see behind a veil—behind the stage set most people had to accept as reality.

The truth was harder. But somebody had to police the boundary between the truth and the lie. Thomas had not named him Thosho, "the one who helps others," for nothing. He would do it.

Other times, Christo privately sensed aspects of his military training were a little much. Later, at another base, a commander hung a diagram on the blackboard depicting the ANC's hierarchy. "KNOW YOUR ENEMY," the chart said in all-caps. At the top was Nelson Mandela's name—though, by then, Mandela had been in prison for twenty years.

Christo's superiors told him he might spend years undercover taking covert photographs of ANC safe houses or gathering information on the sly, and they asked him to create an alias. But they gave him little guidance as to how to do it other than to concoct names for a fake father, a fake mother, and fake best friends. That seemed a little ill-thought-out, as if somebody in the Politburo watched a James Bond movie and tried to copy it. Christo came up with the alias "Charles James Dalton," a cattle farmer. The comic thing was that "Dalton" was of English heritage, but Christo could barely speak English. His efforts were tainted by a heavy Afrikaans accent. In any real-world situation, the alias would never fly.

His superiors approved nonetheless. Christo laughed with his friends about how puffed-up his instructors could seem, as if they were strategizing for a war whose absolute intensity and ruthless terms existed principally in their own heads.

Instead of making him cynical, though, the faint ridiculousness of some of the training made Christo feel more affectionate toward it, in the way some people love most the family member who's the hardest to deal with. Dealing with that person makes them aware of their own strength and capacity for reason—makes them feel generous and strong. And anyway, in life, we are often most urgently pressed to find a way to justify the efforts we make that are most ridiculous or wasted. Oudtshoorn's drudgery made the few pleasures Christo encountered feel sweeter. Like the shared, secret jokes about the Politburo or the time he got dumped by Ichelle, a girl he'd started seeing before he left the farm.

Ichelle had written him a perfunctory "Dear John" letter. When he read it, he felt shocked and dismayed. But his platoon-mates went to great lengths to console him. They pulled his mattress off his bed, placed the offending letter on top of it, and lifted it up like a coffin, bearing it out of the barracks like pallbearers and burying it—the symbol of his hopes for romance—in a field while singing funeral dirges. Christo couldn't help but laugh. Their prank punctured the spell of his grief.

He fell in love with *them*, the other soldiers. I used to talk to Christo in the office where he now works as a lawyer, and he'd frequently pull a manila envelope containing photographs out of his desk. Its edges were dark and greasy, as if it had been handled hundreds of times. "Danie Langer," he said affectionately, pointing out a blurry figure in an image of young men in fatigues. "I never saw him without that shirt. And look at Raath!" He giggled.

Raath was his sadistic platoon sergeant. But Christo even felt affection for him, in retrospect—for the experience of dealing with that crazy Neanderthal. "Look. He had such a heavy brow-bone."

The climax of his officer training was called *vasbyt*. It's both a noun and a verb, like the English word "party," but it loosely translates to something like "bite hard and hold on." It reflects an action you see in the South African wilderness when a small animal, like a meerkat, threatened by a larger predator, jumps at its adversary's leg and just refuses to let go. It's a spirit the Afrikaners liked to see in themselves—an unwillingness to give up, or even an impulse to rush toward tough situations.

In officer training school, *vasbyt* referred to an experience three months in. Near Oudtshoorn stands one of South Africa's most forbidding mountains. Sentried by stinging plants, its knife-sharp boulders could shear you in half if you stumbled. Its heat at midday popped thermometers. The Afrikaner village in the valley beyond was just named "Hell."

For three days, Christo's commanders made his platoon hike the mountain draped in every possible piece of their gear: assault rifles, heavy boots, and seventy-pound backpacks stuffed with cans of food. The young men sweated so much that, by late afternoon, their uniforms became waterlogged; at night, as the temperature plummeted, walking felt more like wading upstream in a freezing river.

"It separated the wheat from the chaff," Christo told me. "Who was leadership material and who was not. Who was strong and who was not. Who could stay and who could not." Christo felt desperately worried about his performance. But on the third day, as he struggled up a rise, he came upon a brilliant view of the town of Oudtshoorn—its red-roofed houses and white churches nestled into rocky hills. One of his superiors handed him a cup of beer, and he realized he had made it.

The officers had designed *vasbyt* to end with that vista. "This is the reason why we are doing all this," one officer said, gesturing out toward the town. It hadn't been clear why hauling seventy pounds of canned food was preparation for anything useful. But, suddenly, Christo felt he got it. His family came from Oudtshoorn. They'd built it, in a way, though nobody was an architect. They'd sustained it just by having faith in it.

It looked so vulnerable from that height. Life in small towns could be absorbing, but from the cliff he saw just how tiny these towns were, how improbable. Places like that, he felt, needed defenders with a kind of final loyalty. A willingness to do things that sometimes went past rationality.

That first cup of beer, Christo remembered, tasted like "the sweetest nectar. And you're so fucked up from *vasbyt* that you're drunk after a cup." His family in Africa: he'd been deemed worthy of protecting it.

8

Christo

CHRISTO'S DREAM WAS TO FLY straight to Angola. He knew Soviet allies, like Cuba, were helping the Angolan government. He considered himself a fighter for democracy. The real TV footage from the border looked like something out of the movies he'd loved: helicopters tearing through the underbrush while men in camouflage camped out beneath camel thorn trees.

Soon after Christo completed *vasbyt*, his sergeant told him and his platoon-mates to pack their bags and wait for their plane. The men waited a day and a night on the tarmac. It was the beginning of winter, and Christo struggled to sleep. But the stars were beautiful, the wind was quiet, and he contemplated all he was leaving and all he wanted to come home to.

The next morning, though, a commander showed up to the tarmac and told the young men their cargo plane wasn't coming. Planes like that—to take men to the border—would never come to Oudtshoorn again, he said. The whole time Christo had been training, it turned out "the war had actually stopped."

By the late '80s, many people in the higher echelons of the apartheid government realized the regime couldn't sustain itself much longer. The Organization of Petroleum Exporting Countries had long prohibited its members from exporting oil to South

Africa; Iran flouted the embargo, but it, too, stopped sending oil after the 1979 Iranian Revolution.

In 1982, the ANC recruited a captivating young preacher to run a new mineworkers' union. The preacher's signature sermon was called "The Trial of Trials," about the guilt incurred by those who killed Jesus; alarmed, the white authorities prohibited him from delivering it. But as union leader, he quickly enrolled more than half the mines' black workforce. The strikes he called were crippling the economy. And, as awareness of apartheid grew overseas, foreign lenders insisted on giving South Africa shorter and shorter-term loans. These were less likely to be publicized and to be an embarrassment. But the pressure to repay them was crushing.

Then Europe and America imposed economic sanctions on South Africa. A friend of mine was the government aide responsible for presenting economic data to the South African president. He recalled the 1987 day the two strings on his presentation chart "crossed," with the "debt" string outpacing the "growth" one.

He didn't say it out loud. But he knew, in that moment, apartheid was over.

In the political sphere, Eastern Europeans were revolting against their repressive communist regimes. Perestroika had begun in the Soviet Union. If the communist bloc weakened or dissolved, that would pose a big strategic problem for South Africa. Western governments condemned apartheid publicly. But behind the scenes, some of them still substantially assisted white-run South Africa insofar as it represented itself as a bulwark against communism. I remember talking to a former U.S. diplomat about the West's secret support of South Africa. "Even France, throughout the '70s, was selling [South Africa] advanced weapons," he recalled—tens of millions of dollars' worth of them, routed through Chile to circumvent sanctions. "Every Western power that criticized white South Africa was so hypocritical." The United Nations had a mandatory arms embargo against South Africa, but many U.N. member states had paid it little heed. The American government also sold South Africa missiles, rationalizing it internally by noting the apartheid regime's animosity toward Moscow. The decline of communism would strip away that rationale, leaving no excuse for anyone to support South Africa besides a naked affection for white supremacy.

In late 1985, the apartheid minister of justice began to meet with Mandela in secret in prison, effectively beginning negotiations toward majority rule. Two years later, a group of liberal white politicians, anti-apartheid journalists, and white businessmen—deeply alarmed by the economic sanctions—arranged a series of secret meetings with top ANC leaders starting in Dakar, Senegal. These meetings were nicknamed the "Dakar Safaris." At one meeting with white elites, Thabo Mbeki, an ANC exile, broke the ice in the hotel bar by cracking a joke. "Yes, here we are, the terrorists," he told the white men, grinning broadly while pouring them glasses of Scotch. "And, for all you know, fucking communists, too!"

After a second, everybody dissolved into belly laughs. It was like checking for the monster under the bed you'd been afraid of your whole childhood and finding nothing there. For one white journalist, it was incredible to consider all the problems he'd been told were intractable—like the black desire for vengeance and the unbridgeable cultural gulf between black and white people—might be overcome over a couple of whiskies. The hope of the Enlightenment, a philosopher once wrote, was that it would eventually reveal that all of our enemies—from sickness to misunderstanding—were "no more than phantoms of our own conjuring." The Dakar Safaris felt like that: the implosion of demons just at the moment you dare to look at them.

By the middle of the '80s, the South African military apparatus consumed 20 percent of the national budget. One of the easiest steps the apartheid government could take toward dismantling itself was to end the costly "border war." And so one minute, the South African government was rebuffing U.N. efforts to mediate and sending fresh waves of soldiers to Angola. The next, the government was accepting international mediation and pulling all its troops out. A conflict that flared for more than a decade, and which had seemed so existential to Christo as to likely be eternal, was wrapped up in less than a year.

Christo hadn't known, though, that any of this was happening. "We were—how would you say it? Stunned," he told me. Christo hadn't been told white South African elites were privately reversing their opinion of the dangers posed by communism and black liberation. He wasn't told that on the tarmac, either. Instead, the commander who came to fetch Christo and his platoon-mates told them something different. Something chilling.

"There's an even more severe threat *in* the country now," he said. "It's within our own borders, and we need to sort it out." It was permeating South African cities and suburbs, he went on. "The threat is amongst ourselves."

Six months later, a sergeant major came to visit Christo's base. He was "a serious man," Christo remembered. "He made a strong impression, one of authority. You got the sense you could trust him. He was a black guy, but that didn't matter." The man told Christo that if he wanted to do serious reconnaissance work— if he wanted an ultimate challenge—he could join a special unit called the 32 Battalion.

The 32 Battalion was an unusual corps comprised of a few dozen top white officers and seven hundred black soldiers recruited from Angola's long-running civil war. Ranging in age from their late teens to their fifties, some of these men had been forced to kill people while they were still children. That made them appealing recruits. The conflict they experienced had raged for so long that many of them—unlike South African farm boys such as Christo—seemed inured to brutal violence.

Christo badly wanted an ultimate challenge. So he traveled to the 32 Battalion's base in a town called Pomfret, ninety miles farther into the Kalahari from his father's farm. The base had been rapidly assembled after the unit pulled out of Angola. Because it was designed from scratch, it resembled a Monopoly board for Afrikaner heroism: its streets were named for famous South African military commanders; its rugby field was enormous. And the training there was even more extreme.

Some mornings, a helicopter dropped Christo thirty miles away in the desert and he had to creep back to the base without being spotted while a "tracker platoon" of Angolan soldiers tailed him. He was given crackers as sustenance, but halfway through the walks, he'd discover they were inedible; his commanders had soaked them in gasoline. The Angolans teased Christo, challenging him to foot races. "You could never beat them," Christo said. One refugee had acquired the nickname "No Drink Water" because the only liquid he seemed to need was alcohol.

Christo was quick to pick up Portuguese. He kept dozens of photographs that show him with three Angolans nicknamed Mamba, Ngoma, and Joaquim Cabinda. In one of them, Christo sits atop an armored vehicle while Joaquim Cabinda perches on his haunches beside him. In another, Mamba nestles his head affectionately against Christo's shoulder.

Christo didn't think of himself as racist. Shortly before he joined it, the South African military incorporated colored soldiers into the white soldiers' camps. He became close to a colored officer-in-training at Oudtshoorn. On their way back from another base, they stopped at a beach together; at one point, they tried to enter a bar. Christo hadn't thought about the fact that it was a white bar. But the bar owner refused his friend entry.

"He's willing to die alongside me," Christo thought angrily, "so why not drink alongside me?" Christo chewed the owner out in front of his patrons, bought beers for himself and his friend, and brought them out to the sand to drink while watching the sunset.

The white commanders at Pomfret, though, used the term "total onslaught" to refer to what black South Africans planned for white people. They said black people's fundamental goal was to hurt civilians. White men didn't do that, the commanders stressed. They followed "proper rules" of conflict engagement, only targeting combatants. ANC militants, on the other hand, did things like burn tires on highway off-ramps or stow bombs under tables at fast-food restaurants, killing women and children, even their fellow black people.

Christo was taught how to cover his body in black paint to "blend in" with black South Africans. Sometimes, a 32 Battalion officer would lock Christo in a cage and tell the Angolans to spit on him. "This is how *they*"—black South Africans—"will do it," the officer would shout.

During his reconnaissance training, Christo also had to study photography. He showed me some of the pictures he'd taken for practice. He was supposed to be honing long-range photography skills with a telephoto lens.

But almost all the images he showed me were close-ups of Nicolene, the girl who'd beaten him in his high school history exams. On a break from training, he happened to travel to her college town and met up with her and her friends. In one of the photos, Nicolene fiddles with her hair. In another, she angles her shoulder away from the lens and looks back at Christo with coy, searching eyes. The pictures were so achingly tender that I wondered if Christo had ever felt ambivalent about his training. If he'd ever wished he could get away to college, to dating—to a more ordinary, domestic life.

When I asked, though, Christo's jaw just tightened. He shoved the photos of Nicolene back into his desk drawer. "I just wanted to do my job," he said.

9

Dipuo

As an activist, Dipuo told herself her mission was to "kill every white person I saw." Lots of activists took on war-style aliases; hers was "Stalin." "I hated whites," she said frankly, when I asked her about the name. "I would have killed any white person if I had seen one. They deserved to die. If you threatened our freedom, you did not deserve to live."

But that wasn't easy. Imprisoned in Soweto, she almost never saw white people. So she and her People's Committee directed their energies toward rooting out black collaborators with the white regime, whom they called *impimpis*, or "spies."

"We had a store called Maponya," Dipuo recalled. Richard Maponya was a prominent Soweto businessman. In the '50s, he'd started a series of grocery stores. One was a half-hour walk from Meadowlands, Dipuo's Soweto neighborhood. When Dipuo was seventeen, her People's Committee began to use it as a secret meeting place.

In the absence of on-the-ground leadership from the ANC, they picked up tactics from the war and spy movies that aired on the state television channel. One was to gather discreetly over the course of a day so the police wouldn't realize a planned meeting was happening. But one evening, as Dipuo's People's Committee reconnoitered outside Maponya's shop, a sniper shot and killed one of their members.

Dipuo was furious. Who told somebody they were activists, assembling for an illegal political meeting? "We decided there and then," she said, "that Maponya was a spy."

In the '80s, the townships and the homelands developed a dark complexity. You didn't always know who was a friend and who was an enemy. "There was so much mistrust, then, between black people," Gadifele told me sadly.

The night her brother Kgadi left for Angola, a group of police officers came to the People's House. They showed Kgadi's photograph to Gadifele and her younger brother Direlo. "Someone who knew Kgadi must have tipped off the police that he was headed for the training camps," Gadifele thought. Whoever it was probably "thought the Afrikaners would give him money."

Gadifele had already warned Direlo, who was only fifteen, that if this happened, they would have to disown their brother in their own minds. In the space of a few seconds, they'd have to convince themselves, internally, that they'd never loved their brother so they could effectively convince a policeman. When the policeman lifted her brother's photograph, she smothered her recognition with the instant thought: *This man is not your brother. You have never before seen his face.*

"We don't know this person," she brightly told the cop.

He gave her a look, then glanced at Direlo. "Well, if he comes here," the policeman said, "invite him in and follow him."

Gadifele had been lying in bed with Direlo, a blanket pulled up tightly around both of their chins. The policeman leaned down and inserted a bill worth $5 in between Gadifele's clenched knuckles. "Then you will get more."

After the police came to look for Kgadi, Gadifele worried Direlo might begin to distrust her. She felt anxious that he thought the reason the police showed up was because "Gadifele has already told them something."

I had a friend named Elliot who grew up in a homeland. In the '70s his father, Elias, attained a supervisory position on an asbestos mine. Elias handed out the miners' headlamps when their shifts began and checked them back in when they were finished. That meant he worked aboveground, in an airy storeroom, and there was a status divide on the mines between those who worked underground and those who got to work in the light. Unfortunately, one of the men who came to work underground was white.

That technically ranked him below Elias. "And that white person," Elias reckoned, "was not feeling good about that. He was jealous." He taunted Elias, failing to turn back in his headlamp—a lapse he knew administrators would blame on Elias—and, other times, dancing a strange, provocative circle around Elias in the storeroom. Elias recounted for me his thought process at the time. "They bring in this white person. He doesn't know anything about this mine. He comes from zero knowledge. Me, as a black person, I know the mine jobs very well. But I also know that now I'm going to be compelled to teach him how to do *my* job. And then, at the end of the day, he will become my supervisor and lash out at me: 'Go and do this. Why haven't you done this?' But *I* will have been the one who taught *him*." The next time the white man did the taunting dance, Elias snapped, punching him so hard he fell unconscious to the floor.

A black man who hit a white man at that time was in deep trouble. Elias fled into the mountains, drinking from streams and tucking himself into the erosion ditches called *dongas*. He hid for two whole days until a policeman shouted his name, commanding him to emerge from the *donga* where he was hiding. When he did, he saw his captor was not white, but black.

The majority of policemen in the late '80s were actually black. Many black South Africans found work with the white regime or the puppet governments in the homelands. Speaking with Elias and Elliot, I was intrigued by how many different modes of engaging with the white regime could exist within a single family. A milestone in their family's lore was the day one of Elias's four wives got arrested for the "crime" of brewing traditional sorghum beer. The apartheid government had made that illegal as an excuse to raid black homes for weapons. After she was caught, the police forced her to do four months of heavy labor cutting sisal, a type of agave used to make twine. She spoke about white people with anger the rest of her life.

On the other hand, Elliot said black men who worked for white police commanders were often treated with respect. Civilians suspected of ratting out local ANC underground activists were condemned, but, paradoxically, those who *officially* worked for the white state could be honored. Power was power. Even dark power conveyed allure.

One particularly handsome black policeman stationed near his house, Elliot remembered, was named Lebara. The whole family esteemed him. "Lebara was a person with a high profile," Elliot said. "He was much better than us." When I asked him to elaborate, Elliot told me Lebara "got all the women." Even after apartheid ended, Elias and his family treasured the invitations they got to eat at Lebara's house.

Lebara was also the police officer who'd arrested him.

First, Dipuo's People's Committee announced a boycott of Maponya's shop. Such boycotts became common in Soweto in the late '80s. Since it took a permit from the white government to run a grocery, in the search for collaborators, People's Committees often targeted such shop owners. "Nobody was allowed to buy" at Maponya's grocery, Dipuo remembered. When shoppers emerged, she and her friends would grab their bags and dump their contents into the dirt.

But it didn't feel like enough. Dipuo was so angry about her friend's death. So, she said, "we burned that shop."

The People's Committee gathered again outside Maponya's shop—this time, carrying jugs of gasoline. As midnight approached, they threw the gasoline over the stoop, lit matches, and tossed them in. "When the shop caught fire, it burned so quickly," Dipuo remembered. In the space of forty minutes, nothing was left but the foundation, offering a newly stark vista over the rest of the township. She'd seen an uninterrupted view like that from only one place before: the top of the hundred-foot-high slag heap that cordoned Meadowlands off from Johannesburg's downtown. Dipuo's friends called the heap "Rand Mine" for a company that ran a gold dig nearby.

Soweto's streets—which were mostly numbered, not named— were a cramped grid with intersections marked only by lone, too-small garbage bins, and there were almost no trees. Her neighbors had tried to create a more natural look by heaping rocks at the intersections to serve as benches on which women operated hair salons or men sat to throw dice in the dust.

But Rand Mine was different. Dipuo sometimes climbed it at night to be by herself. The summit was a weird idyll. Ten-foot reeds provided cover from the wind and glades of volunteer olive trees concealed magical surprises: a pop of blue-raspberry-lollipop-colored flowers; a slick of emerald grass. People said you could see all the way to Pretoria, South Africa's capital. That wasn't quite true. But at midnight, when the coal smoke had mostly dissipated, you *could* see so many white neighborhoods, their lights glowing like the beacons of fishing skiffs out on an open sea.

Elliot had mixed feelings about Dipuo's style of anti-apartheid activism. "The ANC comrades were really contributing" to the liberation struggle, he said, by confronting the white police. As a child in the mid-'80s, Elliot remembered running in terror from white policemen who would "beat you to hell" if you were found nosing around the shops in a nearby white village.

"But," he added, "the problem was, the activists were *also* positioning themselves like those police." Some of the People's Committees ran their own trials for murderers, thieves, and rapists, with legalistic pomp. "If you stole something, the comrades could cut off your hand. If they found you guilty, you would really learn something. You'd end up in a wheelchair. You would have to run away if you did anything they didn't like. I'm telling you, you would have to run and run from them and never stop."

To Dipuo, though, it felt as if black South Africans had been engaging in protests that could feel so hollowly symbolic. Mounting bus boycotts that only got their participants jailed. Organizing peaceful mine strikes and discovering that the white regime could always bus poorer, more desperate black men in from farther-flung places, even from foreign countries like Mozambique.

The conflagration that leveled Maponya's shop was unsettling. But it felt breathtaking, too, even awe-inspiring. Dipuo felt a raw shock at the exercise, finally, of physical power. The vistas from Rand Mine were an accidental gift, bestowed on her unintentionally by white people. The clarity in the air after Maponya's shop burned, however, was something she had made.

In July 1988, a bomb exploded at a Soweto meeting of politicians who collaborated with the white regime. That September and October, forty more bomb attacks throughout the country targeted other collaborators. At least ten thousand black South Africans are believed to have perished at the hands of other black South

Africans between 1987 and 1992; two leading South African criminologists estimate that in the early '90s, the country's murder rate
was "almost or entirely without peer" in the entire world.

Gadifele's other little brother, Direlo, actually died in this violence. "Direlo didn't have a history," Gadifele told me when I met
her. By that, she meant he was too young to have gotten as caught
up as she and Kgadi had in the anti-apartheid struggle. He seemed
to avoid politics. And then, when he was eighteen, he fell in love
with a woman who lived in Katlehong.

Katlehong was the Johannesburg township most affected
by internal violence. Northeast of Soweto, it was created when
Soweto ran out of space. In the '60s, it acquired a somewhat burnished image; jazz heroes came from there. But in the early '90s
it erupted. An academic researcher who interviewed Katlehong
residents in the 2000s found they were still haunted by "desperate stories of running a gauntlet" of gun-wielding teens to get to
work. "I did not want to fight, that is not in my personality," one
interviewee said. "But I found myself carrying weapons because I
had to. Who was supposed to fight for me? I am a man, and I had
to fight for my life."

Direlo's love affair "was strange to watch," Gadifele said. She
wasn't used to seeing young men her age driven by something
other than the struggle for racial justice. The poetry he gushed
about his beloved served as a faint rebuke to the way she, Kgadi,
and Dipuo had suppressed their own crushes. They told themselves that to dwell on love in a township was not only unseri-
ous but impossible, so joyless were their circumstances. As long
as apartheid persisted, they were consigned to live dull or bitter
lives—or *had* to live them, actually, in order to prove apartheid's
injustice.

Direlo's feelings undermined that conviction. If he could fall
deeply in love in *Katlehong*, a grimmer township than Soweto,
then was it true what Gadifele and Dipuo told themselves? That

township life stripped black people of their humanity—and, perhaps, that their circumstances forgave them for acting brutally, like they had when they burned Maponya's shop?

But his love was also inspiring. Gadifele loved listening to Direlo talk about his love affair. His deep enchantment defied white people's claim the black soul was somehow stunted. "He was a man in love," Gadifele repeated a couple of times, shaking her head and smiling.

Direlo bought a car to visit his lover. But as he stopped at a gas station one night on his way into Katlehong, "shots were fired," a witness told Gadifele later that night. Direlo was "caught in the crossfire" and died instantly.

The three-year-old who rode a tricycle around Gadifele's front yard while I talked to Kgadi? That was Direlo's grandson. Direlo hadn't even learned his lover was pregnant when he was killed.

Gadifele showed me Direlo's funeral program. She still keeps a copy in a Tupperware container in her living room display case. The cardstock was as stiff and its fragrance as woody as if it had been printed yesterday.

In life, Direlo might not have had "a history." But he had been assigned one in death. In recognition of the violence that martyred him, Gadifele had printed, on the cover, a Portuguese battle slogan black Angolans used before they liberated their country. *A luta continua*, it went. The fight carries on.

10

Christo

Katlehong was the first place Christo's 32 Battalion unit got deployed. His superiors told him he was heading there as a "peace-keeper." But immediately, he found it cripplingly difficult to feel and perform as he'd hoped he might. The deployment often felt weirdly boring. His platoon was housed in metal hangars just outside the township, and some days he'd wait inside all day with no orders, just sweating in his uniform like a fish baking in foil. He arrived right before Christmas. "Outside the base, I could see people dressed nice, carrying presents," he told me. "I actually longed for that. But I couldn't have it."

One of his early briefs was to put on blackface and find whoever had been shooting from inside an old miners' dormitory. Walking toward the dorm, he heard a noise that confused him. "Remember when you were a kid and you got those paper caps?" he told me. "The ones that made a little gunpowder pop?" It sounded like that. Christo was disturbed to find he didn't recognize the sound of live rounds when they were trained *at* him, although he'd handled ammunition all the time.

Soon he was under a shower of gunfire. He heard bullets *pff*-ing in the dust by his ankles and tearing leaves apart in the trees. The Angolan walking ahead of him fell to the ground. Desperately, Christo radioed for a "hot extraction." This was when an armored vehicle came in and visibly pulled soldiers out, blowing their cover.

A hot extraction meant the mission was a failure. Back at the remote base, Christo took responsibility, suggesting he might have been the one who gave the group away—though he knew it was probably the soldier who had collapsed in fear. Some of his Angolan friends said black people walked with a different roll of the hips. Maybe, Christo offered, he'd failed to "walk like a black man."

But the truth was he had also been terrified—and ashamed that he felt terrified. He'd expected fear, intellectually. But this was a visceral, gut-wrenching fear, the kind that makes you want to drop to your knees and put your hands behind your head and surrender to anybody, anybody, just to make the gunfire and the running-around and the chaos stop.

The way Christo tried to manage his subsequent missions was to put himself in a kind of trance. Sometimes he felt he was floating through the township in slow motion, scanning, disinterested in anything except the silver flash of a gun. The problem was that such a flash could be anywhere. He was not facing a traditional uniformed enemy. Many afternoons, Katlehong's streets filled up with kids in burgundy uniforms coming home from school; they laughed and tossed candy packets back and forth while, in the waning sun, women hawked bunches of green spinach and colorful flip-flops at wooden stalls. Sometimes the place could look cunningly bucolic. He'd been told a gun could be poking out of the children's backpacks or under the crooked arm of a grandmother sweeping her front steps. When he complained about the complexity of identifying his true enemy to a commanding officer, the officer just told him tersely, "Shoot the ones who need to be shot."

He was aware he was beginning to associate danger with any black face. The most enjoyable part of his stay at the Katlehong remote base was when Thomas came to visit. "They called me from the gate and said, 'Look, there's an informant here for you,'" Christo remembered. "When I get out, I see it's Thomas!" He was giddy at the memory. "He was looking me up."

He believed Thomas had come out of simple friendship. Actually, Trudie had asked Thomas to go check up on Christo. Frequently, she couldn't even reach him. Whenever Trudie would try to call him at Pomfret, the soldier who answered the phone would just say, "He's not here."

"Where is he?" she would ask.

"Auntie, he's just gone," he would reply curtly—and then with an almost smug satisfaction: "We can't tell you where he is."

As a civilian and a black South African, Thomas wasn't allowed into the hangars. But Christo sat with him by the gate and Thomas called him by his old name, Thosho. Christo had never felt more relieved to hear that word.

He said he worried Katlehong was "making me racist." On one mission, he remembered, "we found one guy, his head was cut open. His brains were on the concrete. And there were children playing around it. There were people around, but it didn't seem like they were troubled by what they saw." He had the thought, "It is only animals who do this kind of thing." One morning, he was sent into Katlehong to stand between two gigantic groups of men waving sharpened sticks.

His army superiors said they were members of two tribes having it out and his aim was to prevent the factions from attacking each other. This time, Christo was wearing a full uniform and a helmet. But "there were hundreds of them." Pinned between the groups, equally afraid to shoot and to lower his rifle, he remembered thinking: "If they want to kill me, they can just kill me."

And then: "Somebody is going to get hurt in Katlehong. And if somebody has to get hurt, it should be *them*."

Them. When I got to South Africa, I was struck by the way almost all white South Africans, even self-identified progressives, used that word to describe black people. One friend, a left-wing political activist, woke up one morning to find his car was stolen. He called me in a fury. "*They* stole my car!" he screamed.

"You know who did it?" I asked.

"No," he said, sounding perplexed. "What do you mean?" It went without saying there was a *they* out there, waiting to strip him of his things, and it also went unspoken this *they* were black people. He didn't have to know who'd stolen his car, specifically. It had never occurred to him it was a strange thing to say.

It wasn't only Christo who began to develop an antipathy toward the residents of Katlehong. I met a black South African who lived there at the same time Christo patrolled it. Wally Mbhele went on to become a prominent newspaper editor; a broad-chested man, he met me in his office in a blue pinstriped shirt whose crispness contrasted with his loose and jowly face. He greeted me with a smile; at the beginning of the conversation we laughed heartily.

As soon as we turned to Katlehong, though, his look grew distant, as if forced to contemplate something transfixing which he also didn't want to look at. "I had loved the idea of going to live in Katlehong," Mbhele told me sadly.

He'd had a relatively quiet childhood in a small, mountainous homeland, chasing his father's sheep up remote peaks. When he enrolled at a black-only university, he got involved in the campus Black Consciousness movement. Young women and men would sing at meetings, anticipating the day black people got their country back. At twenty-one, he got a job as a cub reporter for an anti-apartheid newspaper in Johannesburg. Many of its staffers lived in a hip, integrating neighborhood near a politically progressive university; white people there had begun to sign leases on behalf of black renters as a form of political protest. But Mbhele wanted to live in a township. His Black Consciousness mentors described townships as places where people were waging the most idealistic battles.

So he moved to Katlehong. Less than two weeks into his time there, though, the township exploded. The apartheid government's line had always been that black people were primitives who, given the opportunity, would butcher each other. Before Mbhele's eyes, it seemed to be coming true.

He began to cover the violence for the newspaper. One morning, he and a photographer went to a squatter camp. An opposing faction had "arrived in the middle of the night" and slaughtered the camp's inhabitants, including women and children, he told me. "We walked over piles of bodies."

He struggled to figure the violence out. Some people were calling it "taxi violence," chalking it up to "thuggishness" by the men who owned minibus taxis. Others declared it "the ANC-Inkatha rivalry," for an ethnically Zulu political party that was trying to challenge the ANC's dominance among black people, sometimes violently.

But all that couldn't account for even a fraction of what Mbhele was seeing. Practically everybody Mbhele met in Katlehong had a gun—and often not an ordinary pistol but a semiautomatic rifle. "The way this thing developed, it became suspicious that it was political," Mbhele said. "You didn't know where such heavy rifles came from. Only a fool would not realize there was a hidden hand behind this thing."

"A hidden hand?" I asked.

"The government," he said, his mouth twisting into a bitter smile.

In the final years of the white regime, long after its leaders knew they were giving up power, some in the government helped inflame the "black-on-black violence" by smuggling arms to black people. The idea was to win concessions in a negotiated transfer of power—and to make a final statement about black people's capacity to lead. If white elites had to step down, they were at least going to try to ensure some doubt would linger in everyone's minds about whether they had been right in their original adjudication that black people were too barbaric to run a stable country.

And then the government sent in the white-led military to do "peacekeeping" to prove, Mbhele said, that only "these people"—white people—"can save us from the mayhem that is our daily black lives."

Throughout our conversation, Mbhele managed to speak evenly. Only when I mentioned F. W. de Klerk, South Africa's last white president, did he allow himself a burst of anger. De Klerk won the Nobel Peace Prize in 1993, along with Mandela, for helping shepherd the transition to democracy. "But I will never say he deserved it," Mbhele spat, wiping tears from his eyes. "I will never forgive him."

Never forgive De Klerk for what his regime did to his countrymen. But most of all, never forgive him for what he did to *him*, Wally Mbhele. For the doubts De Klerk sowed in his own mind about his decency as a black man.

One morning in Katlehong, Mbhele became aware *he* was in danger. Sitting alone in a minibus taxi, he noticed the driver was looking at him strangely. A lump showed in the driver's sock: a gun.

The fact that Mbhele suspected, by then, that the white government was behind the township violence didn't ameliorate the raw fear he felt at the sight of an armed black man. He still fears black minibus taxi drivers, decades later.

After apartheid's end, Mbhele moved to a formerly white neighborhood. In pubs, he sometimes encountered white men who served in the apartheid police or army, and occasionally they'd fall into conversation. He didn't expect *them* to be haunted.

But they were. They'd tell him they had nightmares about Katlehong—nightmares whose violence bled into their everyday lives. Cruelly, Mbhele said he realized, the late-stage violence the white government fomented also "taught the white guys that black people were savages just at the moment they were going to have to be ruled by them."

11

Dipuo

ON A WEDNESDAY MORNING IN early February 1990, Dipuo heard a rumor. De Klerk had taken over after his predecessor suffered a stroke, and he seemed determined to shift the country's position. He'd already rolled back the law prohibiting the ANC from meeting in public. Now people were whispering he was about to release Mandela from jail.

Mandela. Dipuo and her comrades had doubted the ANC. But they had never entirely broken faith, and especially not with Mandela. His name cropped up all the time in their freedom song lyrics. He'd been the ANC's golden boy before his imprisonment—young and eloquent, simultaneously poised and pugnacious. Over his twenty-seven-year incarceration, his stature had, in some ways, grown. His absence meant he was one of the only black leaders who seemed totally pure. Nobody could question his decision to, say, call off a mine strike, because he wasn't making decisions.

After De Klerk unbanned the ANC, *Time* magazine immediately released an age-progressed cover image of Mandela. It only served to highlight just how insane the idea was that he would return to public life. The image looked like a fifty-year-old Muhammad Ali, as if the editors couldn't visualize any other kind of black champion.

Every night that week, Dipuo went to the People's House to listen to Kgadi's radio. The chatter on the street was getting louder. And then, on Sunday evening, the DJ reported that black South Africans were streaming in from Cape Town's outlying townships and converging on its Grand Parade.

The Grand Parade was Cape Town's white heart—a bustling commercial square designed to feel like a European plaza. For decades, white soldiers paraded beneath a City Hall made of limestone imported from England and white *madams* trotted the cobblestones buying fruit and flowers at a flea market. But incredibly, Dipuo and Gadifele heard the DJ say the next day Mandela would be driven to that white place, ascend a dais, and address a crowd that included *black* people.

At those words, Dipuo flew out of the house into the street. Others were coming out, too. Describing that night, Dipuo called the mood "exotic." At first I thought I'd misheard and she meant "exciting." But no, she reiterated: she meant "exotic." Soweto seemed completely transfigured. The train conductors, who normally feared disappointing their white bosses by running late, slowed to a creep and hooted their horns. The minibus taxi drivers, who were usually only motivated to roar through the streets as fast as possible to get the maximum number of fares, just parked their vehicles at the curbs and danced. In all the hubbub, a white police officer shot a black man outside a Soweto station.

Dipuo almost enjoyed that. Not because the victim's injury was funny, but because it proved the police *had* never known them. They couldn't even distinguish black anger from black joy.

Gadifele ran out of her house, too. She had babies of her own by then. But "I just abandoned them," she said. Gadifele never got the chance to be a child. She raised Mandla and Direlo while she was still young; she had kept so many secrets. Now another parent was entering the scene. Mandela would protect her children now. And not just Mandela, but something bigger: history itself and the flow of time. She left her kids without a second thought because "I knew for the first time that they would be for the future."

Liberation had unfurled its sails. Its anchor was up, its hold bailed out, its deck tied with ribbons. Battered, Gadifele could finally stand on the dock and pass her offspring into the hands of history, which would do right by them.

Two mornings later, a comrade with a car picked Dipuo and Gadifele up and took them to a stadium. After Cape Town, Mandela flew to Johannesburg and came straight to Soweto. "They made T-shirts so quickly," Gadifele remembered, printed with Mandela's face at twenty-eight.

When the women got to the stadium it was raining. Some people had umbrellas, but the arena grew so packed they had to fold them and stand shoulder to shoulder. Journalists had put up hundred-foot towers for their satellite dishes, and well-wishers climbed them, belting out freedom songs as they waited.

And then the sun came out. You can see it in the archival footage. A wave of light rolls across the stadium as Mandela emerges from the players' tunnel. His handlers were only holding him underground until the rain stopped, but from the perspective of an onlooker, it seemed as if nature had acknowledged a human miracle. An ANC leader in a ratty baseball cap—nobody had time to buy new clothes for the occasion—began shouting into a microphone, his voice cracking: "Welcome, our Leader! Welcome, our Leader!"

Gadifele craned her neck—and then recoiled. Mandela was almost unrecognizable: a "lean, tall man with a gray suit." He wore a dandy white pocket square and his hair was a frosty halo. The heavy eyelids that, as a young man, made him look fierce now made him look grandfatherly, almost gentle. "And he was walking, like this—" Gadifele bent over slightly to mimic a stiff, unsteady walk.

You can hear it in the footage, too—a brief collapse of the mood. Instinctively, people looked at their T-shirts to check for an imposter. But by definition, Mandela was goodness, so this man would be their role model now. "Today, my return to Soweto fills my heart with joy," he said, and the crowd roared.

After his speech, Mandela walked off the stage and into the crowd. Without being aware of the impulse, Gadifele began shoving other people to push forward. "I am inside the picture," she kept thinking wonderingly. When she got to the front, she saw reporters train their bug-eyed cameras on *her*. "That's what I told myself, over and over. 'This day has come. I am inside the picture.'"

And then, suddenly, she was face-to-face with Mandela. The crowd's noise died like the hissing of a burbling pot vanishes when its lid makes a seal. It was as if she, Gadifele, was the only woman in the world besides him. He reached out, gripped her hand, "and my heart," she said, "left my body."

Flashbulbs brought her back to her senses. She realized she had lost so much time to an entaglement that warped both black and white South Africans' humanity. Now she was being reborn. "I am inside the picture," she whispered again to herself as she cried.

In Gadifele's house, she, Dipuo, and their friend Jacobetta talked a little more, then fell silent. It was as if there had been no day, afterward, quite as meaningful as that day. Our spoons tinkled against our coffee cups.

"Did you think you would leave Soweto?" I asked.

"We thought freedom was coming tomorrow," Jacobetta said, after a pause. I noticed she said *tomorrow*. Mandela's release had been cathartic, but it was not the full liberation.

"We wanted apartheid to end," Gadifele added. "We wanted Mandela to be released and to take over this country that was taken away from our forebears by our enemies."

"We had dreams," Dipuo cut in. "We wanted to have a better life. But there were no details. We actually had no idea of the perils that would come."

12

Christo

In mid-1991, around his twenty-first birthday, Christo finally got the deployment he'd been waiting for. This was going to be a straight-up reconnaissance mission like he dreamed of doing as a boy. His superiors told him they believed the ANC was using a mine dump near Soweto as a secret training ground. It was the slag heap Sowetans called Rand Mine.

A Land Rover dropped Christo off at ten at night. He'd been instructed to take two Angolan soldiers and set up an observation post to watch the dump's summit. In the dark, Christo and the Angolans did a swift dogleg—a clamber up the side and then a 90-degree turn at the top. His pack was so heavy with provisions a strap broke as he climbed.

But grasses and saplings broke under his feet, too, and he was suddenly brought back to his father's farm. The ground there had a special smell in the winter—flinty as well as a little musty and sweet from the summer's wild herbs that had dried in the dust. Christo inhaled deeply. It wasn't Angola, but it felt like a momentary inhabiting of the life's work he had imagined.

The men settled down in some bushes. As the sun rose, though, one of the Angolans pointed to the dirt: fresh footsteps. Christo traced them to a glade of trees and tugged at a branch. And then he heard a loud rustle. Fifteen feet ahead, he saw a hand jut out of the brush—and what he thought was the flash of a knife.

Shoot the ones who need to be shot, his commander had said. He lifted his gun and fired.

Christo's Angolan colleagues dragged the man out of the brush. As soon as Christo saw his victim, he recognized the man was probably no trained combatant but a homeless person—a *bosslaper*, as people called them in Afrikaans, or "someone who sleeps in the bushes." The man was tall, with dirty clothes and tangled dreadlocks, and he was bleeding from the stomach.

"I don't remember much after that," Christo told me. He'd pulled a rubber band out of a desk drawer and was absently wrapping it around his thumb so tightly the thumb had turned an angry red. He said he'd wanted to ask the man, "What are you doing here?" Actually, he wanted to go back—to rewind the tape.

He went on autopilot, digging through his backpack for an IV bag of saline and poking at the man's arm to find a vein. One of his Angolan companions had to shake his shoulder for a full ten seconds before he stopped. The Angolan pointed at the man's open, unblinking eyes.

"I'd never seen it"—death—"close up before," Christo explained. The Angolan told him his victim was already gone.

It was the worst possible moment in history for Christo to have pulled the trigger. A year or two earlier, he might have been hailed by the government as a hero. Instead, after he reported the event over the radio, the police arrived. A policewoman asked him testily: "Why did you confront that guy?" And she wondered why he was painted black and wearing civilian clothing, as he usually was on reconnaissance missions.

The public definition of heroism and goodness in South Africa had rapidly altered, faster than Christo's own personal understanding, emotions, habits, and, indeed, his military orders could catch up to it. In the early 1990s, conflicts broke out *within* white power structures over how to act. Some people continued to operate from a belief black liberation would destroy South Africa and had to be stopped.

President De Klerk, though, badly wanted to demonstrate his government's reformed mores before the world. And so he swiftly changed laws as well as the way the civilian government enforced existing ones, fundamentally altering in a space of months the kinds of acts that were and were not acceptable. Back in 1988, a police commander who ordered a weapons bust that led to the deaths of eleven black civilians was protected: he was doing his job. In 1991, though, around the same time Christo climbed Rand Mine, the South African government opened a criminal investigation into that commander.

Fighting terrorists had been Christo's mission in life. But his reconnaissance mission on the mine berm fell outside the official rules about security force engagements, since he hadn't been wearing the correct military attire. "In terms of the new way the rules were applied," he explained, "*I* was identified as the 'terrorist.'" And then his own white government charged him with murder.

13

Dipuo

ONE EVENT SHORTLY AFTER MANDELA'S release *did* put Dipuo's life on a different trajectory. It began with an encounter with a young man in her People's Committee. "Eve," Dipuo said flatly. "We didn't have a 'relationship.' We were having a meeting. Going through some notes. And then it was just the two of us."

Her mother had always tried to make sex sound fearsome. "You touch a boy," she'd say, "and you will get a child!" Dipuo didn't know what that meant. Touch him how? Along with little talk of romantic love, in the People's Committees there was little discussion of sexuality.

Dipuo had a crush, but she didn't know what she wanted. She didn't know *how* to know what she wanted. Nevertheless, she and the boy met one evening on top of Rand Mine. "The first encounter," she said dryly, "lasted fifteen minutes."

She met him again there anyway. Only five months later—in mid-1991—did she realize, "I am in deep trouble."

The young man took care not to be seen with her in public. "He didn't want to be known for having had sex and having fun when he was supposed to be fighting apartheid," Dipuo told me sadly. So "it was never a romance of two people holding hands." When her friends saw her growing belly, "only then did they ask"—she arched her eyebrows suggestively—"*so-ooo!* There was more with you and that comrade, huh?"

Like Dipuo's father did, her own baby's father initially denied paternity. He was known to be brilliant, and everybody told him "he was university material," anointed for an exciting post-apartheid destiny. Dipuo told me his parents angrily claimed she didn't even know who the father was and only identified their son because their family was a little bit richer than hers.

Abortion by choice was illegal, but it was also common in Soweto. At the government-built maternity clinic in Meadowlands—a woebegone place whose architecture resembled a prison's—midwives performed illicit abortions over the weekends. Dipuo had the impression the white government *wanted* black women to abort their babies. Not only would that reduce the number of black births, it would underscore white people's claim that black people were brutal and thought nothing of killing an unborn child.

She decided to keep her baby. In 1991, that choice felt both political and intuitive, like it wasn't a choice at all. She was terrified: her mother conceived around the same time and became so absorbed in her own pregnancy she couldn't help much. But the loosening of Dipuo's hip joints and the swelling of her belly also corresponded, somehow, with the loosening and swelling of black people's hopes all around her. If South Africans could figure out how to give birth to a new country, then she reckoned she, Dipuo, could figure out how to be a mother.

She went into labor a day before her twentieth birthday. The midwives openly insulted her for getting pregnant with no guarantee of help from the father. "You should be at school," they cackled as they laid her body on a thin mattress on the clinic's floor and spread open her knees. "You should be studying. But *you* were busy sleeping with boys. And now look at the problem you have!"

The baby's head was unusually large, and Dipuo's vagina tore during the delivery. This was another, unexpected thing, and she burst into tears. But after the midwives sewed her up, Dipuo told me she "slept like it was her last night on earth."

When she awoke, a midwife informed her the baby had come out "covered in its placenta." In her mother's relatives' villages, this was a tremendously auspicious sign. It meant the infant was destined to be a special person, like a healer or a great warrior. "Children who are born covered in a placenta—they are the luckiest people," Dipuo explained. "Things that don't happen to other people happen to them."

She had actually never liked hearing her mother recount these kinds of village tales. She associated them with the superstition that kept her mother unwilling even to utter Nelson Mandela's name. But when Dipuo brought her baby home, "it was such a strange thing. It was as if she"—the newborn—"was telling *me*: Now you feed me. Now you rock me. Now you put me to sleep."

Dipuo's baby daughter barely cried. She stared at the ceiling, as if—Dipuo imagined—she was philosophizing. Sometimes the baby stared right at her, like she was determined to communicate something she already knew but Dipuo didn't. For years, thanks to her activism, Dipuo hadn't kept a regular sleep schedule. But the baby somehow "just *knew* that at 9 p.m., normal people are supposed to sleep, and only wake up the following day."

In the pain-racked days right after the birth, Dipuo forgot to clean the dried-up pistil of the baby's umbilical cord. She told me she woke up to find her daughter pointing intently at the cord stub. "It was as if she was teaching me. It was as if she was *my* mother. No matter how sophisticated I am, and I don't want to believe every piece of junk that comes with our traditions, I thought to myself, 'So could it'—the theory about the placenta—'be true?'"

She went on, "You know when you are a first-time parent—on Facebook? Everybody, they all write, '*My* child was smiling in a different way.'" She laughed. "Every parent believes there is something unique about their child. But," she went on firmly, "this child really was different."

Dipuo named her daughter Lesego. It's a traditional name meaning "a blessing." But a few years later, the child told her she wanted to be called by her second name: Malaika.

Malaika is a name much more commonly used in East Africa. It connotes purity and blamelessness. In Swahili, a newborn baby is often called a *malaika*, an innocent little messenger sent straight from Heaven. It can also mean "avenging angel."

PART
2

14

Malaika

MALAIKA'S FIRST MEMORY IS OF South Africa's victory in the 1995 Rugby World Cup. She was nearly four years old. It was the first Rugby World Cup to which her country had been invited since its decades-long ban from most international sports tournaments, and it still seemed extraordinary the event was occurring at all. In the late '80s, international newspapers covered South Africa as if every event—a strike, a protest, a death—was the harbinger of the inevitable, bloody racial apocalypse. "International correspondents were very anxious not to miss out on the start of the Great South African Race War," Jan-Ad Stemmet, a historian of South Africa in the '80s, told me.

Elites might accept the notion of black majority rule, the thinking went, but the regular Afrikaner and the ordinary township activist would never. *The New York Times* depicted the early-'90s townships as a "Stygian" maze of "bombed-out buildings" presided over by violent, power-hungry strongmen with "thick fingers folded over [their] ample bellies" and South Africa's white farming towns as places whose residents tarred and feathered their own mayors after they proposed tiny relaxations in the pass laws.

But after Mandela walked free, De Klerk arranged a referendum among white voters to decide whether to replace the country's constitution with a majoritarian one. In other words, he was asking white South Africans to abdicate their political advantage voluntarily. In 1992, white voters accepted the change with a two-thirds majority, a margin De Klerk said flabbergasted him.

The ANC and the apartheid regime began negotiating a new, one-man-one-vote constitution. "Astonishingly and almost overnight," Mark Shaw and Anine Kriegler—the top criminologists—wrote, "the escalation in [political] violence" in places like Katlehong "halted and began a steady reversal." And at the end of April 1994, South Africans stood in miles-long lines to elect Nelson Mandela their country's first black president.

Mandela showed up to the Rugby World Cup final, which was held in Johannesburg. After the South African team won, he marched onto the field in a rugby jersey and clasped the hand of the team captain, a white man. The captain clasped Mandela's hand back lovingly.

In Soweto, when word came over the radio that the South African team had won, the minibus taxis just "stopped," Malaika remembered. Historically, black South Africans didn't like rugby. The South African team had only one black player, and rugby was considered an "Afrikaner" sport while black people preferred soccer. In the '80s, the few black people who did enjoy rugby openly backed New Zealand.

But that day, the minibus taxis pulled to the curbs and just honked in joy. "People were standing here"—Malaika and I were walking around Meadowlands, and she pointed to a pile of rocks—"and singing." She saw her neighbors' protective instincts suspended in favor of risking belief in the miraculous. "Our families normally never allowed us out of the house at night," she said. "That night they let us out onto the street."

At school a few years later, Malaika's teachers insisted she and her peers remember and recite the particulars of the South African "miracle," as people called the democratic transition. They taught that its truth was like mathematics, amazing but incontrovertible. One teacher would grow angry and hit the students on their hands with a wooden rod, Malaika remembered, "if we forgot how many years Mandela spent in prison. We were taught four things in school: religion, mathematics, reading, and Mandela."

She remembered another teacher quizzing them like a priest quizzes altar boys on Jesus's works. "Who is the premier"—the governor—"of Gauteng?" she'd ask, a newly named province.

"Mbhazima Shilowa!" the two dozen children would chorus.

"And who is the premier of the Northern Cape?"

"Manne Dipico!"

"And who is our minister of education?"

"Kader Asmal!" one girl piped up.

Malaika remembered the teacher frowning. She marched over to the girl's desk and rapped her twice sharply on the back of her hand with a ruler.

"But I know that is correct," Malaika thought.

As student after student hesitantly offered the name Kader Asmal, each one, in turn, was "given two lashes."

"It *is* Kader Asmal," Malaika finally said. She was a leader in her township elementary school. When she and her friends skipped rope after class over a pair of old pantyhose, Malaika would tell the other kids that she, like Mandela, would be South Africa's president someday.

But the teacher gave her a lash, too.

After Malaika got hit, the other children fell into frightened silence. Then the teacher raised her voice and told them she was disappointed in their "collective stupidity," which she said they must have inherited from their parents. The only right answer, the teacher said, was *Professor* Kader Asmal.

The apartheid government prohibited white-run South African universities from admitting almost any black students. Now that all universities were open to black people, Malaika's teacher said black children had to be especially proud of their black PhDs. "A professor is not just an ordinary person!"

This insistence on the miraculous, though, cut against Malaika's daily reality in a way that was perplexing. The way her mother and grandmother talked about their lives under apartheid didn't make them sound that different from her own. Unable to afford an umbrella, she often walked to school in the rain. And she'd often feel so hungry. Whenever she heard the gate squeak in the afternoon, Malaika would run out of her shack. That noise meant the *madam*—what Dipuo called their landlady in the house in front—had arrived home, possibly with leftover pastries from her job cleaning a corporate office.

Matshediso had delivered Tshepiso—the aunt Malaika called her sister—eight months before Malaika was born. Tshepiso was a frail toddler, and she slept on the shack's small couch while Malaika slept on the floor beneath her. Their *madam* had an outhouse, just a brick structure set over a dark hole in the earth, but the girls weren't supposed to leave the shack after dark. If Malaika needed to pee in the middle of the night, she had to creep around Tshepiso to a bucket that sat in a corner.

"You know Converse sneakers?" Malaika asked me. "When it is cold, that sneaker is very cold. When it's hot, the sneaker is very hot." The shack was like that. "In the winter, it could be colder inside than outside." To heat the shack, her grandmother placed a piece of corrugated iron across her two-plate stove so the heat would radiate. Tshepiso loved the heat, and she often stumbled over the searing metal. Her legs are still covered with scars.

Ever since she could remember, Malaika craved periods of alone time. But even thirty minutes alone wasn't something Soweto often afforded. People were gregarious in Meadowlands, and they claimed not to understand somebody who wanted to be by herself. It seemed to Malaika that, in order to diminish the shame of their unchosen, cramped circumstances, Sowetans had decided garrulousness and constant noise would be things they would celebrate. People were always stopping by, and when neighbors got home, if they had a car, they'd open its doors and pump music late into the night. Sometimes, Malaika locked herself in the outhouse for an hour at a time. Tshepiso teased her that she must have digestive problems, but it was one of the only places Malaika could hear herself think.

She took her mother's old books in there. Dipuo kept hundreds of books in suitcases beneath the shack's only bed. Malaika found she really loved Danielle Steel.

"It wasn't so much the romance," she recalled. "It was the imagery that she used when she described the places." The fresh-cut flowers. The burnished leather furniture in people's "home libraries." The huge meadows full of horses. The people in the novels seemed to have so much *space*—physical space to live in and imaginative space to live out their dreams.

15

Christo

BACK AT THE 32 BATTALION's main base, Christo's military superiors initially told him not to worry about what happened on Rand Mine. He was a soldier, after all—the opposite of a criminal. But a few months later, as winter gave way to summer, they served him with papers: six criminal charges including "terrorism" and murder.

Panicked, he called his father, who picked him up and drove him back to the farm. Johannes had gotten a premonition his name could go public. But on the Sunday-night honor roll on TV, not in *this* way. On the drive, he told Christo he had no idea what he should do except never go back to the army. So, in early 1992, Christo quit the 32 Battalion and enrolled at the University of the Free State (UFS), in corn-farming country.

He still had to travel back to Johannesburg for court appearances. The neighborhood around the courthouse had once been racially mixed, but in the '50s the government cleared it, bulldozing tenements to make room for an all-white neighborhood they audaciously called *Triomf*, or "Triumph." But not too many white people ever moved in. It had a forlorn, bombed-out look; some of the razed houses were never rebuilt. Bars covered the stunted courthouse's windows. The foyer Christo had to walk through to get to the "Accused Waiting Room" was decorated with incongruously cheery '80s-era inspirational posters: "Great Success Always Comes at the Risk of Enormous Failure!"

In the courtroom, an elderly judge in a black robe "threatened" Christo, he told me, trying to get him "to confess to things in all this legal language I wasn't used to. It was so intimidating to go into there."

But after several appearances, a military superior got Christo's murder charge dismissed. There were so many issues to be resolved as apartheid drew to a close. Some government officials were furiously burning records in their department buildings' courtyards, worried about their own prosecutions. That provided cover for lesser problems to fade away.

Bloemfontein, where Christo's university was located, had been the capital of one of the biggest Afrikaner republics. In the twentieth century, it became a laboratory for the formation of Afrikaner identity. UFS became the first South African university to conduct classes in Afrikaans. Its campus was Elysian: promenades lined with purple African lilies led to august brick buildings named after quintessential South African plants like the *soetdoring*—an acacia with yellow puffball flowers—and Afrikaner historical leaders. By night, a breeze knitted its twenty dormitories together with the scent of hay from the farmlands a few miles away.

But Christo immediately felt more tormented there than he ever remembered feeling in Katlehong. He flunked his exams and told his dorm father, a law professor named Teuns Verschoor, that he was having disturbing dreams. At first, Christo thought it was a kind of straightforward posttraumatic stress disorder. A branch would snap in a tree and he'd hear a gunshot. A group of crowlike birds would waddle across his dorm's courtyard and he'd hear gunmen creeping around.

But soon he began to think he was angriest at the judge who'd presided over his murder hearings—and at other white South

Africans. That judge, presumably, spent most of his life enforcing apartheid law. And then he designated *Christo* the "terrorist"?

Shortly after Christo got to Bloemfontein, De Klerk made a big show of disbanding the 32 Battalion. During the negotiations over a new constitution, the ANC agreed to halt Umkhonto we Sizwe's armed struggle. But its negotiators rankled that no such disarmament had been expected of the white regime. And then, three months after Christo enrolled at UFS, a group of 32 Battalion soldiers went on a rampage in a squatter camp in Katlehong. The media carried reports that Angolan soldiers raped women in cold blood.

De Klerk declared the 32 a national humiliation, calling it "out of control." He ordered the unit's officers to pull out of the base at Pomfret, making little arrangement for the Angolan soldiers who'd lived there with Christo. These men weren't welcome back in Angola because they'd resisted the faction that dominated the country's civil war. They were distrusted by black South Africans for collaborating with white people. Within months, vandals from neighboring towns invaded Pomfret and stole its copper wires and plumbing pipes, leaving Christo's old friends without electricity or drinking water.

In the military code of ethics, a commander isn't supposed to flee a hot zone before he guarantees the safety of all his subordinates. Christo thought the military's abandonment of Pomfret was dishonorable—and he felt that way about a lot of the behavior he was beginning to see in white people. On campus, white administrators and kids were suddenly getting hip with black culture, as if it was some kind of cool new style and not a political force they had recently feared. Mandela—the man who topped the "KNOW YOUR ENEMY" chart Christo's commanders gave him just two years earlier—was invited to campus with fanfare, as if only his visit, now, would make the hundred-year-old university worthy. South Africa's military began to wind down conscription in 1991, and white boys just young enough not to have served bumped each other's fists and shouted "Yebo!," a Zulu greeting.

A young man named Francois was one of these boys. A couple years younger than Christo, Francois had envied the black kids his father—a liberal-minded professor who did work in a township—occasionally brought to their house. "Have you ever seen the way they"—black people—"hold hands?" Francois reminisced to me. He thought black kids' way of expressing themselves, their strong emotions and their open intimacy, was "wonderful."

He had dreaded the idea of serving in the army, not—he felt—because he was a wimp, but because he didn't want to kill on behalf of a system he wasn't even sure made *white* South Africans happy. In the '80s, the apartheid regime presented white South African communities as idealized spaces where everyone white was absurdly blissful. The lived truth felt different to some white South Africans. Alongside reports of township protests, in the '80s white-run newspapers began to highlight a phenomenon reporters called "family murders": when a white man killed his wife and children and then, often, himself.

Another white South African told me about the day his school-teacher informed his class that one of their peers had been killed by his father with a crossbow. It made my friend—who was about twelve—feel there was a "sickness" *within* white society, and not only in white people's relations with other races. "There's something wrong with us," he thought. "Why is this happening?"

As colonialism in Africa receded—and as the apartheid regime's claim that white people were the only ones able to run the country came under more scrutiny—the line a white South African had to walk narrowed, and those who stumbled were alienated. White policemen who broke up protests often saved their utmost venom for the handful of *white* protesters. Matter-of-factly, my friend's teacher told his class that their murdered classmate's father had become despondent after a business venture failed. It was the dark flip side to that rugged-individualist, nobody-else-tells-us-what-to-do mentality: if a white South African man felt he'd let his community down, he could become so humiliated he decided he had to commit suicide—while retaining the right to take his family with him.

In that friend's view, white South Africans' judgment of black people—and their insistence that violence in the name of self-defense was legitimate—could morph into an acceptance of judgment and violence in all areas of their lives. Some white parents beat their children with the same kind of whips the white regime's police used against black protesters, purportedly to toughen them up. But it seemed to my friend that white elders *embodied* the anger they ascribed to black South Africans, either unconsciously or out of the belief they would only prevail if they matched their enemy in viciousness.

Francois, Christo's classmate, felt an overwhelming relief to enroll at UFS in 1992, the year the university began to admit black students. He felt liberated to talk to anyone however he liked and to espouse any beliefs he wanted. "I took the opportunity to start to call myself a communist overnight," he told me, laughing.

He particularly relished his friendship with a young black man named Lebohang. He and Lebohang founded a social club in which black and white students sang and watched movies together, like the Marlon Brando classic *Julius Caesar*. "It was as if a threat perception dating from all the way back in the 1700s suddenly went away. The faces of black and white students when we sang each other's music . . ." Francois searched for the term to describe it. "The word in Afrikaans is *opreg*," he finally said, which means both "earnest" and "righted," like a ship that finally finds its keel. "It was amazing to see that on people's faces. I don't want to sound overly religious, but it was magic."

UFS also integrated its dormitories. Campus administrators predicted this would be a problem. The dormitories were historically more like fraternities. They had legacy admission—if your father was in a dorm, you'd enter that one, too—and a family-like culture based around customs everybody called "the traditions." Each dorm had a mascot: one had a pig and another a chicken. Live versions of the mascots trotted the corridors. In some dorms, freshmen wore special outfits. In others, freshmen bowed to the seniors, calling them "uncle," and walked in through the back door. There were elaborate, weeks-long hazing rituals.

These traditions were often arbitrary. But they fostered a deep sense of group pride and belonging, and administrators feared white students would be reluctant to let black kids partake. So ahead of integration, the UFS president polled the student body, giving them the option of temporarily preferring racially segregated housing. To his surprise, 86 percent of students said they welcomed housing black students in their dorms.

Lebohang, Francois's friend, told me he fell in love with "the traditions" after he was placed into a dorm. His favorite, he recalled, was freshman hazing. He broke into peals of laughter as he described the ritual, because he recognized it seemed an unlikely memory to cherish. "We queued blindfolded and half-naked." Seniors painted the freshmen's bodies in black and yellow stripes to resemble his dorm's mascot, a bee. They made each one drink tomato juice from a toilet bowl. "It was horrible! Guys were really getting sick!" Finally, the freshmen were led to a "huge drum filled with water, cow dung, and grass." A senior shouted at them to *dyk*—dive! "Then you get out. You're dripping and smelling like cow dung."

Afterward, the black and white freshmen were instructed to shower, change into a jacket and tie, and head to the courtyard, where seniors awaited to hand them a plate of barbecued meat and a beer. "You are a member now," they informed Lebohang. "Color doesn't count."

"I felt proud," he remembered.

What Christo noticed, though, was how many black students on campus were wearing ANC T-shirts. That made him feel lonely. He couldn't show off what *he'd* been a part of. He was, in a sense, still undercover—but now in a different way. His military superiors instructed him not to mention his service in the 32 Battalion. In fact, he gathered they'd destroyed some of his military records, just in case.

Christo knew Francois. He knew Francois hadn't been in the military. He disliked this young man who was now respected for his "daring," for befriending black kids, but who made no sacrifice—it seemed to Christo—in a time when physical sacrifices were demanded of Afrikaner boys. The way he called himself a "communist" with little regard for the way self-described communists killed South African men in Angola made Christo feel bitter. To Christo, the verb encapsulating the behavior of men like Francois was *gatkruip*. It means, literally, "to crawl up someone's asshole"—to suck up.

It was embarrassing, this new swooning over black people. For so long, Afrikaners resisted the desire to look acceptable to the world. Independence, pride, and resistance had been essential to their identity. And now they were giving it up—for what? What were they getting in return?

People claimed white South Africans were getting an extraordinary gift unparalleled in history: the opportunity to live alongside people they had oppressed, basically unmolested. The constitutional negotiations allowed De Klerk to govern initially with Mandela in a partnership, left statues of Afrikaner heroes standing, and sketched out a blueprint for the Truth and Reconciliation Commission, the famous hearings that allowed some perpetrators of apartheid-era political crimes to receive amnesty. In theory, if Christo didn't repeat parts of his past—like the killing on Rand Mine—then that past could vanish. It was like a Christian tale: he could be washed clean, baptized.

What it *felt* like, though, was a subtle degradation. "We're giving you something conquered tyrants aren't usually given," was the message he took from the black South African approach to the transition. "Other people in our position might have marched you along the avenues in chains. We will not do that."

We're better than you, in other words. By not acting toward you as *you* acted toward *us*, we're showing you up. And, by not extracting a material debt, you'll owe us an intangible debt of gratitude forever. You'll be burdened with the knowledge you were never proportionately punished.

Others felt this way. I once walked with an Afrikaner professor to a Pretoria graveyard containing the graves of Afrikaner political leaders; as a young man, he visited it every Sunday. He fully expected it to be "graffitied, burnt, and destroyed" if white people ever lost power, he told me. It had been left intact. Yet he didn't visit anymore. "Maybe the reason," he confessed, "is precisely because it's so clear that nothing happened." That made everything he'd ever believed about what black people could do to him feel that much more shameful.

The Afrikaner journalist Rian Malan acknowledged that, in the lead-up to apartheid's end and just afterward, things went better than almost any white person might have imagined. Under President Mandela, Afrikaners could still read Afrikaans newspapers and get Afrikaans programming on TV. It remained a lot easier for white university graduates to get jobs than black ones.

Many white South Africans, in fact, got richer. Foreign countries dropped their economic sanctions, opening new markets, and aid money poured into the country. People who already had capital were the ones who could immediately take advantage of these developments. White businesspeople started to export wines and $10,000 ostrich-leather sofas to Europe while white-run safari lodges welcomed floods of new tourists. The average white household income increased 15 percent in the half-decade after apartheid ended, much more than the average black household income did. Afrikaner people's share of the Johannesburg Stock Exchange grew over the '90s, from 24 percent to 35 percent; throughout that whole decade, 98 percent of listed companies' CEOs were white.

Malan lived in an upscale Cape Town neighborhood. Most mornings, he walked down to an upscale, tourist-focused seaside café—the kind of cosmopolitan place that hadn't really existed under apartheid—to drink well-brewed macchiatos. "The sea is warm and the figs are ripe," he wrote. Then he went on to describe this existence as "unbearable."

He just couldn't forgive black people for forgiving him. That might sound strange, but "the laws of poetic symmetry," he wrote, dictate that the Afrikaners "should have been wiped out." Paradoxically, being left undisturbed left him with an ever-present reminder of his guilt, of how wrongly he had treated his maid and other black people he met under apartheid on the premise that, if he ever treated them properly, they would hurt him. "The Bible was right about a thing or two. It is infinitely worse to receive than to give, especially if . . . the gift is mercy."

Christo's whole training—all of Afrikaner culture—was about outwitting enemies. Now he felt black South Africans had beaten the Afrikaners at their own game—and De Klerk had helped them.

A few years after Christo started at UFS, an Afrikaner named Chris Louw wrote an open letter to Wimpie de Klerk, a writer and F. W. de Klerk's brother. In the '90s, both brothers became vocal advocates for racial integration. Wimpie penned a preachy book advising young Afrikaners to accept that apartheid had been a "lie" and to undertake urgent efforts to prove their worth to black people by tackling poverty.

Louw had opposed apartheid. As a young journalist, he'd

attended the Dakar Safaris. Yet his letter was brutally angry. It suggested Wimpie touted the pleasures of racial reconciliation because he was in a position to profit off it—materially and psychologically. His brother parlayed his Nobel Peace Prize into overseas speaking gigs and corporate board seats; before apartheid ended, F.W. incorporated Wimpie into the thrill of negotiating South Africa's democratic transition. Wimpie recalled the delight of traveling in secret to meet exiled ANC leaders: "It meant a great deal to me personally . . . the luxury trips and accommodation, the experience of sitting close to a fire and engaging in political breakthrough work . . . the access to confidential information . . . I am convinced [our meetings] greatly improved mutual understanding."

For Wimpie, paradoxically, bringing apartheid to an end—some white officials privately called it "liquidating our firm"—was his life's utmost experience of privilege and power. Louw didn't have that experience. Like Christo, he served in the military. "Do you remember the guns *you*"—white leaders—"gave us to shoot the shit out of 'terrorists'?" Louw wrote. "Shut up," his white elders told him if he "asked questions. 'Get your head back into the scrum. Bow your head and thank God for your blessings.' . . . *You* told us Afrikaners are a people of achievement and a brave history. Those of us who did not want to defend your dreams with the weapons you issued us were jailed. . . . And now you order a new world with a flap of your hands. You mint vigorous new words and riveting phrases. And now you say [again], 'Come, little boys. Pay attention.' But wouldn't you say you're speaking for the benefit of *your* reputation while leaving your children abandoned in a forest? You're telling us to take your advice now, but you imply we should have been smart enough to reject your original advice. . . . *Fuck you*."

The worst thing, though, about the dreams that woke Christo from his sleep was that they weren't really nightmares. They were good dreams. Dreams from which he'd wake up feeling happy.

They were dreams about his army life. He found he keenly missed it: the intensity, the discipline, the bonding, the glory—the *idea* of glory in Angola. He still felt disappointed he hadn't been able to go there. He was also aware these feelings were potentially sick. They kept him awake; they ate at him as he tried to concentrate on his studies. How could he miss something that had been so bad?

Christo started to get into fights with black men on campus. Sometimes, he heard his victims were trying to steal white boys' bicycles. But other times, he found himself punching them for no reason. Verschoor, his dorm father, was given to gamboling around campus in a brown suede jacket and old-fashioned wool tie, parrying with students. Everyone liked him, and it unsettled him he couldn't get through to Christo.

Mostly, Christo seemed "extremely quiet," Verschoor told me. But then he'd blow up without warning. "During one June exam period, I heard a student outside the dormitory swearing like nothing else. And then two solid fist blows. And then silence. That," he said grimly, "was Christo."

Christo would get back to his dorm room after a fight and wonder: *Why did I do that?* But then he'd think about the fact that *he* had to initiate the fights. That made him resentful, actually. *How dare you pretend you don't hate me anymore?* he'd think. How dare you hold up a mirror of graciousness that shows me the reflection of a worse man than you? Every time a black man tried *not* to fight him, it made him angrier.

16

Dipuo

DIPUO VOLUNTEERED TO HELP AT a Soweto voting precinct on election day in 1994. Some grandmothers joyfully wept as she inked their fingers after they voted. But when I asked her about it, she just said distantly that the day was "nice," and that "we had high hopes, as a community."

The reality was that, by then, her own feelings had gone strangely flat. After she gave birth to Malaika, Dipuo went back to high school at night, graduated, and got a job at an American-supported NGO in Pretoria, the capital. Foreigners and their money were pouring into South Africa, and she bought herself a fridge and a long table like the ones she remembered from the white people's dining rooms in which her mother worked. On the weekends, she and Gadifele hosted what they called "kitchen parties." They served salads with slivered carrot and cucumber, cool, crunchy things they never could have stored before.

But it wasn't lost on her that she still didn't have a "kitchen," not really. Not like white people had. After all, a "kitchen," in South Africa, wasn't just a kitchen. It was a whole lifestyle. It meant having a kitchen big enough to have a "scullery," the room in which a maid would do the dishes; it meant good wine and extra meat in the fridge. It meant a long, hedged driveway from which guests came and went in cars. Dipuo couldn't afford a car, and her commute to the NGO took an hour and a half on three different minibus taxis.

Soon after Mandela's election, South Africa began to prepare for the Truth and Reconciliation Commission (TRC). Local and international reporters were thrilled, branding the hearings the redemptive last act of a long-running, captivating TV series. Many high-level apartheid leaders, though, just decided not to show up. De Klerk stormed out, alleging the hearings were biased.

Black people who committed violence under apartheid as well as black victims spoke. But it unsettled Dipuo that observers seemed most interested in what white people had to say. Reporters celebrated an Afrikaner poet, Antjie Krog, who anguished over all the new information emerging about the sins perpetrated by her government.

"*Who hadn't known?*" Dipuo thought with disgust. If not the details, then the gist of how horrible apartheid was? The words of the TRC's white participants were often ostensibly self-deprecating. But somehow it seemed their dominance remained cunningly intact via the sheer amount of attention paid to them.

For the first time in her life, Dipuo felt comfortable walking down Khumalo Street, Katlehong's main drag. She had the sense her country's streets were at least getting a little safer, and she was right. Under Mandela, the police logged an uptick in robberies, especially in white-dominated farming areas. But self-reported victimization rates—the number of crimes people told academic surveys they'd experienced—didn't rise nearly as much, suggesting a lot of the increase in crime represented South Africans' new willingness to report incidents to a more trustworthy police force. By the end of the '90s, the police were recording only half as many incidents of crime as they did in the early '90s, despite a population growth of nearly 40 percent.

Yet some white South Africans were starting to talk as if the country was already falling apart. Shortly before Mandela's election, white-owned businesses began to flee Johannesburg's integrating downtown to a new, heavily guarded suburb. In residential areas, white homeowners erected high, electrified concrete walls. The criminologists Shaw and Kriegler calculated that "the safest parts of South Africa"—formerly white urban suburbs—remained "as safe as anywhere in Western Europe." Yet one such suburb dweller told *The New York Times* that she constantly "visualized a vivid scenario in which she faces black gunmen"—and the paper reported this concern as if it was totally legitimate. The still white-run local TV station Dipuo watched didn't often air crime statistics. Instead, it reported things like a poll result in which a majority of white South Africans said they *believed* they were "very unsafe at night."

The widow of the novelist Alan Paton, whose 1948 novel, *Cry, the Beloved Country*, communicated the injustice of apartheid to the world, wrote an essay claiming she and her husband had looked forward to racial integration. But thanks mainly to "black-on-white crime," she wrote, "I cannot live here anymore. I am tired of being constantly on the alert, having that sudden frisson of fear at the sight of a shadow by the gate—[by] a group of youths approaching." Black South Africans barely had a year or two to right things, yet the letter was passed around as evidence they wouldn't.

It reminded Dipuo of how, just before the 1994 election, a rumor had circulated that people in Katlehong were going to murder their voting officials. That didn't pan out. Yet rumors like these didn't die. When one didn't materialize, the essence of the warning would just attach itself to some new possibility. As the '90s wore on, a videotape went around claiming black South Africans were secretly plotting a massacre code-named "The Night of the Long Knives." On the night of Mandela's death, the video alleged, black people would stream in phalanxes to the suburbs and machete every white person they saw.

It felt painful because she, Dipuo, was trying so hard. She thought she was being so friendly to her new white colleagues at the NGO. She read that the president of the ANC called the head of a white-led labor union to ask his opinion on how to fix problems in the country. The union leader complained, insisting the phone call revealed that the ANC didn't have a clue what it was doing.

Dipuo thought the remarkable thing was that *the head of the ANC still called up a random white guy for advice*. After everything white people did to black people—after they banned the ANC and imprisoned Mandela. What more evidence could anyone ask for that black people were willing to let bygones be bygones?

Dipuo had begun to feel uneasy about Mandela himself, actually. Months after she and Gadifele saw him speak at the Soweto stadium, she thought more coolly about what he'd said. After his greeting, his speech had taken a strangely hectoring, patronizing turn. "The fears of whites . . . are an obstacle we must understand and address," he lectured the crowd. "We must clearly demonstrate our goodwill to our white compatriots and convince them by our conduct [that a democratic] South Africa . . . will be better." He said he'd been "greatly disturbed" by what he'd read in prison about the township violence, the "setting alight of vehicles, the harassment of innocent people. . . . I call, in the strongest possible way, for us to act [with] dignity and discipline."

Now that stung. The ANC's leader in the '80s, Oliver Tambo, *asked* people like Dipuo to be violent. He encouraged them! "As far as many South Africans are concerned," he said in one Radio Freedom broadcast, "violence is happening only in some black backyard. All must be made to experience the struggle"—which Dipuo had taken to mean that everyone, including white people and black collaborators, should have to witness the devastating material consequences of apartheid. To experience the chaos it bred. ANC documents explicitly directed the People's Committees to undertake the "elimination of agents"—black informants. "Every patriot a combatant," Tambo said. "Every combatant a patriot."

But after Mandela became free, he began to act as if *black* people were most likely to be South Africa's problem going forward. His implication seemed to be that white people's fears, their anger and suspicion, had to be catered to and the burden to be reassuring—the bigger people—would fall on black South Africans. It felt wrong to think that white people's previous behavior created the expectation they'd be dissatisfied and that they would have a freedom she might not have: the freedom to admit you were unhappy.

At a rally just before the 1994 election, a group of young black men excitedly tore down a homeland flag hanging on the dais. Homeland flags were an artifact of apartheid, and Dipuo felt they should be removed. But Mandela attacked the black men as if they were common thugs. "What right do you have to act like hooligans?" he screamed. "I cannot stand that! . . . You behave like animals!"

Sometimes Mandela seemed more afraid of black people than white ones. Driving to Cape Town's Grand Parade from prison, well-wishers had beaten joyfully on his car windows. He'd asked his driver to detour to a "safe house," where he cowered for a couple of hours. "I was afraid," he explained later, that *"they"*—his black fans—"might kill [me] with their love."

"They"? Retreating to a "safe house"? These were things *white* people said and did.

After apartheid's end, Dipuo had also expected a substantial turn toward economic redistribution. Like many black South African activists, she considered herself a socialist. ANC leaders had to avoid too many openly socialist declarations lest they lose Western sympathy. But over the decades, they'd advocated nationalizing South Africa's financial, mining, and agricultural industries so—as the movement's charter put it—"the people [can] share in the country's wealth." An illicit magazine the ANC published quoted

Marx and the communist Vietnamese general Võ Nguyên Giáp all the time.

In 1995, though, Mandela revealed that South Africa's white finance minister "appealed to . . . us to ensure that we do not make remarks which have the effect of frightening away investors"— comments that sounded too angry, too redistributive, too "African." He went on: "I accept this without hesitation."

It was as if the depiction of what black people were capable of had gotten to Mandela. As if the fall of apartheid had let the gas of white people's ideas into the highest echelons of black leadership—kinds of ideas from which segregation, paradoxically, had previously insulated them.

Vishnu Padayachee, an economist, worked with the ANC on its economic plans during the transition. In a conversation, he remembered feeling tremendously trapped by "our insecurities." He and his colleagues had been told for so long they were unfit to run a modern nation. They *felt* unsure. After his release, Mandela dispatched his top brass to do "training sessions" at the mega–investment bank Goldman Sachs.

This could be interpreted as a simple wish to cozy up to a powerful firm. But Padayachee felt these kinds of moves arose "directly from our terror." His colleagues often talked about South Africa's democratic transition in language that implied it was a gift they hadn't earned and, perhaps, didn't really deserve. One ANC leader marveled that, in the early '90s, De Klerk gave black people "much more than we expected. If De Klerk had given us more, we wouldn't have known what to do with it!" Another leader begged well-off white South Africans not to flee. "We say to whites: Don't run away. . . . You know when we will become a banana republic? When [you] people go."

By the '90s, no other sub-Saharan African nation was considered a straightforward success story. Many, like Ghana, appeard to come out of colonialism strong only to see their economies decline; others fought civil wars. "One shouldn't underrate the depth of unspoken disillusionment about post-colonial Africa," the Reagan-era U.S. diplomat told me apologetically. "When Ghana became independent, I remember the glowing hopes." In the '50s, he said, the political scientist David Apter "wrote a book predicting that in Ghana, there will be a completely new flowering of human possibilities. There was this idea that this could be the start of a new Renaissance or something. The letdown was very big. I hated the idea of apartheid," the diplomat confessed. "But deep down, I assumed there was no realistic alternative." In fact, a 1992 *New York Times* essay suggested post-colonial Africa was disappointing *mainly* to progressive Westerners who'd believed in it: "Something has gone horribly wrong with Africa, and anyone who knows and loves the continent [has] wondered what."

South Africa's position as the last liberated pressured it to prove at least *one* of sub-Saharan Africa's then nearly fifty nations would be an unqualified success. Some on Padayachee's economic team wanted more redistributive economic policies. They said the fact that white corporate elites opposed this change was an argument in its favor. When had black people had reason to trust anything white people advised them?

Others, though, pointed out black people were taking responsibility for a system designed by white people and it would only give white people satisfaction to see them break it. Therefore, the black-led government should do everything white economists and businessmen said. To Padayachee, it was crazy-making, this absolute inability to shake free of what white people thought of their actions.

It wasn't practically easy to confront the country's problems, either. Take land. In the early '90s, white people owned fully

90 percent of South Africa's prime agricultural land. White people had always been anxious about their legal and emotional right to the land, and the extent to which they improved it was supposed to be their justification for keeping it. A 1971 government pamphlet on the homelands laid out the rationale for legalized racism:

> [With] their . . . African way of life, [the Blacks] did not take possession of the land as private property . . . they did not develop the country's natural resources . . . or establish an infrastructure. The Whites, driven by a determination to improve their position . . . practically overran the Blacks, who did not display the same ambitious urges. The Whites took the initiative and have maintained it ever since.

This was not true, even as a so-called neutral observation. It was a proposition—one white people subsequently had to prove. During apartheid, the white government systematically differentiated rural white from rural black land, stripping black South Africans' right to privately own farms while pouring money into assistance programs for white farmers.

No foreign country ever recognized the demarcation between white South Africa and the black homelands as real. But over time it *became* real. By the '90s, white and black South Africa had literally different climates. During segregation, most of South Africa's fertile, rain-washed plains were given to white people and its barren peaks and dusty, hot, malarial lowlands to black people. The borders between "white" and "black" South Africa could be seen from an airplane: it looked as if a child cut up travel magazine pictures of pastoral English fantasies and the Sahel desert and spliced them together in a mad, bicolor collage. Green was white South Africa. Brown was black South Africa.

When the ANC took over the agriculture portfolio, it set a goal to transfer at least 30 percent of South Africa's commercial farmland to black people within a couple of decades. Michael Buys, a colored man, was put in charge of "land reform" in a northerly province. When an ad for the job appeared in the newspaper, he felt a thrill, though he was working as a school principal. "I loved the idea of giving land back," Buys told me in a hotel lounge in Pretoria. He smiled conspiratorially. "Even of *taking* it back."

As part of its effort to racially purify urban neighborhoods, when Buys was twelve, the apartheid government relocated his parents into a house occupied by a black couple. This was, theoretically, a win. It was a decent house. But Buys had to stand on a curb and watch as the black couple loaded their possessions onto a military truck. The husband was crying. Even so young, Buys felt it was wrong.

Yet as a land-reform official, Buys immediately began to feel alarmed by the people coming to apply for previously white-owned farms. "Their business plans were way out there," he grimaced. They envisioned immediately owning fleets of tractors and raking in incomes in the millions. "We would say: you are only just starting out! We would explain to them that even white farmers who have tractors and delivery vehicles and center pivots"—irrigation systems that sprinkled water in a perfect circle—"didn't get to that level overnight."

The applicants didn't accept this. They would retort: "This is our time. You are a black government. You are our people. You should help us get these things so we can be like the ones for whom we once worked."

Early on, the ANC government focused on buying farms from white people and giving them to the direct descendants of black people removed from what became white-owned estates. In theory, this was the most direct reparation. In practice, it begat huge problems. One was that, many generations later, there were often tenfold more offspring than there had been original victims. Groups numbering in the hundreds were resettled on small plots recently owned by a single white man to quarrel over its direction, sometimes to the death.

Another problem was that the descendants of those most deprived by colonization were also the least likely to have gotten the kind of education necessary to run a high-tech farm in a globalized commodity marketplace. Some were illiterate; many hadn't finished high school. Buys compared giving a property that immediately demanded the implementation of a complex spraying-and-harvesting program and a marketing plan for exporting to Europe to stealing someone's car, refashioning it into an airplane, and then returning it and saying, "Good luck! And don't crash."

Many of these "beneficiaries," as the government called them, were on the older side and came to the heartbreaking conclusion, after having lived most of their lives arbitrarily condemned to servitude, that servitude was indeed what they had deserved. "We are grateful we got the farm," Daniel, a seventy-something former mineworker and the de facto manager of a now black-owned fruit plantation, told me when I visited his farm, though he never figured out how to make it generate revenue and was now practically starving. He went on with a grimace of self-reproach: "We know we are suffering because we ourselves are not correctly utilizing the land."

Daniel's plantation sat in the middle of a corridor of farms stretching from Johannesburg to the Zimbabwe border. The government bought the farms in the mid-'90s and transferred them to black people. Not long after, the landscape looked hit by an apocalyptic event. Lychee and mango trees still grew along the sides of the road, but their leaves were brown and dry, and whatever withered fruit they produced was left on the tree to be gnawed by monkeys. Most of the buildings—sheds, farmhouses, packhouses

136

for drying fruit—had collapsed and been stripped by vandals of their roofing and electrical wiring.

Speaking to me sitting on his farmhouse stoop, his thin arms and ankles swaddled in a threadbare shirt and hiking boots leaking their stuffing, Daniel told me the missing object standing between him and being a real farmer was a John Deere tractor. If he only had a tractor like the ones he had seen on TV, he could be in business.

"You're in luck," I said. I had just come from a farm down the road whose managers wanted to get rid of an unneeded tractor. I said we could drive it over that afternoon.

Daniel paused for a long moment and then shook his head sadly. It actually didn't seem to him it would really solve the problem, he said.

Apartheid told black people they didn't have a magic touch necessary to operate a farm, and that notion still operated powerfully. Daniel and the other land reform beneficiaries on his farm weren't lazy. They had lots of energy. The whole time we spoke on his farmhouse stoop, a trio of men was vigorously hacking at a patch of soil behind him with hoes. "Are they planting something?" I asked Daniel.

"No, they're weeding the yard," he replied. Gardening: now that was something black people had long felt confident they could do. "We do it every day."

Michael Buys felt viscerally angry at people like Daniel. But he also knew his anger was a projection of his own shame. Of course many land reform beneficiaries were underskilled. That was what the apartheid regime intended. "I was also embarrassed for myself," he said. "Because I knew these people's grandiose fantasies were due to the promises *we* had been making."

We meaning the new black-led government. Just before the '94 election, the ANC assured South Africans that appropriate housing would be "provided to all" and that there'd be "proper" new schools, roads, and health clinics. It unveiled an economic policy that promised GDP growth of 6 percent and 500,000 new jobs every year. Even black elites returning from exile with PhDs didn't adequately question "how all these things were going to be possible."

Elliot, my friend who grew up in a homeland, was one of the people who believed in these promises. After he graduated high school in 1998, "everyone was telling me: 'Go to Johannesburg,'" he told me. "Because we knew we came from the dark places."

He used this phrase often to describe his homeland. It was dark for lack of electricity, but also dark for lack of knowledge, sophistication, and opportunity. "We all assumed Johannesburg had become the bright area." So, at twenty, Elliot left his parents and younger siblings and beat a path to the city.

The end of apartheid actually ruined his father, Elias, financially. Startlingly, Elliot calls black liberation his family's "collapse." After the police arrested Elias for punching the white man at the mine where he worked, the mine's supervisor fought for Elias not to get jailed. Elias had impressed the supervisor in the past. The white man should not have provoked Elias, the supervisor declared: "Elias is not his boy."

Elias wasn't jailed. From that day on, he decided he would have to study hard how white people thought and what qualities in black men they respected. He would have to learn how to work with white people: not to become a "spy," but to work with them like clay, massaging their egos and their fears until they took the shape that would further his goals.

Cultivating the goodwill of the white mine managers, he won an appointment to teach other mine chefs how to cook, a position that came with a chauffeur. Back in the homeland, he began to buy up cattle for $40 each; his fame there burgeoned. He built four stucco homes, one for each of his wives. Admiring locals clustered their thatched-roof houses around his estate. He was seen as both traditionally wealthy—cattle were the barometer for prosperity—and forward-thinking, working with something new to the country-side: cash. Elias used his capital to open grocery stores.

Starting in the late '70s, the apartheid government handed out copious business permits in the homelands to try to prevent black people from migrating to the white-run cities. "My father," Elliot told me proudly, "was the first one to bring serious money back to his village."

But in the early '90s, in the space of a year, Elias's grocery shops went from bustling to empty. Apartheid's restrictions on movement benefited some businesses in the homelands; after they were removed, people preferred to go to the mall in a formerly white area nearby. "One day, I just found the shops with nothing in them," Elliot recalled. "I couldn't find out, then, why it closed. A kid of twelve can't ask: Why are things no longer like before? I was habituated to eating stuff from the shop. In the morning I would get bread with peanut butter and jelly. We would drink Cokes! We would put sweets in our pockets. We would open the fridge and think, 'White meat or red meat?'"

But after "the collapse," everything changed. The family sub-sisted on cornmeal porridge and *morogo*, or cooked wild leaves. The locals moved their houses away from Elias's estate, carrying the walls away to other places stone by stone. In a final blow, fifty-nine of the sixty-eight cattle Elias pastured in the mountains disappeared. "We wanted to believe they were just lost," Elliot remembered, not stolen. Every day for a month, a group of boys from the extended family combed the mountains for the missing herd. It was nowhere to be found. After a month, "my father sat down and said, 'I surrender.'" Elias took ill and didn't get out of bed for a year.

At least Elliot had his older brother, Sam. Throughout Elliot's childhood he dwelled happily in the long shadow his brother cast. Sam was a ray of light, a twinkling fairy of a child among the men in Elliot's family, who were generally known for their rectitude. Tall, slender, and playful, he loved to dance, joining a local troupe and taking Elliot to concerts on a stage an hour's walk away.

In the cool of the afternoons, Elias's sons liked to climb the wild fruit trees on their father's estate and gorge themselves on sticky mangoes, papayas, and figs. One day, Sam spied some ripe figs hanging from an especially high tree hanging over a river. He said he was going to climb it and pass them down to his younger brothers. "Take these," he shouted. "They're for you." But then a branch snapped and Sam fell.

After Sam's frightened brothers retrieved him from the water, he wouldn't stop crying, not for days. His mother salved his external wounds, but "he was damaged inside," Elliot told me. One Saturday a few months later, Elliot woke up in the middle of the night to his mother shaking his shoulders. She told him to gather his sisters and brothers and take them out of the house. In the local culture, children weren't supposed to stay in the presence of the deceased. And Elliot knew that his brother was dead.

That whole day he reeled around the estate bewildered. He felt afraid for Sam, gone into that other, unknowable world. But he also felt afraid for himself. "I knew: 'I'm the elder person now.'"

The realization was a blow. In the homeland, a family unit's eldest brother had special duties. "With an elder brother, I always knew I couldn't suffer. If our eldest brother can go get a job in Johannesburg, we knew he would come back and take care of us, buy us clothes and something nice at the grocery. But if you are the firstborn, you have to advise your younger brothers and sisters so they can have a better life. You have a bitter life. You have to taste everything, no matter how bitter, so you can go and tell your younger brothers, 'This one is good and this one is not good.' "

Before Elliot traveled to Johannesburg, he arranged to stay with a cousin who already lived there. He had a plan. "I would work for two years to buy a new house for my parents and my siblings. The third year, I would marry." I asked him what kind of job he had imagined for himself. "Being at a desk," he said. Then he laughed.

Because it hadn't worked out that way. His cousin turned out to live in a squatter camp for people streaming from rural areas to look for jobs. Just like the homeland, though, the squatter camp lacked electricity. The streets were unpaved and the houses were shacks. It all had a shambolically pastoral look, stalks of corn poking up between the shacks on the muddied pathways.

The end of apartheid opened the cities to black people, but it didn't create many new roles within them, so many new black entrants remained visitors, condemned to standing in endless queues as if locked in some eternal process of immigration. In an industrial area, Elliot joined huge lines of jobless people. He tried to develop a strategy. He'd arrive at a factory gate at six in the morning, when the night watchman switched with the morning guard. He'd sidle up to the watchman and ask if he would take him in to see a manager. Some watchmen took a sadistic pleasure in tormenting their unluckier comrades. "Sometimes there would be a board on the gate: NO JOB," Elliot told me. "They would taunt me: 'My man, can't you read English? What does that board say to you?'

"And I'd say, 'No job.' And then the guard would have a smirk."

Other guards were more humane, but there was little they could do. They would whisper sadly, "My man, they are not employing here. It is too dark."

"Too dark," in the local slang, "meant just that," said Elliot. "Nothing. There's no job." The image was painfully reminiscent of the darkness he'd tried to escape.

He searched for two whole years. In that time, he landed just one day of work in a cold-storage facility. He and the other new hires lumbered around shelving pallets of frozen beef, clad in spacesuits complete with masks and rubber gloves. At the end of the day, though, all the new hires were fired. Management decided it didn't need the extra hands.

Michael Buys, the land-reform official, confessed to me what felt like a dirty, shameful secret. Under apartheid, "we were always looking at the white areas," he said. "It looked like they had everything! There was a sense among us that the country that had been bequeathed to us was the white country. But it wasn't."

He dropped his voice. *"It was the whole country."*

Every fucked-up element that had existed under apartheid, in other words.

Buys's superiors told him not to grill the land reform applicants too hard. Asking probing questions implied black people ought to worry about their abilities. "A black man comes in with an application for a farm," his bosses would challenge him. "Why do you ask all these questions? You don't think he'll be able to do what the white people did?"

Buys was often the man tasked with dropping the "beneficiaries" off at the gates of their new farms. Sometimes, driving home, he would find himself gripping his steering wheel and blinking back tears. "As I'm driving away, I would be very sad in the knowledge that this thing—I already know it's not going to work for them," he said. "I could feel it. It is not going to work."

He began to worry everyone around him was flirting with magical thinking. With the hope that, much like apartheid laws seemed to vanish overnight, everything in the country would be similarly wondrously transformed. That the sweat and tears black people poured into the anti-apartheid struggle would be converted, without too much more painful struggle, into the capacity to steward, to grow, and, most of all, to enjoy the country they had inherited. Black people deserved a well-functioning country, was the thinking. Some of his colleagues openly complained they deserved to rest and have good things to flow their way.

This was understandable. If black South Africans didn't deserve this, at least for a little while, who did? But Buys also wondered if this wish wasn't another by-product of pressure from the outside world. The world was so impatient for South Africa to be a "miracle"—maybe even more than black South Africans were.

The story of the twentieth century was supposed to be one of the triumph of peace and human understanding. But its final decade took uneasy turns, with authoritarian backslides in post-Soviet states and genocides in Rwanda and the Balkans. Buys felt the world was looking to South Africa to accomplish what it had failed to show elsewhere: that humanity had exorcised primitive demons like racism and tribalism.

And they wanted South Africans to offer them evidence their faith in black people hadn't been misplaced. They wanted proof that the efforts *they* mounted to help end apartheid—the sanctions, the anti-apartheid concerts at Wembley Stadium—hadn't been for nothing. In celebrating the South African miracle—and, then, intensively scrutinizing its aftermath—Buys sensed foreigners wanted to be shown they had done something really significant for the earth's poor and marginalized. And that perhaps not much more than what they did for black South Africans would be demanded of them to dispatch their duty toward all formerly colonized peoples.

On a flight from America to South Africa, I once overheard a conversation between a black South African flight attendant and a younger black passenger. The flight attendant was admitting she hated Afrikaans. South African Airways pilots still made announcements in the language, which was a constant, painful reminder of her youth. "I hope one day soon it will be gone," she said.

That statement, though, made the younger black passenger upset. "*We* shouldn't say that," he lectured her. Trying to stamp out cultures they didn't like was something white people did. "Progressive people," he informed the flight attendant, "have a duty to preserve the things they hate." He turned toward me and smiled. "*EK* HOU *VAN AFRIKAANS!*" he bellowed. I *love* Afrikaans!

I heard this kind of self-policing to be better than white people all the time. In 2016, a prominent white real estate agent posted an incredibly racist rant on social media—"I shall address the blacks of South Africa as monkeys"—and refused to apologize. But when she died a few years later, black South Africans warned each other not to dance on her grave. "[She] said some racist shit, but I can never celebrate her death," one woman tweeted. "That's what white people do."

A historic Soweto neighborhood began to get wealthier in the '90s, and there I met an internationally touring jazz musician who had razed his whole house to rebuild. There was almost no furniture, but the aspect of the house he was concentrating on, he said, were its fourteen bathrooms.

He shook his head with a mix of faux-irritation and pride. The remodel was killing him, he said. Did I *know* what fourteen imported European toilets cost?

I asked him if he ever anticipated a scenario in which fourteen people would need to take a crap in his house at the same time. That wasn't the point, he said. He visited Italian manors on his tours, and the parts that most impressed him were the bathrooms. The gleam of the chrome faucets, the tiles, the gilded wallpapers. To make it, he decided, was to have beautiful bathrooms. So he was prioritizing his bathrooms first.

When I recounted that to Dipuo, she said it could have been a metaphor for the new ANC government—that it began to abandon a focus on redistribution and justice in favor of designing beautiful bathrooms, of mimicking the apparent sheen of so-called first-world countries. The government refurbished the Johannesburg airport to be "world-class" while parts of Soweto still had open sewage canals. Thabo Mbeki, Mandela's deputy president, took over stewarding the economy and adopted a corporate-friendly mien. He instituted an affirmative action program that incentivized large corporations to do deals with already-successful black businesspeople—often Western-educated former exiles—who dressed and talked in a polished way or who already had money.

Rapidly, a group began to emerge that people called the "black diamonds." White journalists doggedly investigated the sources of their wealth, reporting that black businessmen who drove Audis or wore TAG Heuer watches made their money off shady arrangements with the government. Government ministers themselves began to drive high-end cars—a behavior many black South Africans both criticized and wanted to emulate. Often, the first thing a university graduate did with his paycheck was make a down payment on a shiny new Peugeot. The townships filled up with informal driving schools; Soweto's vacant plots sprouted cones and overturned plastic chairs to demarcate the training courses.

I had a white friend who rarely complained about South Africa. But he became strangely irate when he saw black officials driving BMWs. "I know it sounds stupid and naive," he confessed. "But I was bitterly disappointed when black people started buying BMWs. I hoped they would be better than us."

In the '80s, this man came to hate almost everything he associated with white life—from its hypocritical democratic pretenses down to the cloyingly sweet food. White society prized uniformity. There was no such thing as a minor disagreement with white culture. If you broke with one aspect—if, say, you dabbled in recreational drugs, stopped believing in God, or came out as gay—you were presumed to oppose apartheid. And if you opposed apartheid, you might be called gay or be accused of doing drugs. In his teens, this friend tried to grow a beard. It came in too thin; actually, it looked terrible. But he couldn't shave it, because when he shaved it and looked in the mirror, he saw his father, who supported apartheid.

In the early '90s, he moved to a shabby "commune" on the edge of Johannesburg's downtown. It seemed to him the nuclear family was also for racists. White people's conspicuous consumption, their materialism and "house pride," disgusted him.

That disgust was matched by an equal awe for black South Africans. He felt admiration for how much music and art black South Africans made under apartheid—for what he considered their cool in warped circumstances. For the way they'd made space for pride, even joy, while the white regime strove to crush them under the boot. By "I hoped they would be better than us," my friend meant he hoped they would import the qualities they'd evinced under oppression into leadership. He hoped they would be both completely different from white leaders *and* prudent, economically responsible, and not too revolutionary.

"You were hoping the new leaders would be like the Princeton economics department crossed with Bob Marley?" I joked.

He didn't laugh. "Basically," he said.

This hope, though, also permeated black society. In the '80s, describing white South Africans, Oliver Tambo said, "*They* shoot children. That's *their* morality." Police shootings under apartheid were terrible, but they had also somehow come to be expected, while police shootings afterward were seen as shocking and unnatural. Some black South Africans asserted that it would not be possible, existentially, for black people in power to turn out like white people. A black sociologist wrote that "given their tolerance and inclusivity, black people may turn out to be the true guardians of a properly contextualized and progressive liberalism. . . . Grace, dignity, and self-worth have always been the defining characteristics of the black world."

From time to time, allegations surfaced that some leading post-apartheid black luminary or politician was a "spy." As juicy as these allegations were—and as important as they might be to investigate, since a secret history as a collaborator could make a leader vulnerable to blackmail—they tended to be suppressed; after apartheid, it was as if this ambiguity had to be erased. In 2019, a black listener called into a top talk radio show to ask why there were rumors that ex-collaborators held high government positions. There were terribly powerful incentives, under apartheid, to collaborate; it didn't take an evil person to do it. But the host began to shout to drown out the caller. *"Calm down!"* he hissed. *"Calm down!"*—as if even to suggest a black person could behave dishonorably was, now, the graver kind of treason.

Dipuo told me she also hoped her "personal life would resume" after 1994. "I realized my childhood was gone," she said. "There weren't fun things I'd done in my youth, like ordinary people. A huge chunk of my life just hadn't happened for me."

But it turned out there was nothing to resume. She had never been around many men, and she found dating excruciatingly awkward. Meanwhile, the men and women in Soweto who were seizing the opportunity to fall in love and have sex were dying.

By 1996, epidemiologists estimate 15 percent of South Africans in their twenties were HIV-positive. Epidemiologists said the fact that HIV flared just after black liberation was a coincidence, or even an unfortunate corollary to more freedom of movement.

But it seemed wrong to Dipuo that the people who had the most to gain from the end of apartheid were being struck down when they began to do the things they had never been permitted: to flirt, to make love, just to live. White people were contracting HIV, too. But the awareness campaigns—murals with brown-faced stick figures juggling condoms—obviously targeted black people.

She noticed a friend in Meadowlands was dropping weight. One day, Dipuo saw her friend standing in front of her house, tears streaming down her face. Dipuo realized she'd unconsciously assumed apartheid's aftermath would entail no more tears.

Later that night, an acquaintance came to tell Dipuo that her friend had gone inside, collapsed, and died of HIV-related complications. Dipuo went to look at the body before it was taken to the funeral home. She wept to see a woman who was supposed to have a future but, so soon, had ended up a corpse.

17

Christo

A BLOND RUGBY PLAYER NAMED Monte arrived on the UFS campus around the same time Christo did. When he got there, Monte told me, he felt tremendously afraid. Like Christo, Monte served in the army. In the early '90s, his uncles told him point-blank that the purpose of his military service was to annihilate any hope of black rule. They warned him that under a black-led regime, "they didn't even know whether there'd be structures for us to live in."

Jaco, Christo's brother, also enrolled at UFS shortly after Christo did. He told me he felt confused, too. "We were kind of lost boys in this Peter Pan situation. I'm not saying there was anything *wrong* with our fathers. But they had no idea what we were going through. The Afrikaner authorities we trusted—they just suddenly decided, 'Oh, we've been wrong all along.'"

Most of the black students in Monte's dorm were initially basically nice. "You don't even know what you're afraid of," he said. But he found himself flicking pencil shavings at them from the window of his dorm room anyway.

Heartened by the apparent success of UFS's early integration efforts, in 1994 its administrators began to recruit black students much more aggressively. Billyboy Ramahlele, the first black dorm father UFS ever appointed, took the lead, running radio campaigns to encourage black students to apply. *He* had been wary of UFS, he told me in his campus office.

In the township outside Bloemfontein where he grew up, the white city was considered the epitome of evil. "I'd go in to buy clothes," Ramahlele remembered, "and I'd come back and tell my people, 'I wish I had an AK-47 to shoot all those whites.'" But the way his attitudes softened in the mid-'90s surprised him. A liberal administrator had recruited him to campus, and Ramahlele loved meeting fascinating international scholars. He liked the quiet of the early mornings on the main quad, when the only noise was the clucking of crowlike birds as they snuffled through the Styrofoam trays students had left the night before.

White campus leaders tended to attribute changes on campus to their decisions—to white people's choices. Ramahlele, though, thought *he* was the one who'd made the difference. He felt proud he'd charmed the pants off the white administrators. "I was smuggled in [to management]," he told me, but white adults and young people alike soon came to trust him. "Whenever there was a soccer match"—historically the "black" sport—he took vans full of both black *and* white students to watch. "Every year," he told me, the black cohort at UFS "doubled, doubled, doubled."

One night, though, some of the new black students got together with Lebohang, Francois's friend, in his dorm room. Lebohang was relating how a white student had pulled him aside and marveled, "Hey, where did you learn to speak such beautiful Afrikaans? You are definitely going to make it here."

That had made Lebohang feel happy. But another boy named Shadrack disagreed. He wondered why speaking "beautiful Afrikaans" was still a condition for "making it" after apartheid. Their parents fought the curriculum that required black students to study in Afrikaans. Shouldn't the white boys have to learn *black* people's languages now?

Shadrack also called attention to the way the dormitory traditions Lebohang liked actually mimicked—and subtly perpetuated—classic South African power dynamics. The way black freshmen were required to walk through back doors. The way they had to bow to seniors and call them "uncle"—and the seniors were all still white. Black men had to grovel before white people under apartheid. Why should black youth now do it voluntarily? "This whole thing," Shadrack concluded before a rapt audience in Lebohang's dorm room, "amounts to shit."

"We started off with 10 percent [black students] in the dorms," Teuns Verschoor, Christo's dorm father, told me. "That was really something. They fell in with the [dorm] cultures. They even decided to start playing rugby." When the black student population reached 30 percent, though, "they started establishing their own identities."

Ramahlele and Verschoor often mentioned the number 30 percent. It seemed like a demographic hot line—when the unhappy feelings of black students like Shadrack became dominant. When a dormitory became more than 30 percent black, black students started to feel far more empowered to request that a dorm's culture reflect *their* preferences. Verschoor's rumpled approachability made him a natural confidant, and "a lot of black students started asking me questions. Why do we have to do this tradition or that tradition?"

He held meetings to discuss tweaking the practices that most bothered black students. The first black woman on the UFS student council fielded a huge number of black complaints. "In one dorm, when you turned twenty-one, you had to run naked," she told me. "For black guys, the culture does not allow a twenty-one-year-old guy to run around naked with his penis out." But when black students started criticizing the traditions, white students closed ranks around them. "Even white students who actually didn't like running around naked—it became important to them."

Monte's dorm mascot was a chicken. If a freshman encountered the chicken in the hallway, he had to wait for it to pass before he continued. The black students in his dorm began to object to the chicken at dorm meetings, saying that waiting on it reminded them of the humiliations black people suffered—and continued to suffer—on white-run farms.

As their objections mounted, Monte became more devoted to the chicken. "The chicken tradition was awesome," he told me defiantly. "And then *they* said it was racist. A lot of the things we thought were just discipline"—like requiring freshmen to wear special uniforms—"were said to be racism. Some black people began to say only a racist would play rugby." He opened a yearbook and turned to a page with picture of his dorm-mates. He stubbed at the faces of several white boys who'd played rugby with his pointer finger, as if to erase their identities. "*You're* a racist. *You're* a racist."

After flicking the pencil shavings at black students from his dorm room window, Monte graduated to throwing pebbles at them. Administrators disciplined him. But *this* created a feedback loop that started to clarify for him the roots of his distress: shame—specifically, a degree of shame he was being forced to feel that was disproportionate to his personal sins. Administrators suggested his reactions to black students' criticism arose from irrational psychological afflictions like "posttraumatic stress" or "pathological white pride."

He guessed this was a stab at empathy. But a black education professor's book on integrating universities used the word "emotional" dozens of times to characterize complaints Monte felt were real and legitimate, like that black students in his dorm aggressively switched the common room TV from rugby to soccer and then wouldn't switch it back. The academic concluded anxious young white people were merely experiencing what he called "the sensitive cultural properties of white emotion" or "one of their right-wing fits."

Monte found this kind of thing patronizing. It was clear he was somehow pitied. But it was also clear he was expected to come to Jesus—to become less "emotional" and more "reasonable," which seemed to mean to acquiesce entirely to black people's depiction of their now shared universe.

And it wasn't true that nothing was changing. Things were changing *slowly*, yes. But more important than the rate of change was Monte's perception they were only changing in one direction. And that, in the future, they could only ever change in one direction. Most public schools had operated in Afrikaans. After apartheid, the government shifted a number of them to English instruction. And the ANC government began to rename things: South Africa's three main airports had been named after Afrikaner political leaders. That was a point of pride for white South Africans, representing how they thought of themselves not just as rugged pioneers but as technological innovators. But the new government renamed them all.

Many streets and schools named for Prime Minister Hendrik Verwoerd, the "architect of apartheid," were renamed, too. After Mandela became president, the name Verwoerd was expunged even from places like Verwoerdburg, the largest town between Johannesburg and Pretoria. The ANC government boasted that Verwoerdburg's residents would get to pick their new name in a democratic vote. But Monte noted they weren't given any choice to retain Verwoerdburg. Wasn't that rigged, actually? Rumors circulated that this was just a beginning—a testing of the waters to gauge white people's capacity to resist. And that in ten or fifteen years black people would rename *every* street and city and take their farmland by force. Meanwhile, Monte knew there would never be another new South African town founded with an Afrikaans name.

Contemplating South Africa in the '90s, an *Economist* correspondent observed that "the lives of many whites exude sadness." It perplexed him. In so many material ways, white life remained more or less untouched or had even improved. But as time wore on, even wealthy white South Africans began to radiate a degree of anxiety that didn't match any simple economic analysis of their situation.

A startling number of formerly anti-apartheid white journalists began to voice bitter criticisms. One told *The Wall Street Journal* that post-apartheid South Africa was "worse than anything under apartheid." An Afrikaner poet who did prison time under apartheid for aiding the black-liberation cause wrote a major essay pronouncing the new black-led country "a sewer of betrayed expectations and thievery, fear and unbridled greed."

People became distressed by things like potholes in the roads. The theory was that they were emerging at a faster and faster clip. Compared to other, less developed parts of Africa, the roads in South Africa were pretty good. But "the roads are all going," people would say mournfully. "It's because *they* don't care."

Potholes became a potent symbol: a sign that the veneer of reconciliation or, indeed, of civilization in South Africa was fragile and something darker was going to erupt through it. Sometimes, when I told white South Africans about my travels in rural areas, they'd ask me about the potholes. They seemed disappointed if I said I hadn't encountered any. That potholes were getting worse was something it seemed they *wanted* to believe.

Hermann Giliomee, the historian of Afrikaner culture, went on the Dakar Safaris. He told me he thought what dogged Afrikaners after apartheid was less a concern for their physical safety than the deep sense of being irrelevant. A political scientist he knew was invited to make a presentation to the government on the Afrikaners' sentiments about the new South Africa. The academic wrote that their greatest grievance was a feeling of superfluousness. "We would like to assure [you] that the Afrikaners are . . . deeply involved in the affairs of this country. [Our] withdrawal . . . from education, the economy, agriculture, technology, sport, etc., will lead to serious consequences."

Progressive white South Africans, in particular, had the sense under apartheid that they were a vanguard. One of Giliomee's friends, a liberal white politician, left the Dakar Safaris believing he and Thabo Mbeki were "best friends." Without articulating it to himself, he expected the aftermath of apartheid to be an exciting time, full of the same adventures with black thinkers and thrilling work helping redesign the country. When apartheid fell, though, Mbeki just stopped returning his calls. He had no more use for him.

The sidelined politician fired off policy proposals to Mbeki's office. Mbeki gave no signal he even read them. His friend "started drinking heavily," Giliomee said. "He drank himself to death."

White people weren't supposed to cling to the past. But in subtle ways, they weren't fully welcomed into the future, either. Some did feel eager to change their priorities. One engineer I knew slept only a couple of hours a night in order to design and test an extraordinarily complicated, computer-run water-tank and filtration system that "could have great implications for the lives of the black poor," he told me excitedly. Another pair of white engineers attempted to design an eco-friendly house with built-in solar panels for poor South Africans.

They built a hundred. But few black families moved in. Bereft, the engineers couldn't understand it. Dipuo thought she knew why. The eco-houses resembled igloos, and "what African wants to live in a fucking igloo?" she asked me, howling with laughter. That might seem cool to a white hipster, but for black people, "a shack is better."

Francois, the UFS student who founded a club with his friend Lebohang, confessed he always wondered if Lebohang wasn't really "looking down at me from a skeptical distance." Dipuo and Malaika *did* make private comedy of white people who claimed to be their "allies," mocking their poorly done dreadlocks or their pseudo-African-patterned shirts.

Dipuo recalled a pair of young white people who came to live in Meadowlands for a few months. "They said they had been vegetarians before, but in Soweto, they wanted to eat meat with their bare hands, to be 'with the people.' They used language we don't use. Violent language. They had this poster—'Fuck White Supremacists!'"

She burst out laughing again. They seemed to expect Dipuo and her friends would be progressive robots that spouted race theory every time you wound them up.

"Do you remember that white woman," Malaika broke in, "who thought she could take a selfie with a lion?" She started to laugh, too.

She was referring to a white woman who was killed by a lion while on safari. It was a freak accident. The woman only rolled her Jeep window a quarter of the way down.

But the two black women were cracking up. Then Dipuo turned serious. "There is no white person in the world," she said, "not a single one, who will ever legitimately be a part of us."

Another white friend told me, with unease, about taking a hike in a remote area. He hired a pair of local guides who said they wanted to show him a rock pillar the "locals" used for "authentic worship rituals." The guides insisted my friend pose for pictures touching the pillar, assuring him that was how they did it. When the man got home and looked through his camera roll, though, he realized the stance they made him adopt made it look unmistakably like he was stroking a giant penis.

He would have found the prank funny if he had been overseas, he allowed—a perhaps well-deserved caper at the expense of a naive or arrogant tourist. But he wasn't a foreigner. He was one of the guides' countrymen.

Little things like that made white South Africans wonder if there was a far deeper well of antagonism toward them waiting to be uncovered. A white man who studied with Christo at UFS explained how conflict arose in his dormitory over "telephone service," a tradition in which freshmen had to man a telephone in the lobby in shifts. As a freshman, he hadn't enjoyed the job. But he experienced black students' refusal to do telephone service as an assault on something holy. "Why should a white freshman do an extra hour of telephone service just because somebody else thinks it's below him?" he asked.

And he wondered if the black stand against telephone service was about much more than just the irritation of answering telephones. "I thought there was some sort of broad intent against Afrikaner things," he said. "I remember one black guy told me, 'It's discriminatory that this university teaches in Afrikaans at all.'"

In 2016, Shaw and Kriegler—the criminologists—noticed something fascinating in the crime data they studied. When white South Africans answered a survey about the crimes they'd experienced, their responses contradicted what they reported to police stations. To the police, they reported twice as many carjackings as home invasions, a media-notorious crime in which robbers entered a house, tied up its inhabitants, and sometimes killed them. But to the academic surveyors, they reported they'd been the victims of twice as many home invasions as carjackings.

A carjacking is an easier crime to fake for insurance fraud. But the disparity was so stark it suggested another explanation: that a number of white South Africans had a memory of being assaulted in their homes when it never happened.

On some level, I found white South Africans simply expected to have their homes invaded someday by black burglars. The journalist Mark Gevisser has called this "Mau Mau anxiety," after the violent rebellion that helped drive white colonials out of Kenya in the 1950s. It lurks even "in a bleeding-heart liberal like myself," he wrote.

Perhaps the survey respondents heard frightening reports of home invasions on the news and came to imagine the memory was theirs. But some of the respondents may have imagined they had been attacked in their homes simply because they could not understand how they would *not* be.

Many white South Africans suspected that, if *they* were in black people's shoes, they would not be so forgiving. I knew a white woman who was haunted by the memory of a car accident. The crash had been another driver's fault. On the scene, the other driver acknowledged responsibility. But then, a few days later, my friend's insurance called. The other driver was formally denying culpability.

The insurance rep explained it wasn't going to make a difference; all the damage would be covered. But my friend found herself possessed by an unquenchable rage. The infuriating thing was that the other driver *acknowledged the truth* to her and was now tactically denying it. The bait-and-switch had informed my friend's behavior. Right after the accident, she didn't bother to take photographs because she took the driver at her word.

Bitterly Facebook-stalking the driver a few days later, my friend had a chilling thought: "This is the position black South Africans find themselves in every day." They accepted the guarantee implicit in white people's embrace of a constitutional change that they regretted apartheid. And that, if necessary, they would pay.

Now white authority figures were claiming South Africa's problems were black people's fault. And so black South Africans were denied the opportunity to dwell in a truth everybody knew, deep down. Given the blinding fury my friend felt after being put in this position over a *car*, she told me that "I just cannot believe black South Africans are not quietly going mad."

In apartheid's aftermath, Chris Louw—the journalist who wrote F. W. de Klerk's brother the bitter open letter—moved to an Afrikaner-dominated town outside Pretoria. He wrote that he felt an omnipresent sense of dread. The lake nearby was blissful, with teens cavorting on Jet Skis and grandparents watching from waterside bars. But the kinds of robberies that, in the '80s, were the township thugs' specialty had spread to formerly white, less-well-policed rural areas, and his neighbors reported break-ins.

Louw began to feel petrified something much worse than a break-in—a murder, a rape—could happen to him or his wife. The town's white residents had established a neighborhood watch. In its operational style, it mimicked the old white military. Its volunteers kept their radios on 24/7 and formed tracker platoons to trail unfamiliar black pedestrians.

Partly that felt like overkill to Louw, even a tiny bit embarrassing. But it also felt reassuring and familiar to join it, almost joyful. Louw wrote that listening to the neighborhood watch's radio made him feel he'd been living in an illusion. Not the old illusion that black people were out to get white people, but the post-apartheid illusion that they *weren't*. South African life still constituted "a low-scale war," he told his wife. "We have to take sides."

Several years later, Louw was found dead on his estate. Weeks earlier he told his wife he'd found a gun buried in a corner of their property. It was all unfolding just like Christo's father's military friend warned it would: black people would hide weapons on white people's land so they could come back for them later.

But Louw's death actually turned out to be a suicide. I had a friend who happened to be one of Louw's good buddies. He told me he believed Louw essentially tried to stage his own murder to expiate a feeling of guilt. In his open letter, Louw referred obliquely to the violence he'd been sent to commit as a soldier— and the bind in which that personal history put him. Now "I'm nothing but an old sinner, tainted with gun-oil [and] the blood of black children. I'm too innocent to beg for forgiveness, [but] I'm too guilty to wash clean my hands."

My friend said he thought Louw's anxiety arose partly out of a *wish* to be attacked, not only a fear of it. Louw wanted his guilt expunged by a black man drawing *his* blood. Driven to agony by waiting, he did it himself.

In America, we think of white "deaths of despair" as driven by a straightforward sense of downward social trajectory. But I wondered if some aren't prompted by guilt and the lack of resolution inherent in having escaped proper judgment. Like many South African men who died by suicide, Louw also had financial problems. But—paradoxically—Louw's friend said he believed Louw committed suicide so the younger version of himself, the one who mistreated black people so they wouldn't hurt him first, could be redeemed. Louw even planted the gun on his property himself.

18

Malaika

WHEN MALAIKA TURNED ELEVEN, DIPUO told her she was going to attend an elementary school in a formerly white neighborhood. Some of these schools were actively recruiting black students, and Dipuo spent significant money to buy Malaika new things: the black skirt and the turquoise sweater, a new backpack, even a cutely decorated plastic lunchbox. She braved a mega-mall in Soweto to buy what people in Meadowlands called a "white person's lunch." This was different from the messy, fragrant mounds of corn porridge slathered with gravy Sowetans enjoyed. A "white person's lunch" was a bouquet of colorful cylinders, cubes, and pyramids individually wrapped in plastic. Fingers of celery, apple wedges, and sandwiches on white, pillowy bread.

Malaika still had to wear shoes with holes on the bottom. But her grandmother exhorted her to polish the tops extra hard. "Even when your shoe is a problem, shine the top. People can't see underneath your shoe."

But somehow it seemed to Malaika they could. Melpark Primary was much bigger than the school Malaika had attended in Soweto. There was a "piano room" and a "computer laboratory" with twenty desktop computers. In Soweto, she had to buy snacks at recess from informal street vendors. The schoolgrounds were encased by metal bars, and kids had to claw through the fence for treats like they were in a zoo. Her new school had a dedicated snack bar right on site.

Yet Malaika's new uniform felt baggy and tight in all the wrong places. The slender white girls gliding through the halls bumped into her, as if they hadn't seen her, despite what she felt was her considerable bulk. Those girls smelled amazing, like gardenia perfume or lavender shampoo. Malaika thought she smelled like bus exhaust.

Months passed before most of her classmates ever heard her speak. On that day, Malaika's fourth-grade English teacher came into class weeping. "Mrs. Martin had very smooth skin," Malaika remembered. "She was a sweet teacher . . . and she was crying and crying."

Some students cried out, "Ma'am! What's wrong?"

"My dog is missing," Mrs. Martin wept.

Sitting in the back of the class, Malaika felt something rising in her chest she couldn't control. A tickle. It was going to be a laugh. "My laughter is actually very insensitive," she told me. "The snot streams out, and I start to choke."

She knew it was wrong to laugh. Mrs. Martin looked so upset—disheveled and pitiful, in fact. "I felt sad for her," Malaika told me. Yet the urge to laugh also filled her like air inflating a balloon until the pressure was too much. She knew this was going to be one of her worst laughs ever. She laughed until she cried.

The classroom fell silent.

"Why are you laughing?" Mrs. Martin said crossly.

"It's just a dog!" Malaika choked out. "Who cries about a dog?"

"The girls were throwing daggers at me" with their eyes, Malaika remembered. But "the more they looked at me, the more I laughed. In my world, a dog is not something serious. A black person—when he goes missing, it's like, 'Okay, one of those.' But when you say a *dog* is missing, they"—white people—"act like it's a moral thing."

"You should hear them talking about their animals," Dipuo added. "They call them their 'babies.' The same white man who will make a black person ride in the back of a pickup truck, in the rain and the wind, will put his dog in the passenger seat."

It's true. When I moved from Cape Town to Johannesburg, I rented a cottage behind a house in a predominantly white neighborhood. My neighbors there frequently sent tear-jerking appeals over WhatsApp about rabbit sanctuaries that needed funding, dog-blanket drives, or wounded lizards. Compared to people, animals were easy to love. They couldn't talk back or inform you that you were loving them wrong. It felt as if white South Africans' ostentatious love for animals served as a proxy for the tenderness they knew they ought to extend toward black people. The language they used about animals echoed the language black South Africans often begged them to use about black people—language about their vulnerability and fundamental rights. On my neighborhood Facebook page, a woman posted that she'd discovered a terrifying spider in her bathroom.

Spiders are "gentle, shy creatures," native to the land and deserving respect, a commenter reprimanded her. "Please educate yourself to be less fearful." Black people who moved to formerly white neighborhoods traded grim stories about white landlords who, upon meeting them, claimed the property was taken. But another white commenter said it was virtuous to allow spiders to live in your house. "They are very good tenants, you'll see."

Mrs. Martin stared at Malaika while she laughed—less out of distaste, though, than fascination. She, too, was surprised to hear Malaika speak good English. Many white Melpark Primary teachers didn't push Malaika too hard out of a sense it was a miracle she was at the formerly white school in the first place and she shouldn't be expected to do *well* on top of that. Once, a math teacher asked her to stay after class when she scored high on a test. The teacher went through each question, requizzing her and asking, "How did you get that?"

The teacher didn't seem angry, just perplexed. "She's puzzled," Malaika realized, that "a black child got 99 percent."

After the missing dog episode, Mrs. Martin became more solicitous of Malaika. She began to praise her essays; she'd tell Malaika's white classmates that a girl from Soweto was beating them at *English*, and wasn't that grand? Sometimes, Mrs. Martin would ask Malaika to stay after class just to talk. "She always wanted to hear my thoughts," Malaika remembered. "Always wanted to be with me."

Malaika had anticipated this would be better than being ignored. But unexpectedly, she began to feel uneasy. The love she knew had always been fraught. From her grandmother, love went along with scoldings. From her sister Tshepiso, it went along with arguments and pinches. Mrs. Martin's love was sugar-sweet. She began to invite Malaika to her house after school, where her husband would fix them elaborate snacks. "She put me on a pedestal," Malaika remembered. "I could do no wrong."

Malaika found herself acting out, testing Mrs. Martin's love. But it seemed unconnected to her behavior. If she talked out of turn or cracked jokes in class, Mrs. Martin just smiled benignly. If she showed up hours late to school, Mrs. Martin would accompany her to the principal's office to defend her. "It got to a point where I was like, 'Can you really *not* love me? Even my own mother doesn't love me like this.'"

Malaika started to wonder if that was, in fact, the point. When she acted out, Mrs. Martin would say compassionately that, if anyone ever made her feel wrong or undeserving, that person was to blame. By *that person*, though, even if indirectly, Mrs.

Martin implicated Dipuo—who, indeed, picked fights with Malaika. Mrs. Martin's comment made Malaika feel defensive of her mother. "She deserves to be *my* child," is what she felt Mrs. Martin was thinking. "This child is too good for black people."

"You may love me, ma'am," she imagined herself responding. "But I have a *black* mother. I am a *black* child."

Perhaps Mrs. Martin's efforts were not a hundred percent altruistic. They might be an effort to refurbish her self-image—to prove to *herself* that, although she grew up under apartheid, if she had been in power she would have behaved differently.

"With white people—when they love you, it's revolting how they love you so extremely," Malaika reflected. "If anything happens to me, the first people who will come to my aid are white people. The most generosity I ever get is from whites." Malaika said this contemptuously. By the time I met her, she was in college, and she wrote popular essays on Facebook. Invitations came her way from the very people—white elites—she often targeted with the most withering criticism. "The rich ones, if they hate my views, they'll say, 'Please come to our company and share your views with us. We will pay you!'"

Once, Malaika published an essay lambasting a South African literary festival as racially prejudiced. The next day she awoke to an email from the festival's white organizer. "Please come speak to us," the organizer begged. So she went and "basically" told the white audience: "Go fuck yourselves! All you white people are doing terrible things!" The crowd broke into frenzied applause.

It had briefly felt baffling. Didn't these people have any self-respect? But then she realized they were clapping for themselves—celebrating their own willingness to take a punch.

At Melpark Primary, she made a white friend named Charlie. But when she told him she fantasized about going on vacation to the banks of the Fish River—a remote place where you had to camp in a tent—his jaw dropped. White South Africans historically liked camping while black South Africans who could afford vacations stayed in hotels. "Wow!" Charlie said. "You always want to go to these white places! It's so cool!"

"What does that mean?" Malaika asked.

"I just mean, you're different from the rest of *them*," Charlie replied.

"The 'rest of them,'" Malaika told me hotly, "were people like my mother, my uncles, and my grandmother." Whenever Charlie told Malaika what he liked about her, he juxtaposed it against an expectation that black people, on the whole, would be uneducated, unimaginative, or inscrutable.

Her new white friends could be so kind. Almost painfully kind. They paid for outings to places she'd never gone, like the zoo. "Black people," she thought unhappily, "didn't do that." They didn't seem to do the things white people did: go to lectures and the theater, dream up entrepreneurial schemes, artistically decorate their homes, travel through Africa.

It gave Malaika a queasy feeling when she returned home from school. She'd get back to Soweto and wonder, "Why are these people not *doing* anything?" In the neighborhood around Melpark Primary, "you'd see white people in the coffee shops, working on their laptops. Busy." White people didn't look like they sat at intersections throwing dice, like her uncle Ali did.

It seemed to her the white people she saw had purpose, which unnerved her, given her difficult experiences with some of her fellow white students. Sometimes, she tried to go into the white-dominated cafés, but she felt uncomfortable. "Nobody was going to say anything," she said. "Under apartheid, it was explicit. 'Can I see your pass?' Now, there was no one saying, 'Can I see your pass?'" But her hand-me-down clothes and the way she hurriedly paid her bill when she saw a battered minibus taxi pull to the curb felt like a chorus of mocking voices continually whispering, "You don't belong here."

The thing that hurt the most was that she couldn't tell how much the message that she didn't belong was sent by white people, or engineered by them, and how much of it was her own insecurity or her imagination. When she missed the school bus home, she had to take a minibus taxi through a formerly white neighborhood. In the '70s, it had been a desirable address of high, granite apartment buildings, but in the '90s it rapidly became much blacker and poorer. The buildings fell into disrepair. Trash fluttered everywhere and threadbare undergarments hung off the balconies like SOS flags.

"It's dirty," Malaika would think. "And white people are clean. So maybe it means black people are fundamentally dirty. It would make me think, 'What's wrong with us?' As a black person, you begin to think something is not quite right with your own nature."

At one point, Dipuo enrolled Malaika in a formerly all-white theater club. The teachers talked about something called an "inner monologue." But it felt like what Malaika had in *her* head was a dialogue. A dialogue between her own voice and that of a white person saying, "You are savage." Sometimes, the voices argued. Other times, their murmurs blended together until she couldn't tell them apart. "So it becomes your own voice saying, 'You don't belong in all those pretty, proper places.'"

Later, though, she thought harder about the difference between her white peers and her black community. "We are a big family," she considered. "My mom, my gran, me, Vina, Ali, Tshepiso. There are six of us in a shack. There isn't space to move! So we go onto the streets. The older ones go into bars. We don't have money to buy washing machines."

She wondered if part of the point of white people's generosity was to underscore—wordlessly—black people's insufficiencies. To justify the status white people still occupied in South Africa by subjecting aspirational black South Africans to the constant, unhappy comparison between a sparkling, glorious version of white society and the gritty, enduring reality of black people's communities.

"What kind of experience," I once asked Dipuo, "do you think Malaika was having at the school?"

"Malaika never gave me major issues about it," Dipuo said proudly. The two of us once drove past Melpark Primary together, and Dipuo asked me to stop so she could take a selfie in front of the steepled main building, as if it had been a seminal place in her own story.

Malaika rarely had the heart to tell Dipuo her real experience. Dipuo's friends sometimes joked to Malaika about what a radical her mother was. That her nickname was "Stalin." That when other black women were using chemicals or weaves to sport a smooth "white" hairstyle, Dipuo went to her NGO job in long dreadlocks. She knew her mother gave herself, body and soul, to the struggle against apartheid. At a time when the white government tacitly encouraged abortions among black women, she felt thankful Dipuo stubbornly insisted on having her.

Dipuo still attended ANC meetings in Soweto, and sometimes she brought Malaika. Their leaders kicked them off with lusty rounds of old apartheid-era struggle songs:

Shona malanga, shona
Sesizo dibana, nge bazooka ehlathini.

Let the sun go down
Until we meet again and bazooka them in the forest.

Yet Malaika sensed that if she didn't take advantage of Melpark Primary—of "white" opportunities—she might crush some fragile hope lurking inside of her mother. When Malaika came home, Dipuo would ask her, with excitement, how it felt to take the bus to the formerly white neighborhoods. She would say, "You will be my struggle's beneficiary."

For a performance of *Sleeping Beauty*, the theater club's white director cast Malaika as a slave. Malaika came home and told her mother she wanted to quit. But her mother lashed out. "Not only will you return," she snapped, "you will learn to *enjoy* it."

After the director shouted at Malaika in front of the whole club, though, Malaika had enough. She informed Dipuo she wouldn't return even if her mother whipped her. "I am sick and tired of acting in plays about white sleeping beauties!" Malaika screamed. "Take me to a community theater where I can at least act out *our* stories! Not these things of white people!"

When she put it this way, Malaika assumed Dipuo would understand. But her mother just withered in front of her. She averted her eyes as if Malaika had hit her, and said exhaustedly, "Okay, Lesego."

By herself, Malaika paged through the '80s-era books and pamphlets her mother still kept. She found herself brought to tears by the early Black Consciousness thinkers when they said black people suffered both from white people's low expectations and their own self-hatred and self-doubt. Reading that felt like pushing the unmarked gate to Liliesleaf in—discovering something that was still there but that somebody tried to hide from her. She wrote her own poem:

God, we beg You to forgive our sins,
Even though . . .
It was not [black people] who denied [Jesus] . . .
It was not us who sold him . . .
We have never been to Jerusalem.

You have always demanded honesty, God.
And the truth is that Your son Jesus Christ
Did not come to us . . .
He was not killed by us.

While at Melpark Primary, though, Malaika also fell in love with a white-run store. Once, she missed her school bus home and, waiting for the next one, she wandered through a strip mall. Beside a pharmacy was a thrift shop called Bounty Hunters: a long, dark warren lined with knickknacks, apartheid-era coins, clothes, and jewelry. "White people's old stuff," she thought with wonderment.

And there were so many books. Soweto didn't have used bookstores. She flipped through hundreds that afternoon, amazed to learn she could buy hand-me-down novels for the price of a popsicle. She settled on *Blood Oath*, a thriller about a man who avenges his dead relatives while being hunted by vicious assassins.

Malaika started to pay weekly pilgrimages to Bounty Hunters. She used her allowance to buy political novels about Richard Nixon and Danielle Steel romances. Though Malaika felt judged by the people at Melpark Primary, she loved going through their elders' belongings. "The books had little inscriptions: 'To Annabelle, I hope you will enjoy this, Grandma.' I also found a lot of photos," she remembered. "There were pictures of old white grannies. Farms with kids. And love letters. I felt so happy reading those."

And she began to dress more "white." It started with chunky knitted scarves and then T-shirts advertising obscure American punk bands. Dipuo felt perplexed. "It reminded me of how those academic leftist sorts dressed," she told me.

Dipuo's NGO work brought her into contact with the white South Africans who believed themselves to be the most progressive. But faced, for the first time, with colleagues who would *always* be considered more progressive—people of color—these white progressives seemed to drift, fashion-wise, further and further toward the avant-garde, as if determined to convey they were still rebels. The men painted their fingernails. The women wore mohawks or sported oversized, spiky steel jewelry, as if driven to prove their willingness to undertake penitential rites.

It was strange to see Malaika adopt this style. "When everybody in Soweto was getting weaves, she would do Mohawks," Dipuo remembered.

"And in the middle, I'd dye it red!" Malaika chortled. At Bounty Hunters, she scavenged the CDs. Sowetans listened to Kwaito—a township hip hop—or jazz or gospel. But she started to favor heavy metal. "I went through a Bullet for My Valentine phase."

Malaika also started an illicit business selling essays at school for pocket money. "I had different prices for different races," she told me, laughing. It was a form of unspoken payback: black students paid the least, then colored students. White kids paid the most.

"The white students were very lazy," she remembered. "They would say, 'Please write an essay for me, but don't make it too smart. Make it a bit dumb. Otherwise, the teacher will know it's not me.'"

But she actually loved writing the white kids' essays. Her favorites to write were the personal ones, answering prompts like "What Did You Do on Your Vacation?"

Malaika had never been on a "vacation." "I'd never been to the beach," she said. "I'd never flown on a plane." But she nonetheless delivered impressive results. The white students were in awe. "It sounds so realistic!" they would marvel. "You describe it better than I could have. It's as if you really were there, on my vacation."

"I'd just deeply imagine what it would be like," Malaika said. "I'd close my eyes and put myself right into that situation. 'There was this blanket of blue water, climbing very cold over my feet.'"

19

Dipuo

I drove around Soweto often with Malaika and Dipuo. Afterward, I found myself driving back to the places we'd seen by myself. At first, I told myself I was just getting a better feel for the area. But then I realized I *preferred* being in Soweto to the formerly white suburbs. Many of them are Instagram-worthy, but they can also feel desolate. Looking closely, their lush yards turn out to be studded with red, blinking eyes, the ever-watchful lenses of security cameras. Few people walk in them—few white people, that is. Many white households employ a gardener and at least one maid, and these people walk to and from the minibus taxi stops. But when I once took a walk from my cottage, a black boy of about ten wheeled up to me on his bicycle. "Ma'am," he cried out, "why aren't you in your car?" His voice was as bewildered as if he'd seen a horse driving a truck—something that breaks some kind of fundamental, natural rule.

By contrast, people walked in Soweto. Walls weren't so high and you could see to the stoops, where the doors were often open and women sat to chat. A steady stream of children flowed in and out of the shacks and the houses to play hacky-sack on the street.

But Dipuo always insisted on taking the minibus taxis to come meet me at my cottage. She and Malaika claimed I *shouldn't* like to come to Soweto. When I drove with them there, they constantly warned me I was in danger because we were in "a ghetto." "Roll your windows up," they'd snap, lest somebody stick in a hand and steal my cell phone.

In a part of the township they didn't know well, we rolled up to an intersection. Three men were standing there. Dipuo slid down in her seat and checked that her door was locked. "There are the *nyaope* boys," she hissed.

Nyaope, Malaika informed me from the backseat, was a street drug. Its carelessly poisonous composition—heroin cut with random toxins like rat poison—represented the careless, degraded nature of the township, which, in turn, represented how deeply black South Africans had been warped by the white regime that stashed them there. "*They*"—*nyaope* boys—"even steal HIV antiretrovirals from sick people and crush and snort them," Malaika said with disgust.

They—to hear it from Malaika startled me. "Literally all the boys I grew up with are on it," she went on. "My friend was telling me her younger brother was taken far away, back to the rural areas, because she was afraid he was now getting to become like that—a *nyaope* addict." It was queer, she said, but in order to protect the boy's promise—his future—his family felt they had to send him back to the homeland, a thing the white police did twenty years earlier. But that was how dangerous, how poisonous, the township was.

As a child, Malaika decided she wanted to go to a historically white university. She'd tell her friends she intended never to live in a township again. "I am serious," she would say. "I would sell my body on the street before I ever live in one again."

I sometimes got the sense, though, that by resisting me coming to Soweto, she and Dipuo were trying to keep something of the place for themselves. They looked so at home there. One evening, Malaika decided she wanted to find a Sowetan delicacy, a boiled sheep's head. "Oh my God!" she cried thinking about it, shimmying in the backseat.

Sheep's head was sold in un-signed houses—an artifact left over from when it was illegal to run businesses in Soweto. We spent an hour and a half searching, driving farther into "deep Soweto," as people called the township's poorer interior. Malaika kept saying she remembered the best spot. She'd tell me to pull over, jump out of the car, and then come back tight-lipped and empty-handed.

"We are lost," Dipuo finally said crossly. "It's getting late. We don't come from this area. This is not wise."

"I know Soweto," Malaika snapped back hotly. It was a betrayal for a black woman not to know the township in her bones.

She had a theory GPS didn't work in Soweto. Not the way Sowetans' soul-level knowledge worked. After apartheid, Soweto's dismally numbered streets were renamed for black heroes. But I noticed that when Sowetans directed me somewhere, they rarely used those names. They'd direct me either with the old numbers or with landmarks that seemed subconsciously selected to be hard for me to find—like an outdoor driving school, of which there were so many, or a "big rock."

Another night, I drove to Soweto to visit a young friend of mine named Mophethe. He kept calling to ask if I was lost. When I told him I was navigating all right, he sounded disappointed. He kept offering to meet me at a gas station anyway, so he could play the role of guide.

Later, out at his favorite bar, I mentioned I needed to use the bathroom. Mophethe shook his head. "The bathroom is okay for *us*," he said. "But it won't be okay for you."

"What's wrong with it?" I asked.

He just shook his head again sadly.

I went anyway. The bathroom was normal. The toilet's lid was broken, but otherwise it was well equipped, with a fresh roll of toilet paper and a can of air freshener propped up on the windowsill.

At first I wondered if Mophethe assumed white people's standards were so high they'd only shit in a showroom. I'd seen something like that before. One autumn, I went with Elliot to visit his parents in the homeland where he grew up. On the way, we stopped in a town called Penge. "Let me show you the place I found more beautiful than any other when I was a child," Elliot said.

Penge was a white settlement within a black homeland. Usually, these places existed around mines or big factories, because white people did not live in "black" areas unless they had to for business. Penge was for the managers of an asbestos mine.

When we got there, I couldn't understand the town's appeal. The mountains around Elliot's father's homestead are among South Africa's most alluring. Their ten-thousand-foot-high summits play host to the world's second-highest waterfall. By contrast, Penge looked like a total dump. There were small, faded houses with their roofs caved in; parched, balding English box hedges; and a main block of abandoned, doorless shops with broken windows. But Elliot kept insisting on its charm. "Eve, let me tell you," he said. "This was the most beautiful thing in this area."

We got out of the car. "In my childhood, this was a very serious town to me, because only white people were staying there. The white people made it beautiful." It turned out Elliot had admired Penge *because* it was a "white spot." He'd marveled at the characteristics that couldn't be found on his father's estate. "There was grass," he reminisced as we walked down a residential street. "The place was green all year round."

Elliot wasn't the only black child entranced by Penge. Groups of kids from his father's estate walked an hour each way from their homes to scout it out. The white children chased them away nearly as soon as they arrived. "If they caught you, they'd beat you for nothing. You had to make sure you dived and hid in the bushes! Because you're black, you must run!"

He chuckled from the belly as he recounted the torments unleashed by the white children. I got the sense he had incorporated their enmity into his childhood play to defuse its hurt. Elliot said his friends used to giggle as they scattered pell-mell, teasing those who lagged and fell victim to the white children's blows.

After he said it, he furrowed his brow. Now that he was older, he recognized the chilling quality of the scene he had just described. "Apartheid," he mused. "It was good, somehow, when it came to beautifying the area. But on the other hand, it was really a great oppression."

He agreed Penge looked dumpy now. But he ascribed the ugliness to the encroaching influence of black people. In the late '80s, he said, black mineworkers—emboldened by the awareness their comrades in the People's Committees were escalating the liberation struggle—went on strike to demand more money. As a result, the asbestos mine became unprofitable and had to close.

He pointed to some scraggly trees. "They planted these as a design. The trees' flowers smelled wonderful. But then black people let them go wild."

We turned onto to the main street. "There were many shops. But people destroyed them," he said, selling the window frames as scrap metal. At the end of the block, three men leaned against the shattered window of an empty store, a boom box at their feet. The boom box was blaring a gospel song on repeat, giving the block the air of a deserted carnival. The men stared at us. Elliot stared back with distaste.

"As you see, black people, they don't care for things," he said.

In Elliot's telling, white people's inventions had operated by "design." White people designed, while black people neglected or consumed. The image of black people breaking apart and digesting

Penge like termites fascinated me because it reversed the common sense of who are the parasites in South Africa: white people, living off the resources and labor of the indigenous. In Elliot's account, though, the grandeur of what white people built turned black people into the parasites—squatters, paradoxically, on their own land. Even their quest for freedom, in his tale, turned out to be a destructive one because it resulted in the closure of the mine.

In fact, this account wasn't true. Penge's mine didn't close because black workers demanded higher wages. It closed because the international consensus on asbestos's danger reached South Africa in the '90s. An academic study found "visible asbestos fibers all over the paths" and recommended Penge "be closed to human habitation." In other words, what white people made had been toxic all along. But Elliot either didn't know that story or ignored it. In his mind, the collapse of Penge formed part of a narrative of black incompetence and failure to live up to the responsibilities of freedom.

A now disused pair of long buildings, Penge's high school was surrounded by a chest-high fence. Elliot rested his arms and nose on the arc of the gate. It was locked.

"Is anybody in there?" I wondered.

Suddenly we heard a voice. "There's somebody inside," Elliot whispered. A man emerged. He was sucking the butt of a dead cigarette. Approaching the gate, he pulled the butt from his lips and muttered something. "He says he's the security guard," Elliot translated.

He looked more like a starving Beat poet, his spectrally thin frame clad in a high-necked black sweater and a tattered newsboy cap. After unlocking the gate, the man began to reel around the property, pushing us into one empty schoolroom after the other to show off their cleanliness.

"Who's employing you?" Elliot asked.

"No, I've never been paid," he replied. "I haven't been paid in nine years." He said he had made a bedroom out of the principal's office. "I can barely eat. But I have to protect this building from the others."

By *the others*, he meant the black people who came to Penge after white people left. When these nemeses came in the dark to try to strip the tin roofs off of the school buildings, he told us, he frightened them away with sticks. Stacks of branches lay in piles around the schoolyard. He collected firewood, he said, and sold it on the side of the road to buy bread.

But it seemed he mostly lived on the vaporous honor that came from guarding the white man's creation. As we sat on a bed he'd made for himself in the principal's office, it came out he hoped white people would come back to reclaim the building. That's why he stayed. If they came back, he reasoned, they would be grateful he took care of it and employ him. He took a key out of a Tupperware container and led us to the thing he was proudest of: a bathroom, which he scrubbed regularly to get rid of the spiders and the dust. Its white porcelain fittings gleamed, a wrapped bar of soap sat on the sink, and a plump, neatly folded blue towel hung on the towel bar.

In the years he guarded the property, he said, he had never used this bathroom. He kept it locked. For himself, he had dug a crude pit latrine out back on the soccer field. The bathroom's immaculateness had reserved it, in his head, for white people only, long after the last of them had gone.

I thought there was something else, though, to my friend Mophethe's feelings about the bathroom in his favorite Soweto bar. When I arrived at the intersection he designated for us to meet, another man was standing with him. I got out of my car— and felt a sudden blow to my back. The other man was tackling me from behind. He wrestled my cell phone out of my hand and ran around a corner.

I looked at Mophethe, shocked—but he was doubled over laughing. He explained he'd arranged for a friend to pretend to mug me so I could experience "the real Soweto." Soweto was rough, he said proudly. Although its creation and its continued existence was unjust, it had also been black people's proving ground.

Mophethe wasn't proud of its danger, not quite. But he was proud of the qualities that its hardness revealed in him and his friends. *They* called Soweto the *kasi*, a Zulu twist on the Afrikaans word for township, *lokasie*, or "location."

In the '70s, black people didn't use *kasi* much. Most preferred to call a township a *lokatsheneng*. That still derived from a foreign word—the English "location"—but at least English was a language less intimately linked with black oppression. After 1994, though, among young black South Africans, *kasi* began to make its way anew into the vernacular. It could be a noun—"let's spend the weekend *ekasi*"—or an adjective. "He has *ekasi* vibes" was a way of complimenting somebody's sartorial style. Radio stations and fashion labels branded themselves "from the *kasi*."

The fact that the word derived from Afrikaans was part of its allure. For wrapped up in that word were memories of what black people had endured under racial segregation, which—Mophethe told me frankly—sometimes felt more noteworthy than what they could create afterward.

I once asked a group of schoolchildren in Katlehong to define *kasi* for me. It was an NGO-run school, and all the kids aimed to get away from the township to a university. Yet when I asked them to describe *ekasi*, a few literally screamed with excitement. *A leather jacket!* one shouted. *A gold chain*, cried another, or a prison tattoo and a *chiskop*—another loanword from Afrikaans meaning a closely shaved head.

Their parents, they said, frowned on such outfits because they were what "thugs" wore. But just talking about them gave the students visceral joy because they were describing something that was already theirs, not just a dream. "We have black people who live in the *kasi* and black people, now, who live in the [formerly white] suburbs," one boy explained. "The people who live in the suburbs—other people think they are clean and everything. But I think the people who live in the *kasi* are actually greater, because they're living a harder life. Even breaking the law," he reflected, "is not something just anybody can do."

Malaika once remarked to me that "as the number of black people increased" in formerly white neighborhoods, the black people got "strangely, a little bit more alienated. A little less black." They began, she said, to mimic their white neighbors: to build high walls, to lock their doors, to refuse to answer their doorbells when itinerant black handymen came around.

One woman I met in a formerly white neighborhood had become a life coach. She wrote an advice blog for other black women aspiring to enter the upper class. One post coached women on how to handle maids. Only give them half a loaf of bread for lunch, she advised. A full loaf was too friendly. They could bring home the leftovers, which implied you understood they had families. She warned black women to resist an instinct to treat their maids like sisters. Upwardly mobile black women had to act like white *madams* for maids to respect them, she said. In fact, they might have to act more madam-ish and haughty to signal their authority.

When I read this post to Malaika, she made a hissing noise between her teeth. Hadn't they learned anything, black South Africans? She emphasized, though, she believed black people who lived in formerly white-dominated areas acted like this for their survival, not because they wanted to. "Otherwise, their white neighbors would not trust them."

I got the sense my friend Mophethe set up the mugging prank because he wanted to see me thrown a little off balance—to remind himself that, in Soweto, there was still an unbridgeable gulf between him, a black person, and me, a white one. Mophethe no longer lived in Soweto. He had moved to a lush formerly white suburb. But he insisted he would still live in the *kasi* if his commute to work wouldn't be so long. "Living *ekasi* meant everything to me," he told me sadly. "It's the way we love. The way we talk. The way we dress. You have lived under harsh circumstances. You have survived. You have taken minibus taxis. You have eaten *kota*." (*Kota*, from "quarter"—a quarter-loaf of white bread stuffed with ham, processed cheese, French fries, and sometimes a hot dog— was a township specialty.)

He told me upwardly mobile Sowetans who moved to formerly white neighborhoods returned to Soweto on the weekends. I heard that often. People said you could find Johannesburg's wealthiest black men and women shacking up with their Sowetan cousins on Saturday nights.

I was in Soweto many Saturdays, and I never met people who'd come in from the suburbs. I'm sure some did. But the concept also seemed important as an inoculating idea, suggesting that even increasingly affluent black people never lost their connection to what made them "black."

At first, white people's scornful reaction to the upwardly mobile "black diamonds" made Dipuo want to defend this new, rich black coterie. White businessmen who drove Audis were respected. How come when black people aspired to the same material things they were treated as tasteless or disreputable? But now white people were changing the rules. Their team had been guarding a goal representing success—a certain kind of wealth, a culture, a lifestyle. But as soon as black people became able to drive their ball into that same goal, they began shouting that it was the *wrong* goal, trashy or unethical.

Yet Dipuo also wondered why some of her former comrades and heroes were getting rich so fast while others remained poor. Did they think black liberation was individual, not collective? Unhappily, black South Africans began to perceive they were treated worse, at times, by the so-called black diamonds than they were by white people. Taxicabs that took you door-to-door were much more expensive than the minibus taxis. Their drivers noted that white passengers often tipped well while upper-class black passengers expected them to bow and scrape. A journalist described one exchange: "You [wealthier] black riders are the worst," his driver told him bitterly. "Some rich black chicks expect us to open the door for them or help them put their groceries in the [trunk]."

The journalist fought back, alleging the complaint betrayed a double standard. It seemed to *him* that poorer black people sometimes refused to believe other black people could acquire *any* money legitimately. They saw him like white people did—as corrupt or a faker, with the unmistakable odor of the unwashed still hanging about him. "I bet you open the [trunk] for white women," he retorted hotly. "Why do black service providers not show love to *us*?" Another friend, a corporate manager, told me he'd ridden with a black cab driver who weaved all over the road, distracted by a cell phone conversation.

"Would you have driven like that if your passenger had been white?" my friend asked angrily at the end of the ride. The driver broke into a half-sorry, half-conspiratorial smile.

"Well, I am black, and you, my brother, are also black," he said. "So it is cool, right?"

In 2016, the black South African journalist Sisonke Msimang wrote about taking the front passenger seat in Ubers when she visited South Africa. The daughter of a prominent ANC exile, she had opportunities to go to university in America and then to live in Australia. "It makes me feel more egalitarian," she said. On one ride, her driver was a black man a bit older than her. "He tells you a story about . . . how long he has been driving, [and] you are relieved. . . . You begin to think . . . that Uber is justice . . . because he is chatty and 'smartly dressed' and does not smell like *mahewu*"—fermented corn drink, a subsistence food.

It happened to be the day Muhammad Ali died. The news alert popped up on her smartphone. In the cab, she found herself tearful, overwhelmed by memories of the Rumble in the Jungle, the epic 1974 contest in Kinshasa between Ali and George Foreman. "I re-member[ed] everything," Msimang wrote. "My dad and his friends drinking whiskey in the living room . . . the cloud of smoke curling under the lamplight . . . the crowds screaming and screaming."

She mentioned Ali's death to the Uber driver. He peeked at a picture she'd pulled up on her phone. "Is he from South Africa?" he asked.

It shocked her that the driver didn't recognize Muhammad Ali. It turned out he'd never heard of him. "Like, where have you been, dude?" Msimang wanted to ask mockingly.

But in the same instant, with a sinking heart, she realized: "He has been *here*." Possibly without a TV—without access to the nar-rative black elites were telling themselves about the gains they had won for black people in South Africa and worldwide.

Thinking about it harder, she realized she could not have had memories of the Rumble in the Jungle, because she hadn't been born yet. She must have pieced them together from the tales her father had told her and from video footage. And it occurred to her she might have done so for a psychological reason—to shore up her own sense of black identity when it perhaps was more practically tenuous, more abstract and intellectual, than the daily reality her Uber driver lived. She wondered if the encouraging stories black South African leaders sometimes told themselves about Africa's "rise"—as originally represented by the Rumble in the Jungle, which millions of people around the world watched live—were illusions.

She always assumed she and a black cab driver were "the same," she wrote. "In your mind, you"—she and the black driver—are "like a single being. [But then] you realize that . . . you and he occupy different worlds, and you wonder whether you should count yourself lucky that he does not yet see you as his enemy."

Another friend, Nonhlanhla, grew in post-apartheid Katlehong. An academic superstar, she was the first woman from her township school to attend Johannesburg's premier formerly white university. Her boyfriend there was a white man. When her friends in the township heard that, some claimed to be unsurprised. "We always knew you would go for a white guy," they said.

Nonhlanhla was unsure how to feel about that. These same friends dogged her for something they called her "white tendencies," which they claimed they could detect in her from the first time she visited home. "White tendencies" were the shoes you wore, the words you used, even what you drank. To celebrate her college graduation, she took a group of friends out to a restaurant. They teased her that her selection of champagne was "white." Black people drank beer. They also criticized her for sending an improperly cooked dish back to the kitchen. Black people didn't do that, they said. Complaining about restaurant service was a "white" thing.

She detected a mocking edge in their voices when they quizzed her about her boyfriend. The subtext was she'd been both lucky to land a white boy and somehow weak, not loyal nor deep enough to love a man from her own community.

What they didn't understand was that Nonhlanhla still felt terribly uncomfortable in the white world. Her English was impeccable. Her father never went to school, but when Nonhlanhla entered the first grade he decided to study with her, and in the shack where they lived, they drilled each other on English phrases until their spelling was perfect. Her first week at university, though, she was given an assignment to type. She didn't have a computer. In fact, she had never *used* a computer. She went to the computer lab, but she couldn't figure out the device. And she couldn't erase her errors because she didn't know, yet, that a keyboard has a backspace key.

That felt representative of her broader experience after she left the township. She was constantly making missteps of which she was painfully aware, but she didn't know how to stop making them. She didn't want to tell her white professor why she couldn't complete the assignment. It seemed like making an excuse or whining to stress how deprived her upbringing was—and untrue, because her father's shack had actually felt happy and full of love. It felt better if her professor just thought she was lazy. At least she had control over laziness.

Every day she encountered choices like that. Situations in which she had to choose between revealing herself to be either inherently stupid or a pitiable girl from Katlehong whose mother still told everyone she gestated Nonhlanhla for fourteen months, and she didn't care that Western scientists said this was impossible. There was always this *choosing*, and it was so exhausting.

A couple of months into her relationship with the white man, he gamely told her he'd like to try to master Johannesburg's minibus taxi system. The minibus taxis are still very infrequently taken by white people, and they can be hard to comprehend if you didn't grow up using them. They have no fixed routes and you hail them using complicated hand gestures.

Nonhlanhla's response was visceral. "No!" she heard herself shouting.

"You think I'm too dumb or afraid to get on a minibus taxi?" her boyfriend retorted, hurt.

She was trying to protect him, she protested. The minibus taxis were notoriously rickety.

But later, it occurred to her she might have been trying to protect herself. With her black friends pushing her out of their world and the white environment staunchly resisting her entrance, it was comforting to know there was a place, a realm where she just belonged. Where she was at home. Where she was *more* at home than white people were. With all her boyfriend's other, inborn advantages, now he wanted to master black people's *taxi system*, too?

By the time I met Malaika, she was in college, and she'd already picked out her dream house from the Johannesburg real estate listings. It was in a leafy, formerly white neighborhood, and she'd saved photos of it on her phone. "It's four-bedroom—"

"Double story," Dipuo broke in eagerly.

"A pool," Malaika said.

She showed me the pictures. The house was strikingly modern, with tall windows; a second-story steel railing made its gray facade look like the prow of a cruise-liner. "I like new, modern furniture," she said. "A huge kitchen. And I love the idea of 'upstairs.' My bedroom must be 'upstairs.' See how it's glowing from the inside?" She scrolled to images of the property taken at night. "Some bastard bought it ahead of me," she laughed. Then her tone got fierce. "But I should have been born there. I never should have been born in Soweto. I should have been born in that house."

She told me, though, about a childhood episode that unsettled her a little when it came to her ambition to live in a formerly white neighborhood. While waiting for a minibus taxi in an integrating part of downtown, she noticed a fancy car waiting in the parking lot of a fast-food restaurant. Through the tinted windows, she could just make out a well-dressed white man sitting in the back, possibly waiting for his driver to pick up an order.

He was the kind of man she was supposed to envy. But she was struck by a strange, sudden sense of pity. Around the car, black people came and went and chattered in the parking lot, their poverty necessitating they go on foot. Kids teased each other and swung their backpacks.

It was a beautiful, fresh afternoon, but the white man's car windows were rolled up tight. He stared rigidly ahead at the back of the driver's seat, as if afraid to look at the hubbub around him; maybe he didn't realize everybody was just having a good time. "How alone, how fragile he looks," Malaika thought—and how terribly unhappy that must be, she concluded with surprise.

20

Dipuo

By 1998, Dipuo was earning enough at the NGO to move the family out of their shack and into a four-room brick house. She named it Tlhomedi, or "Our Home." Malaika loved it. She slept on a bed and her uncles had their own bedroom. She still used an outhouse, but it had a real toilet.

It was Dipuo's brother Godfrey, though, who already seemed to live in Danielle Steel's world. He spent a lot of time away from the house. But he always came back looking gorgeous. Other Sowetan men sometimes wore cheap, bright, baggy clothes to cover up their imperfect bodies. To Malaika, these men's efforts to disguise their poverty—their malnutrition or the dirt under their collars from their jobs toiling in white people's gardens—only made it more obvious. Godfrey wore real linen shirts, the kind of nubbly, slightly imperfect fabrics people wore when they could afford to be bored by perfection. He unbuttoned them at the top "so his chest would show," Malaika said, and his skin was like velvet. On weekends, Dipuo loved to play a particular song on a boom box called "Black Is Beautiful." Godfrey embodied the song. His polished leather shoes always glowed.

Malaika didn't know what his job was, exactly. But he brought incredible things back to the shack. Pretty furniture. Food—kinds of food she had only seen on television. When he was away, Malaika used her imagination to fill in her picture of Never-Never, the place Godfrey said he worked. There were no dusty, lonesome bus stops. No outhouses. No hunger. Godfrey said it only ever rained there if a girl as sweet as Malaika wanted it to so she could look outside and daydream as water ran down the windowpanes, as if the world was her fish tank, an amusement designed just for her.

One night, though, policemen showed up at Dipuo's house. They forced their way through the door, saying they were looking for a man named Godfrey. Dipuo hurriedly woke Malaika up and said if the police asked her, she was to deny that her uncle, who was asleep inside, was named Godfrey. Dipuo said to call Godfrey by a different name—"Thabiso."

Dutifully, when a policeman asked, Malaika called Godfrey Thabiso. But the encounter left her confused. The next morning, she woke up to find Godfrey packing a suitcase. Time to go back to Never-Never, he said. The next time he returned to Soweto, he promised he would take her there for good on their own private airplane.

But Godfrey never came back. A couple of months after the police came to Dipuo's house, Malaika was on one of her occasional visits to her father's house when Dipuo showed up. That was even rarer. When her father returned to her, he blurted out that Godfrey was dead.

Later that night, Dipuo told Malaika the full story. Godfrey, Dipuo tried to explain, was a thug. He made his money stealing. He robbed homes and carjacked vehicles, mainly from white people in neighborhoods like the suburb where Malaika's grandmother had toiled in "the kitchens."

"But I know thugs!" Malaika thought in bewilderment. Mago, a local thug, stole cars. He invited Sowetan men to come to a field late at night and watch him turn wheelies. Malaika went

EVE FAIRBANKS

sometimes without her mother's permission. It frightened her, the darkness and the wild strafing of the headlights and Mago doing such risky maneuvers it seemed like he didn't care whether he lived or died or about the lives of the bystanders.

Another flashy and pompous thug, Sihle, owned minibus taxis. Malaika knew some teen girls admired him because he gave them money or made them seem remarkable by letting them ride in his passenger seat. But if the brother of a girl he seduced tried to confront him, he'd beat the boy up beyond recognition. Rumor went, too, he was making his girlfriends sick. That his apparent success—the money, the taxis—was a mirage, and the truth was that *he* was a disease, infecting young black women and killing them.

It made no sense Godfrey was the same kind of man.

And yet Dipuo told Malaika that Godfrey had approached the security guards in a new mall in Soweto to steal their guns. A companion of his got away. But the guards chased Godfrey and shot him multiple times in the back. He ran several hundred feet before falling to the pavement in an upwardly mobile cul-de-sac. Even then, in sight of the police and bleeding out, he crawled into an alley, as if he was trying to protect the cul-de-sac's residents from seeing something they weren't, after apartheid, supposed to have to see.

When Dipuo got to the hospital after Godfrey was shot, her mother was hysterical. "His chest was rising and falling," she cried out, "but the doctors are insisting he is dead!" One nurse had curtly advised her to "pull the plug" on her son. As if he was a television. Just another material asset, like the ones he stole from white people. A plug? Godfrey was a human being. He didn't *have* a plug. He had *been* the plug for their whole family, pumping them a singular, electric current of hope.

190

Leading black South Africans complained, at that time, that they struggled to be seen as something other than thugs or frauds—to be seen as "proper" people, as the phrase went. Mandela's right-hand man, Thabo Mbeki, was a dandy, given to wearing Savile Row suits and quoting from classic literature. He was the one who'd served white elites Scotch on the Dakar Safaris.

They'd appeared to appreciate that in the '80s. Now they approached him with new suspicion, though he'd come by his taste for British clothes and erudition entirely soundly. Mbeki studied economics in England, becoming the first black South African to obtain a master's degree with distinction at Sussex University. He actually wrote many of Mandela's celebrated early-'90s speeches. But when he started to give speeches himself, commentators judged him "angry" and a "typical Afro-Bolshevik." They tittered when he quoted Shakespeare, as if there was now something funny about hearing the Bard coming out of a black man's mouth. Behind the scenes, Mbeki bitterly referred to this phenomenon as the "One Good Native Syndrome," wherein Westerners acknowledged there could be one good African politician—Mandela—but only one.

Ironically, Mbeki's economic policies helped secure the environment in which many white South Africans flourished after apartheid ended. Breaking with what the ANC proposed while it was out of power, he stressed deficit reduction and trade liberalization, and privatized numerous state-owned enterprises. Under his economic stewardship, a media conglomerate that supported the white regime became South Africa's biggest company, expanding into Asia and Latin America; its Afrikaner CEO is now a dollar billionaire. By 1999, when he succeeded Mandela as president, South Africa's annual GDP growth had risen from 2.6 percent in 1992 to more than 4 percent.

And yet white businessmen, Mbeki said, maintained a firm expectation the new South Africa would "fail." As time went on, he began to chafe against white expectations—or whites' seeming inability to see him for who he was—and to wish he'd been less accommodating. Why try, if it didn't make any difference? "Some of us," he said acidly, "wanted to go much harder" on the leaders of the former white regime, jailing them. But "people said there could not be a Nuremberg [in South Africa] because it would muddy an important experiment"—and "because [white] people [do] not trust black Africans to run Nuremberg trials in a just way."

Mbeki's biographer observed something brooding and "alienated" in Mbeki. Other ANC leaders surmised he was cut off from some form of "black roots." In the 2000s, Mbeki broke with Western expectations—but in a way that was devastating.

Mbeki began to question whether the HIV epidemic was what Western epidemiologists said it was. Sometimes he did this incognito, coauthoring an HIV-denialist manifesto under a pseudonym, and sometimes he did it brashly, in public. In a letter to U.S. president Clinton, Mbeki quoted a U.N. official who warned that "the prevalence of [HIV] infection has increased so much in five years that South Africa could [soon] see its life expectancy decline to 47."

"Interestingly," Mbeki noted, "the five years to which [the official] refers coincide . . . with the period since our liberation from apartheid." In another document, he elaborated that "often I have wondered whether [HIV researchers and scientists] did not, in fact, seek to achieve precisely this result." Mbeki was alleging that white people either seized upon the coincidental eruption of HIV in South Africa as a way to demonstrate a black-led country would fall into chaos or—even grimmer—they'd initiated a germ warfare conspiracy to accomplish a destruction of black people they hadn't managed with political maneuvering.

When he succeeded Mandela as president, Mbeki encouraged South Africans to reject Western doctors' and researchers' accounts of HIV's etiology. Positing that AIDS was not a virus but a syndromic "disease of poverty"—produced by malnutrition and thus, by extension, the legacy of colonialism—he delayed the introduction of antiretroviral treatments long after they became available in other developing countries. He pressured South Africans to embrace "African" remedies like garlic paste or a locally manufactured "medicine" called Virodene. Questioning the Western line on HIV, he insisted, was a healthy skepticism akin to questioning white people's claims under apartheid itself. "It is said there exists a scientific view that is supported by the majority, against which dissent is prohibited," he wrote.

He noted the same thing had been said under apartheid to bulwark the claim only white people, biologically speaking, could run a "civilized" country. He alleged the whole AIDS narrative rested on a portrayal of black people as "diseased, corrupt . . . amoral, sexually depraved, [and] rapists. . . . In the very recent past, we had to fix our own eyes on the very face of [a similar] tyranny."

By 2001, HIV accounted for a quarter of all deaths in South Africa. The country's life expectancy had dropped from sixty-four to forty-eight. Before antiretrovirals were finally introduced, thanks to pressure from a South African activist group, epidemiologists estimate more than 300,000 South Africans died unnecessarily due to Mbeki's stance.

Dipuo encouraged her peers to wear condoms. But the complicated thing was the *reasoning* behind Mbeki's AIDS denialism felt true to her. Historically, black South Africans had very good reasons not to trust self-described scientific experts. To make the disease feel beatable while government policy faltered, doctors concentrated on actions ordinary black South Africans could take, like safe sex. That emphasis, at times, seemed to hold black people responsible for their suffering. In the past, white officials and missionaries beat it into black South Africans that their traditional ways of life caused their own degradation only to be followed, in a sense, by HIV experts. And there was a long history of white authorities engaging in cynical, behind-the-scenes manipulation to try to prove black people were unfit to rule. It didn't seem implausible to Dipuo they would do it again.

The HIV epidemic *did* give some white South Africans a way to position themselves again in society as the righteous ones, the ones concerned about practical problems. Virodene, the local HIV treatment Mbeki touted, was concocted by a white medical technician; ANC-linked businessmen funneled the technician thousands of dollars to develop it, even though its main ingredient was a toxic industrial solvent. Toward the end of the '90s, photographs of white South Africans protesting Mbeki's stance or adopting AIDS orphans dotted the newspapers. Seeing these pictures made Dipuo furious. When had white people ever cared about poor black people until they could be their saviors?

In general, Dipuo was starting to believe the attitudes white people held prior to apartheid's end hadn't been eradicated but had gone into hiding, like doctors were saying HIV, even if medicated, retreated into hidden nooks in the body only to roar back if you ever let down your guard. It was incredible to her how quickly they'd seemed to overcome their tarnished reputation and repositioned themselves as South Africa's arbiters of rationality and purveyors of compassion.

"Perhaps," she thought bitterly, "they never conceded this in the first place." They had managed to hold on to it while appearing to hand over the political reins, like an apprehended movie criminal who, halfway through, looks like he's handing over the stolen goods while deftly slipping the only ring of any real value deep into his pocket.

After Godfrey died, Matshediso, Dipuo's mother, decided he must have been the victim of witchcraft. She started training to become a *sangoma*, a traditional healer. The training dragged on for years and ate up money. Dipuo dutifully paid, but her mother's decision frustrated her. The family was struggling to enter the future and her mother was still sacrificing goats beneath an urban overpass?

"If you don't complete the process, the ancestors will come and haunt you," Matshediso would insist. Dipuo wondered privately whether it wouldn't be more distressing for her mother to finish the *sangoma* training, because then she would have to confront the fact there were no rites of passage left to turn to that could make everything all right.

Dipuo wasn't able to tell, either, which of these so-called traditional customs were "real" and which ones black people had to accept as authentic long after their cultures were irrevocably changed by white influence. Like "witch-burning," which rural communities periodically did. There's little conclusive evidence precolonial black South Africans routinely burned so-called witches to death. Some of the first evidence, actually, was a 1957 Witchcraft Suppression Act—a law the *white* government passed to help define black South Africans as savage. But by 1984, a rural black leader was defending immolating his political enemies by telling a magazine that "white people do not understand black magic. We deal with [wrongdoers] according to our custom, the way our ancestors taught us."

During the '80s, members of Dipuo's People's Committee pressed their neighbors to speak black languages instead of Afrikaans or English by taunting them: *Why ukhuluma iEnglish singa, bodarkie?* That last word was what it looked like: a tweak to the Anglophone slur for black people. Even the mocking phrase Dipuo deployed to remind her peers not to become too proximate to their oppressors revealed how entwined they were already.

No written history of precolonial black life existed that wasn't filtered through white people's fears and desires. A black South African historian pointed me to early missionaries' reports that the black teens they encountered liked to recite erotic poetry. She said precolonial black people had a different, much freer attitude toward sexuality. She lamented the loss of a playful eroticism that puritanical Europeans strove to snuff out. But then she admitted that the only way anybody knows black people had that attitude was through the missionaries' own accounts. And maybe the missionaries just made the erotic poems up to bolster their argument that black people were less "civilized."

Meanwhile, a tabloid called the *Daily Sun* launched, targeting the townships. White executives published it, and they started to make millions of dollars off it every year. "Our research shows most *Daily Sun* readers had never bought a newspaper before it was launched," the paper's chief financial officer bragged. It trafficked in loony stories about black people's belief in a demon called a *tokoloshe* who hid under beds and stole men's virility. "Tokoloshe Tracker in My Bum!" ran a typical headline, describing a malevolent and technologically adept *tokoloshe* who'd purportedly embedded a GPS tracking device in his victim's rectum.

The *Daily Sun*'s executives claimed to be listening to its black audience's desires. But were they actually just feeding black people an age-old pejorative image of themselves as haplessly superstitious? Most black people Dipuo knew in the '80s hadn't believed stupid things like that a *tokoloshe* could put a tracking device in your asshole. But she noticed that a lot of black South Africans were suddenly training to become *sangomas*. Black people who were, in other ways, starting to successfully penetrate the white world—PhDs or accountants at international firms—were sporting decorative dots on their cheeks drawn with white eyeliner, a ceremonial makeup some rural black women wore on special occasions.

These upwardly mobile black people, though, wore the cheek

dots to cocktail hours at high-end steakhouses. It struck Dipuo as a corrupt way to signal you were still part of the "masses." A black economist who appeared alongside white men on a financial TV program began to accessorize his business suit with a deer-hide headdress traditionally worn by nineteenth-century Zulu warriors. The deer's hairy, desiccated tail flopped over his eye while he discussed commodities futures. When black elites postured this way, Dipuo thought they made the very notion of a black style look crassly utilitarian.

A friend of mine, a corporate auditor, wore the cheek dots when she went to visit her relatives back in her ancestral village. Her relatives seemed to find her makeup ridiculous. They wanted independence from white oppression, they said frankly, by entering the white world and succeeding in it, buying a car or getting a corporate job. They touted a book called *Capitalist Nigger*. Written by a Nigerian author, it has sold nearly 100,000 copies in South Africa, which qualifies it as a massive bestseller. It exhorts black people to mimic the "devil-may-care, killer instinct attitude of the Caucasian race" and to become "economic warrior[s] who love money. . . . Whatever the Caucasian does," the author advises, "the [black man] must follow him every step of the way."

Dipuo's tone when she recounted her brother's death was almost wry. Godfrey had been *her* favorite brother. She nursed a small hope that his risk taking could somehow lead, eventually, to a good and normal life. Even as Godfrey readied his final heist, the last thing he bought was a double bed. Not long before he died, he confided to her that his ambition was to get married. But before that, he wanted a "proper" job. He didn't want to expose a wife and children to such danger.

"Despite the fact that I knew the truth of the life he was

living," Dipuo said, "and that it was reckless—and that I expected something like this—when it happened, I found I still wanted him to live. I just wanted to go back and remake his whole life from the beginning."

But that was a fleeting emotion. Dipuo didn't even make it to the hospital before Godfrey died. When she told a coworker Godfrey was hurt, he agreed to drive her to the hospital so she wouldn't have to take a string of minibus taxis. But then he balked near the township's entrance, saying he didn't feel safe going into a "black" area, and dumped her under a highway overpass to trek the rest of the way on foot.

That just summed up everything—her society's purported willingness to treat black people with equality and compassion and then the recoil when the chance to do so came.

By the time Godfrey died, Dipuo's faith that an ordinary black man would be let into the formerly white world without twisting the rules had been eroded. She knew how Godfrey got his beautiful clothes. She knew it was "wrong."

But even so, she privately celebrated her thug brother. She and Godfrey would joke that he was "liberating" cars and TVs from their "colonial masters." "They need a break," he would say, and she would laugh wildly. They took pleasure in mocking the bland language ANC leaders sometimes used to characterize the transformation they intended for post-apartheid South Africa—bloodless phrases that made a mockery of their more practical hopes, like "affirmative action" and "broad-based economic empowerment." She and Godfrey referred to his crime sprees as "affirmative re-possession."

She knew that "people in that business, they don't live long." But when I asked Dipuo if she ever tried to do an intervention—knowing his way of life was probably unethical and likely to land him in jail or the morgue—she paused and narrowed her eyes, as if trying to conjure a memory she thought I wanted her to have, but she didn't. "I guess we did," she finally said vaguely. "But I think he was in it too deep to go back."

A number of educated black South Africans I know, like a chef who worked with Anthony Bourdain and a project manager for the Canadian government's foreign-aid bureau, still wonder twenty years later whether Mbeki wasn't right about HIV. Or they *wish* he could have been right. They had been so proud of him, their man who knew Shakespeare and went head-to-head with the most arrogant of white intellectuals. To see a man like him stumble after black people worked so hard for their liberation was brutal. They wish Mbeki could have been right precisely *because* he sought respect from white people. It was terrible to think that the minute he stopped toeing a line he fulfilled the racist expectation that African political leaders always become mad tyrants who kill their people.

Because that's what happened. Every top global newspaper wrote editorials about South Africa's "alarming" turn against science. The *London Review of Books* triumphantly declared Mbeki "crazy" and "macabre"—and therefore "typically African." The predicament he was in seemed like one of those sets of trick ropes magicians use—the ones where, when a bound audience member pulls on any loose thread, he only manages to cinch the bind tighter.

Dipuo occasionally defended Mbeki to me. She'd turn provocatively effusive, as if she half-wanted me to make fun of her or call her crazy, too. So many black people still seemed terrified of running afoul of white people; at least Mbeki hadn't been. In the early 2000s, Dipuo read commentaries she found irritating by a preeminent black South African scholar, William Gumede.

Gumede warned black leaders not to stray too far from Western experts' advice. "There is a moment when many African liberation movements stumble," he told *Newsweek*.

Shortly thereafter, Gumede was accused of plagiarizing parts of a book he wrote. Critics noted he stole from white journalists. It seemed to confirm to Dipuo that nobody, not even a leading black intellectual, felt sure of where he stood without looking toward white people for approval.

It was a strange feeling, but Dipuo was becoming aware she envied white people *their* liberation—as if they had been freed more than black people. She perceived them to have been liberated from their pariah status at little material cost, while black people had been burdened with heavy new expectations. "It is their country now," the white owners of the *Daily Sun* claimed when they advertised the paper. But when a young black fashion designer tried to get in on the fun by developing a line of T-shirts printed with iconic *Daily Sun* headlines, the white executives threatened to sue him.

For her part, the night she heard Godfrey died, Malaika locked herself in the outhouse and wept. What did it mean that Godfrey was a criminal when he was also the only one in her world who seemed truly good? Amid all the increasingly tiresome worship of Mandela, Godfrey had been her Mandela, her generous hero, her real-life "Professor Kader Asmal."

Love and happiness seemed to be such limited resources in Meadowlands. Most of her elders were reluctant to waste the little they had on children who, they hoped, could generate them on their own. Godfrey, on the other hand, had an infinite supply of love and attention. "He got down on the floor and listened to me," Malaika said. "It was a gift."

His death seemed to suggest ordinary black people simply couldn't be like Mandela, so respected and beautiful, without faking it. Without courting shame, even death. And Never-Never, her dream place—it was *"the kitchens"*? Where her grandmother scrubbed white people's dirty dishes? And you had to terrify white children or steal white ladies' cars to get there?

Malaika's grief mixed with disgust, fear, and anger. Godfrey had no right. He had no right to ruin Never-Never. No right not to fulfill his promise to take her there. The depth of her anger terrified her. All she could do, sobbing in the outhouse, was to conclude her tears were the problem. If she could stanch them, the situation would partly go away. So she decided she was never going to cry anymore.

21

Christo

BILLYBOY RAMAHLELE HEARD THE RIOT before he saw it. In February 1996, UFS's first black dormitory head was relaxing in front of a wildlife program on TV with his apartment door open. Suddenly, he became aware of a noise. Could it be the campus's trees, rustling in a gust? No—it was heavier, more like trampling. Could it be his TV? He switched it off. The noise grew louder.

Ramahlele got up and poked his head out the door. There, he saw the black students in his dorm stampeding out of the entryway and running toward the central quad. Some were holding sticks or cricket bats.

They told him they wanted to confront the white boys on campus. Those boys refused to treat them like they should be treated in a democracy, they said. Racing alongside the group, Ramahlele wasn't truly worried until he rounded the corner and saw, under the moonlight, a line of white boys at least as long as his line of black students, standing shoulder-to-shoulder. "It looked like an army flank," he remembered. The white students were also holding cricket bats, cocked over their shoulders like rifles. And their mouths were open: they were singing.

Vivid images flashed in Ramahlele's mind, memories of his own apartheid upbringing. The song the white boys were singing was "Die Stem," the apartheid-era national anthem. Sometimes, when ransacking a shack in his township, white police officers would hum "Die Stem."

Ramahlele's heart sank. "The history was," he told me, "if they're singing that, somebody is going to die."

As the '90s wore on, the kind of violent acts Christo engaged in at UFS became endemic on campus. "Black student leaders would find [white boys] had ejaculated on their blankets," Verschoor recalled grimly. "And the black guys would form *impis*"—a Zulu battle line—"and boom, boom, boom, march through the white corridors. It was war."

The black students who ran out of Ramahlele's dorm to confront the white boys retreated when they glimpsed the army on the quad. But on their way back, Ramahlele said, they "smashed all the white boys' cars" along the campus road. Then they locked themselves in their dorm. Ramahlele's dorm had unofficially become nearly all black. It had extra rooms, which turned into refuges for dissatisfied black students. As black people came to dominate the space, the white students drifted away into private accommodation.

The white boys followed and broke the dorm's windows until "there was no windowpane left." His boys were afraid to go to sleep. "The whole night we slept in the corridors."

Not long after that, a group of black boys went to the black woman on the student council. "If we continue to stay together, we will kill each other," they said. Groups of white boys visited Verschoor and begged, "Please let us move out."

Verschoor and Ramahlele worried there really would be deaths on campus. So, to tamp down the tension, the UFS administrators decided to split the dorms up temporarily by race. In one building, Verschoor let the students put up plywood to separate the black and white corridors.

The east side became white; the west side, black.

Verschoor hoped it was just a short-term emergency solution. But when he removed the white boys from one dorm, as a final act they poured cement into the pipes of the swimming pool. If they—the white boys—couldn't have the dorm, at least they wouldn't let the black boys enjoy it, either.

Christo's friend Monte was one of the boys who poured cement down the swimming pool pipes. He told me he felt guilty about it now. But at the time, he said, it fit the bitter-prankster mood taking hold among his white peers. If they couldn't be seen as honorable, they felt, then why try at all? Why not be bad? Why not suck completely?

It's remarkable how quickly it became cool in young Afrikaner circles to act like a fuck-up. Country music had always been popular among Afrikaners. Under apartheid, it mostly panegyrized upright, successful, God-fearing people. But in the mid-'90s, an opposite kind of song emerged: the ode to being a redneck or a hedonist—a *slapgat*, or "floppy ass," the kind of man Christo's brother Jaco once feared becoming. One star released a song called "Kiss Me on My Beer Belly"; another made a megahit about disrupting a wedding by walking around gripping his testicles. At Afrikaner parties, even in fancy neighborhoods, you could witness something you might call white-trash minstrelsy: young lawyers or business consultants doing Jägermeister shots out of a glass shaped like a woman's breast.

The country's moral context had suddenly come to lionize people who had been victimized. And so for white South Africans to represent themselves as déclassé queerly afforded them a sense of honor. When I asked one of the first Afrikaner friends I made, Cobie, how to say "What's your name?" in Afrikaans, he answered, *"Waar's jou ma se poes,"* which means, "Where's your mother's pussy?" For days, I went around greeting doctors and lawyers in Cape Town by asking, "Where's your mother's pussy?" Usually, these professionals responded by slapping my back and hooting with pleasure.

I met Cobie in a beautiful wine-farming village east of Cape Town. He was wearing pants that looked like they hadn't been washed in years and no shoes. He referred to himself a "poor white" and invited me to see his house. It was nothing but a shipping container. The front door was a shower curtain and the bathroom was a toilet positioned under a tree in the backyard. A chicken pecked around at my ankles while I urinated. The decor looked like a landfill had sneezed: there were stuffing-less carcasses of armchairs, rotting banana peels, and endless disposable mini disco balls. At night, to see what he was cooking over a camp stove, Cobie lit a lamp positioned at the crotch of an old mannequin, uplighting its perky, peeling plastic breasts.

Only later did I learn this wasn't Cobie's real house. Or it wasn't his only house. It was a kind of weekend home: his wife worked at a university, and they also had a normal apartment. His late father ran a profitable mohair farm, turning over several hundred thousand dollars a year in profit. But Cobie preferred to receive me at the shipping container.

It all reminded me eerily of my American youth. My parents, political conservatives, hadn't allowed TV in our house in the '80s. They disliked MTV's sexual innuendo.

That all changed, though, in the '90s, when my parents bought a TV specifically to watch the O. J. Simpson trial *for* its trashiness. My mother loved the dirty-mouthed Kato Kaelin. The conservative radio and magazines they consumed manifested a sudden shift in tone from the prissiness of William F. Buckley to the foul-mouthed rebelliousness of Rush Limbaugh; a new right-wing journal called *The Weekly Standard* published odes to "terrifyingly overweight" truck drivers dancing in bars to "dumpy" bands.

I remember a vacation we took with friends to West Virginia, where my father's uncle had a lake house. He was an affluent railroad executive and the house was a beauty, built of fragrant cedar wood. But we got lost driving out and ended up in a trailer park. My mother's friend got out of the car to ask for directions. She scurried back with a queer look and reported that the trailer owner had brandished a diaper in her face.

After a second, everyone in the car burst into appreciative laughter. The superficial mood was of concern, but below that bubbled a vast magma lake of satisfaction. The '90s, after all, were a decade in which white Americans were starting to be more heavily criticized for clinging to privilege. It was a strange pleasure, then, for my upper-middle-class parents and their friends to reassure themselves that white Americans still had an aspect of the underdog, even of raw stupidity.

The Afrikaner community was torn between presenting itself as down-home and insisting on its extraordinariness, between getting drunk on Jägermeister and innovating $15-a-jar walnut-grappa macrobiotic honey. For, on another level, it was also totally shameful for a white person to be ordinary.

When I lived in Cape Town, I had a roommate named Philippe. His hair always smelled a little, because he rationed shampoo. He was having trouble getting a job, he told me apologetically. His father was a big banana farmer, but he had no major career ambitions. He wanted to be a fry cook.

Yet he was actually unable to achieve this downward social mobility. Every morning, Philippe set out by bicycle to deliver his résumé to the new beachfront tourist cafés. But he never got a bite. It seemed to him it was acceptable, even honorable, for black South Africans to aspire to formerly white-only professions after apartheid's end, but Philippe got the impression society didn't permit white people to step into jobs formerly reserved for black people, even if white people wanted them. When Philippe would present his résumé to restaurant managers, black or white, they would laugh in his face. White people didn't work in kitchens, they told him.

I had lunch once with Hermann Giliomee, the Afrikaner historian, in an upscale café. He pointed to its fantastically large sidewalk umbrellas and its array of expensive organic jellies. That felt new, he said. Under apartheid, he sensed white people often avoided this kind of over-the-top, flamboyant taste. The political situation would have made it obvious such opulence rode on the back of extreme racial oppression. It was important, in the public square, to maintain some impression of restraint.

But after the end of white rule, there was no clear reason anymore for white South Africans *not* to flaunt architecturally braggadocious houses. Homes got bigger and more luxe while white resort towns seeded themselves along the coasts. High-end coffee shops catering almost entirely to white people took over Cape Town, proffering things like $9-a-cup coffee distilled from beans predigested by a rare civet. It was weird, Giliomee mused. But racial progress in South Africa had been accompanied, in his view, by the relinquishing of a certain kind of humility among white people.

The white South Africans I met often claimed to have the most astounding careers. Two men I knew sought corporate sponsors in exchange for filming themselves jumping off thousand-foot cliffs in hand-designed wing suits. I met so many white entrepreneurs who exuded fabulous optimism about their unique-in-the-world cannabis inventions or their 3D-jewelry lines.

White South Africans had always worried they had no natural place on the continent, and that place could theoretically be won by accomplishments. Now, career failures make them feel so vulnerable they are usually denied. These white entrepreneurs *never* admitted financial or operational vulnerability to me. I'd liked some of them. I played with their kids and friended them on Facebook. But I'd turn up at their shops one day and they would be gone. Vanished, a "for sale" sign plastered in the empty storefront windows. When I'd try to contact them, they'd never reply.

My friend Cobie believed he had to create an exceptional business—though I sensed he was, like Philippe, the kind of unambitious guy who would do best as a fry cook. He tried importing granite countertops from India. He tried engineering a new kind of solar panel. None of these ventures made him remotely enough money.

They were all, objectively, long shots, but his family harshly criticized him. They suggested he was betraying the Afrikaner community or even had some kind of psychiatric disorder. "My voicemails over Christmas say, 'We're praying for you,'" Cobie told me bitterly. Unemployed, he began to have crippling panic attacks. A doctor prescribed him benzodiazepines, which he hoarded.

And he became a conspiracy theorist. Over the eight years I knew him, Cobie came to believe not only in the "Night of the Long Knives" conspiracy—that black people, when Mandela died, would stream into white-dominated neighborhoods with machetes—but that Monsanto, the agricultural megacorporation, was spraying chemicals over South Africa to control its citizens' minds. I found these kinds of conspiracy theories unusually widespread among white South Africans. Their believers weren't necessarily uneducated. It struck me that to believe you know strange secrets was one way to be exceptional. If you couldn't *do* something extraordinary with your life, at least you could say you know something extraordinary *about* life—something other people aren't yet perceptive enough to see.

As the unrest at UFS spread, Christo actually drew back from it. He started spending a lot of time at the library. The musty scent of the books and the enveloping presence of history felt calming. One day, he pulled an old green-covered book off the shelf.

It was a biography of a general in the Anglo-Boer War, the early-twentieth-century conflict between the Afrikaners and the British. In the illustration, General Christiaan de Wet eerily resembled Christo, with the same high cheekbones and dark blue eyes. The British captured De Wet, but he escaped and then resisted his own Afrikaner leaders' orders to surrender. "His unit was forcibly disbanded," Christo told me. "It was the same thing that had happened to me."

Christo checked the book out and took it back to his room. He put it on his nightstand and read passages whenever he could. It's been forgotten, but at the turn of the twentieth century, progressives worldwide were charmed by the Afrikaners. Their struggle against British imperialism was likened to the Greek effort at self-determination that attracted romantics like Lord Byron. An American newspaper editor marveled that the way "a tiny people faces death without hesitation to defend its independence presents the world with an aspect of moral beauty which no soul, attuned to the higher things, will disregard."

In Christo's book, De Wet's refusal to give up was depicted not as pathological but as noble, as a mark of strong character. Before his defeat, De Wet was uncannily able to "get out of situations people normally couldn't get out of," Christo told me. The biography said De Wet cultivated his sense of purpose through self-discipline. He'd get up at four in the morning and pray; it was a custom nothing, neither war nor defeat, could disrupt.

Christo liked imagining a world in which consistency was rewarded. De Wet suggested there was a moral code you could follow that would basically guarantee you'd never accidentally betray your people or become a pariah. Even his enemies "respect him," Christo said. Whenever he talked to me about De Wet, he used the present tense, as if De Wet were still alive.

Christo never returned that biography to the library. He started rising earlier and praying, following De Wet's rules. Verschoor noticed Christo was changing. "He calmed down," Verschoor said—a striking development, given all the other troubles on campus.

Christo took over coaching a girls' rugby squad and excelled in his classes. And he started studying law. "My roommate came to me and said, 'I know girls who have good notes in law,'" Christo remembered. Hearing there were classmates who could share notes with him—*girls*—"I decided then and there that was what I was going to do." He laughed.

"But I liked the law," he went on. "It gave me a lot of insight into other things"—into the way people decide what's right and wrong. In his final two years, the UFS students elected Christo to serve on their student council.

"Everybody came to respect him," Verschoor told me. "Gradually—I can't say if ever I knew whether he was totally 'rehabilitated,' but he became a very acceptable person." So acceptable, in fact, that administrators decided to put him in charge of a dorm they were establishing to house the most difficult white students, like the ones who poured cement down their dorm swimming pool's pipes. A black administrator, Benito Khotseng, told me he felt Christo was "sensitive to the black students, and he also understood the fears of whites. We felt we had found someone who—he wouldn't let things go back to the way things were."

He also got married. He'd met Hanlie years earlier on a furlough from the 32 Battalion. After that meeting, he announced to whoever would listen, "I've met my wife!"

His fellow soldiers would usually laugh. He'd taken her on a single date—to the Mel Gibson shoot-'em-up *Bird on a Wire*. "She slept through it," he remembered, laughing.

But one day, his UFS roommate—who served with him in the

military—remarked, "Remember that girl you wanted to marry?" He thought he'd seen her around campus.

It turned out Hanlie was enrolled at UFS, studying music. Jaco was also a music student, and Christo begged him to put him in touch with her. Hanlie was tall, dark-haired, and artistically inclined. She came from a more urbane family, and Christo said she put him through "tests": "It was like *vasbyt* all over again." When he proposed marriage near his father's farm—he thought it was a romantic place—she had him do it over again in an elegant rotating restaurant atop Bloemfontein's tallest building.

But these tests reminded him how his military service helped him grow, to tolerate suffering for the sake of a goal, though De Klerk had deemed it worthless.

Christo held his bachelor party over two nights at his future father-in-law's house. He invited some of his old friends from the military. The reunion, though, ended up being disturbing. "It was like putting [gasoline] on fire to get them together," Christo told me.

The veterans drank to near-blackout and pissed on his father-in-law's bushes. These were things he did occasionally while he was a soldier, but now their pranks had an unbridled edge. The second night of the party, somebody decided it would be funny to steal a chicken from Hanlie's father's neighbor's yard and grill it.

Unfortunately, the animal happened to be an expensive show chicken—and its owner was a policeman. When the cop discovered his beloved pet had been barbecued, he stormed over and threatened to "hold the groom ransom," Christo said, until Hanlie's father paid him a substantial sum of money for a new chicken.

Christo felt embarrassed in front of his future father-in-law. And he worried about his friends. Hanlie challenged him to learn how to express his feelings and control his impulses for a vision. He felt so grown-up when she agreed to his second marriage proposal. He had learned to change and to master himself. Why hadn't his comrades? "These guys are still messed up," he thought. It seemed they'd subconsciously accepted the condemnation, even the contempt, directed at them by post-apartheid society. De Klerk had claimed the 32 was "out of control," and the veterans seemed determined to prove him right.

22

Christo

REITZ, THE DORM VERSCHOOR TAPPED Christo to run, was chaotic at the beginning. The boys struggled in their classes, Christo told me. "They were confused by what's happening around them. There was a new government, and we didn't know where we were going or what's going to happen. Change was happening without us." The father of one of Christo's new charges had been brutally murdered on his farm, and the event angered and frightened the other boys. The murdered man's son, in particular, "sat with an incredibly raw kind of aggression."

Christo's idea was to be present for the boys and not shame them. Instead of talking to them about politics or the future, he spoke to them about their individual struggles—their crushes, their academic problems, or their difficulties at home. Hanlie came to accept that her family life and Reitz life would be entwined. When she gave birth to a baby boy, he ran around the interior quad, like the new dorm's mascot.

Christo told me his other goal was to "put the boys' roots in." He advised them to study the episode in Afrikaner history in which he'd found solace as a student: the Anglo-Boer War, when the Afrikaners were celebrated as moral beacons. He invited a historian to deliver lectures on the war and encouraged the boys to investigate their genealogy to see if they were related

to any Anglo-Boer War heroes. Once or twice a year, the historian took them to a battlefield where some Afrikaners defeated a better-armed, artillery-reinforced British division.

But Christo hadn't stopped dwelling on his personal memories. The hope he had nurtured was that he could somehow become De Wet, possessing De Wet's backstory as his own. But the dreams about his own army life kept coming. To crush the sensations of pleasure and pride these memories triggered—to construct an entire new notion of what honor and glory entailed—would have required the erasure and revision of all of his childhood dreams, the ones that woke him up in his youth in an excited sweat like the young Nikolenka Bolkonsky in *War and Peace*, who awakens from a dream of his battle-slain father and pants happily, "Father! Father! Yes, I'll do something that even he would be pleased with . . ."

So, with the new dorm, he would try to redeem part of his youthful experience from its bad reputation. He went by his army nickname, "Dippies," and instituted rituals from his military training. Every student took part in an early-morning "inspection," just like Christo had done. He examined their toothbrushes and their possessions laid out in a line on the bed; if they screwed up the order of the soap and the toothbrush, they had to do push-ups.

If his boys became disciplined—if they simmered down, excelled in their classes, and became desirable boyfriends for the young women on campus—it would prove *something* in the experience to which he'd devoted his youth wasn't all bad. He even created a *vasbyt*. At the beginning of their freshman and sophomore years, the Reitz men took a bus out to a farm and did an overnight obstacle course. The next day, Christo treated them to a barbecue and a cup of beer, just like he'd gotten in Oudtshoorn.

Verschoor placed Monte into Reitz. Monte adored it. As a dorm leader, Christo was striking, he told me. He seemed to have acquired an unusual inner stillness, a quiet confidence that was comforting. "The headmaster of a secondary school—you will always be afraid of him. But I never got that idea [with Christo]. He had such a calm way of speaking to you. I never heard him shouting at any guy." The dorm felt like a brotherhood. "After graduating, if one guy had a birthday, his year group would send him text messages. People saw [Christo] as a father. Long after they left Reitz, they'd call him up to ask him if they should get married."

A man named Erik also lived in Reitz. Born in 1984, "I never fully understood the whole rigamarole," he told me by phone, by which he meant South Africa's democratic transition. "Please understand what I'm going to tell you now. Growing up after apartheid, my friends and I never had anything we could belong to. We still shouted for the Springboks," the national rugby team. "We felt 'South African.' But Afrikaner culture, everything our fathers talked about"—Erik's father had been in a Special Forces unit—"we didn't have any place to live that out. So for us to be a part of Reitz—it was basically amazing. We felt like some of the [Anglo-Boer War] guys who fought for freedom."

Christo had tapped into a cultural shift. While he ran Reitz, the Anglo-Boer War became a popular subject of study among young Afrikaners. A pop star released a hit song about it; tens of thousands of young Afrikaners filled stadiums to hear the singer belt it out. And a new NGO founded to press for Afrikaner interests decorated its offices with banners of its generals, like Christo's favorite, De Wet.

The NGO, called AfriForum, had its offices in a vast open-plan warehouse with the look of Silicon Valley workplaces before that look existed, all rounded edges and primary colors and funky lower-case fonts. The day I visited, one of the NGO's founders—names Flip Buys—explained the ambiance. It was a hot day, but

215

he wore a tight, James Dean leather motorcycle jacket. Piles of left-wing academic books were strewn across his desk: *The Power of Identity* by the Marxist economist Manuel Castells; *Sources of the Self* by the communitarian philosopher Charles Taylor.

In the early '90s, he said, he and his Afrikaner friends genuinely feared black rule. Around 1994, Flip's wife remarked, "Mandela seems like a nice person." He remembered warning her: "I think they"—black leaders—"have made compromises in order to get power. But after they've consolidated power, they will use it to pursue *their* interests."

But he also felt shame and deep self-doubt. Buys and his college friends wanted to become academics, but they felt embarrassed to identify themselves as white South Africans at international con-ferences. Europeans and Americans subtly distanced themselves from them, as if the young men had forgotten to shower.

He found unexpected refuge in certain left-wing academic theories. Manuel Castells talked about progressives' duty to care for "Fourth World" peoples, a term that described ethnic groups or religious communities that don't have the protection of their own state. Typically, the term referred to profoundly historically marginalized peoples like the Australian Aborigines. "But what if Afrikaners are such a community?" Buys thought.

The idea came as a bolt of inspiration. "I wanted to fight for Afrikaners, but I came to think of myself as a 'liberal internation-alist,' not a white racist," Buys told me, with audible relief in his voice. "I found such inspiration from the struggles of the Catalo-nians and the Basques. Even Tibet."

His college friends studied the history and theory of adver-tising, and he recruited them to envision a sweeping rebrand of the Afrikaners' image from entitled oppressors to a hip, fragile minority facing potential extinction. "We are not a normal mi-nority," he acknowledged. "We are a discredited minority. And yet, as a discredited minority, I think we have to fight extra hard for our rights. Some people think nothing ever changes, and that a group of people who once held power will always be empowered." One of his first projects was to send a mission to the U.N. High Commissioner for Human Rights to argue that Afrikaners deserved protected status as an endangered ethnic minority.

The NGO became enormously popular. By 2016, nearly a quarter of Afrikaners were paying members. Dues gave members access to a charity, an app-based "panic button" that dispatched a private ambulance, and lawyers who helped them pursue claims against the affirmative-action program Mbeki established. AfriForum even declared its intention to establish a system of private prosecutors—parallel to South Africa's state prosecutors—to which you could submit complaints. The NGO gave its members the subtle but pervasive sense that a new, if micro, white-friendly South African state already existed, with its trendy headquarters as an alt-capital. Radio stations and a publishing house operated out of the headquarters, as well as a private Afrikaans-language college.

Another executive took me on a tour. In a room full of cubicles, some fifty young people uploaded posts to social media. "I sought work with AfriForum because I consider myself a liberal and an environmentalist," one employee told me cheerfully. As an example, she mentioned an environmental initiative AfriForum undertook to save threatened hippos. Then she gestured toward a word cloud displayed on one of the room's walls. It depicted AfriForum's characterization of "Afrikaner values": "Constitution-abiding." "Peace." "Civil rights." There was a quote by Martin Luther King Jr.

"I think the whole apartheid thing is something of the past," the young woman went on. "I hate politics, to be honest with you." In her previous job as a TV reporter, "I interviewed ten youngish people and I didn't find one who thought apartheid was still relevant. It's amazing, the absence of feelings about apartheid among the youth." She also said, though, that she hoped Afrikaners would ultimately seize back political administration from the black-led government because "at the moment, everything is falling apart. There's rhino poaching, acid mine drainage, and dumping at landfill sites." The Afrikaners, she said, were "naturally good" at management. "South Africa's environment is very unique. God intended us to look after it. We must maintain it. They don't care about it. That's where we come in." She pointed to the King quote on the wall. "Martin Luther King also fought for a people without much political representation," she concluded with a straight face. "That's why I consider him one of my most important forebears and heroes."

I brought up the encounter later with the executive who gave me the tour. I half-expected *her* to bring it up, to admit it was at least a little awkward. But instead, she challenged me. Technically, wasn't it true King fought for the rights of a "people without much political representation"? What could I complain about? What had anybody at AfriForum said that was *factually wrong*?

One of AfriForum's chief claims is that it doesn't want to bother black South Africans. After losing political dominance, Flip Buys told me, the Afrikaners "just want benign neglect." And yet the group's leaders are totally unable to resist provocation. When they floated the idea of the private prosecutors, they threatened to drag South Africa's president before its lawyers, claiming the current judiciary system had become hopelessly incompetent or biased. They frequently sue the ANC government over headline-grabbing issues like white South Africans' right to display the old, apartheid-era flag—which most white South Africans don't want to do anyway.

In person, the group's leaders didn't act like extremists. They read *The New Yorker*. Sometimes I couldn't tell if they believed their own messaging. They often expressed their rhetoric with a strange smile on their faces. A wink forming in the skin around their eyes. They seemed to relish other people's bafflement or criticism, the more exasperated and contemptuous the better. *Go on*, their smiles said. *Say we're ridiculous. We dare you to mock us. After all, your claim to be better than us only rests on the notion that you're more tolerant.* For if their provocation got them treated badly, *then* they could finally claim equal status as victims, instead of having to live with the apparent evidence of black people's greater capacity for empathy.

I came to understand that inflaming black South African anger was a goal for certain white South Africans. The goading could be cruel. "For those claiming [the] legacy of colonialism was ONLY negative," a top white South African politician tweeted, "think of our independent judiciary, transport infrastructure, piped water etc. Would we have had a transition into specialized health care and medication without colonial influence? Just be honest, please."

A thousand people, mostly black, replied. "That's fucked up," one wrote.

"You mean to say that, without white people, we would be nothing?" said another.

But the politician just would not stop. She doggedly pursued commenters with almost no followers—"Do you think [your] life would be better without infrastructure?"—until the thread devolved and a respondent lashed out, saying he didn't want to kill white people *just yet*. Then the politician triumphantly declared she'd been justified all along in thinking black people wanted to annihilate her.

It reminded me of an experience I had with a boyfriend. He'd failed to do something he said he would do, and it made me seethe with an anger I'd rarely experienced. The next morning, hungover from venting fury, I wondered why I'd gotten so mad. And then I recalled a conversation I'd had with a work supervisor just before

I criticized my boyfriend. She'd asked me why I hadn't turned in a project on time. *Why had I made promises I hadn't kept?* she pressed.

I had behaved toward her exactly as I later accused my boyfriend of behaving toward me. And it became clear to me that I'd shamed him as a proxy for the harder work of confronting my own shame. The thing that struck me was how justified, how totally reasonable, my anger had felt in the moment. I had *reasons* to be upset. But what I was really doing was passing my shame forward like a hot potato to a convenient victim—one I believed, deep down, would not abandon me, no matter how much I criticized him.

Don't white South Africans have reason to imagine that, whatever they do, black people will not forsake them? "You know when we will become a banana republic? When *they* leave," a black politician warned other black people. Analysts both inside and outside South Africa tend to fret single-mindedly over the economic apocalypse that might ensue if white people emigrate, not if skilled people of color do.

Yet I also sensed an undercurrent of desperation in this goading. On the radio, I often heard an Afrikaans pop-country song with a startlingly uncertain lyric: "I'm in love with my country, but does my country still love me?" It expressed an anxiety that underlay some of white people's bitterest accusations about black failures. Do you respect *us*? Do *we* deserve to be here?

It often seemed to me as if the white South Africans who most categorically claimed they didn't care what black people thought actually cared the most, deep down. That *that* claim was a bitter defense against the deeper truth that they longed to be accepted and redeemed in black people's eyes.

At a dinner party I attended in Johannesburg, a colored woman named Thandi told a powerful story. A few years before, her cousin's friend broke his arm, and her cousin accompanied him to the emergency room at Johannesburg's main hospital.

After a while, an orderly emerged from the wards to invite Thandi's cousin in to join his friend in back. "Hoffeldt?" he called out.

Thandi's cousin stood—and so did a white man. The white man frowned. "I think you misheard," he said to Thandi's cousin.

"I didn't," Thandi's cousin replied. "My last name is Hoffeldt."

"But I know my family are the only Hoffeldts in South Africa," the white man said.

Thandi's cousin immediately guessed at the truth, because he grew up hearing it. The truth was that two Hoffeldts, German brothers, immigrated to South Africa in the late nineteenth century. One fell in love with a black woman. But the other became so disgusted by the idea of miscegenation that he disowned his brother.

The children of the German who fell in love with the black woman ultimately entered apartheid South Africa's mixed-race caste—vanishing from white society, but taking with them the richer, deeper version of history. When the anti-miscegenation brother married a white woman, he never told her, nor their children, that he'd even had a brother.

In the emergency room, Thandi's cousin explained all this to the white guy. He acknowledged it might sound fantastical. But the white guy actually didn't seem surprised. "It kind of makes sense," he murmured. "My great-grandfather"—the anti-miscegenation brother—"always seemed lost, like he had a limb missing. Something never seemed right."

In 2008, the Republic of Congo extended an invitation to South African farmers to move there and overhaul its agricultural sector. The Congolese president had heard South Africans were good at farming, and he was anxious about food security. Compared to almost any farming job in South Africa, farming in Congo would be a harrowing prospect. There was little existing infrastructure—no silos or decent roads—and Congolese politics were far less stable.

After a South African farming union announced the opportunity, though, seventy thousand South Africans—nearly exclusively white—contacted the union begging to be relocated, almost twice as many people as already farmed commercially in South Africa. In requesting information, they often said they had to leave because their black countrymen were irremediably prejudiced against them. A farmer named Theo headed the mission.

Theo soon discovered the project wasn't going to be difficult. It was going to be impossible. Congo's humidity caused fungus to sprout on the corn; it was hopeless to dry the harvest enough to grind it properly. The fertilizer he shipped never arrived because the Congolese port authorities demanded a bribe. The project was going to lead its participants to a financial ruin more comprehensive than any they would face in South Africa.

But he didn't want to give up, Theo told me. To explain why, he showed me his cell phone. The Congolese agriculture minister, he revealed—almost shyly, blushing—was text-messaging him. A powerful black man had given him his cell phone number. He had rarely felt so happy in his life.

It reminded me of a story I heard from a white professor, an avowed believer that the Afrikaners had to self-isolate in order to preserve their identity. But when he visited a university in Alabama, "I found that I sought the company of black people," he told me.

He didn't even fully understand why. But he found he wanted to be around black Americans "all the time." He started shooing away his academic handlers in favor of lingering for hours by the front desk of his hotel to chat with the black staff. The pleasure he felt when a black man shouted at him on the street and invited him, in the Southern style, to come up on his stoop and drink iced tea was almost physical, like the feeling of relief you get when you accept a glass of water and only then realize you'd been so thirsty you were almost dead.

"I felt so comfortable with them," the professor told me sadly. Some desire that had been bottled up in him for decades, fermenting, finally got decanted far from home and bubbled over wildly. "I'm not sure what we actually shared. But it was beautiful to meet them each morning and greet each other. In the restaurants, I made such an effort to talk to them. It was wonderful."

When the white professor returned to South Africa, though, he found it no easier to approach his black countrymen. In fact, he got involved with a mission to start an Afrikaners-only city in the desert.

In 1990, a group of conservative Afrikaners bought a mining town wholesale for the equivalent of $500,000. They named it Orania, and the rules were that only people who identified as Afrikaners could live there. Ostensibly, the founders said their goal was to prove, once and for all, that white people deserved a place in Africa by showing they could make it on their own without relying on cheap black labor. Not only would Afrikaners be Orania's elites, they would be its service workers. White people would sweep the streets, sponge down the restaurant tables, and pump the gas.

The weird little enclave with white gas pump operators became a mecca for foreign journalists. Every foreign correspondent did an Orania dispatch, because it was bizarre, but also because it fulfilled a grim expectation: that white people, deep down, will never change. The townspeople would start interviews by reciting academic lingo about marginalized peoples and then, like a record skipping into its more comfortable groove, suddenly spout raw racism. The residents, for instance, craved a rugby team. But because they didn't want black people tarrying in the town, their team couldn't host other teams and couldn't compete nationwide. That's white people for you, the dispatches always concluded. Terminally racist and pitifully self-defeating.

I saw something else, though. On my visit, I met the town's young mayor, a former philosophy student named Carel Boshoff IV. A grandson of Hendrik Verwoerd, Carel was raised well-to-do in Pretoria. In routine conversation, he quoted Tocqueville by heart. It was a hapless thing to see him struggle to brand cattle, one of his jobs in Orania. Dressed in amber Roberto Cavalli loafers and a tweed jacket, he stepped into a manure patch to swat a cow's rear. "Come," he cooed.

Braying loudly, the rest of the cattle began to back toward a gate he'd left open. Carel trotted to block their way. "No, no, you can't do that," he said politely, as if they were misguided undergrads in a logic class. "You're thinking wrong."

The cattle, now spooked, broke into a stampede. "Oh, no, no!" Carel screamed, holding his glasses to his face with one hand. Dashing after the runaways, he got hitched up in barbed wire. In extricating himself, he flipped right over the fence like a cartoon character. "It's not the best image," he said afterward as he dusted himself off. In the rest of South Africa, "this is certainly a thing that, normally, black people would do."

At times, Carel described his choice to live in Orania as simple. He wanted his kids to be taught in Afrikaans. If he showed up to church on Sunday, he wanted to hear a sermon featuring the Afrikaner God he grew up with. At other times, though, he explained his decision to relocate in terms of love. His father, a prominent pastor, "grew up with the idea people loved him," Carel said.

His father did missionary work in townships, and Carel said his life was an unbroken "experience of respect." In fact, Carel's father found it hard to conceive of the idea anybody *wouldn't* love him. But then, during the nationwide conflict in the '80s, a hearse mysteriously showed up in the family's driveway. The phone rang. The pastor picked it up. "We are here to collect your body," a voice said ominously, and hung up.

That event, something between a prank and a threat, suggested a time was coming soon when the pastor's whole understanding of the world would be undermined. "I thought I understood what he felt," Carel said.

He, too, grew up with the sensation of being a prince in the world. "People respected me, even if I did not in any definite way earn it." Partly this was an effect of his special heritage— the honor bestowed upon him, under apartheid, as a grandson of Verwoerd. As a young boy in the Afrikaner version of the Boy Scouts, the other boys tapped him to speak at awards ceremonies, even though he was socially awkward. Strangers came up to him and insisted on recounting where they were when they heard Verwoerd was assassinated.

But feeling loved, Carel reckoned, was also the psychic state of all white people. "That is the way in which we entered this world."

Many white South Africans still claim the black people they knew under apartheid loved them, even if there was bad blood between their political leaders. A major subgenre of white South African literature is devoted to memorializing the purported love between the white child and his black nanny. One night, at a dinner in Johannesburg, a white acquaintance began to talk about the going pay rates for black nannies. The man claimed he felt no guilt about paying his family's nanny, per month, just a quarter of what his new Apple laptop had cost. It wasn't only a job, he argued. As a child, he loved his nanny, and he knew she loved him. Nannies were part of the family.

"Is it really possible to know if our nannies loved us?" another white guest asked, uneasily.

The host turned angry. "I knew," he said loudly. "I knew."

The guest said she wasn't so sure. A friend of hers, she said, employed a black gardener for decades. One evening, he came home to find the gardener had stolen things from his house.

The gardener hadn't taken much. But the woman said her friend wept as inconsolably as if a spouse cheated on him. "He sold the house right afterwards," she said.

It wasn't that he felt unsafe. The gardener never came back. And moving to another house and hiring another gardener would only leave him open to the same vulnerabilities. Her friend experienced the theft as a deeply intimate betrayal. He always believed he'd *shared* his house with the gardener.

He needed to believe that—because otherwise he would be an exploiter. He needed to believe a lie so badly he'd come to believe it, plain and simple. The gardener's theft had shattered a vital illusion. Staying in the house would be an omnipresent reminder of everything he never understood about his environment—or, even more shamefully, a reminder of how cravenly he'd sought to conceal the truth from himself.

Carel told me he reclaimed a sense of being loved in Orania. As Verwoerd's relative, he said, its residents "group around me." But I was struck by how often he ditched town. Carel didn't always go to other predominantly white areas. He often went to *black* neighborhoods. He'd hobnob with black parliamentarians in the provincial capital, who got a kick out of his fashion sense and paid a tailor to weave him a bold African-patterned suit. It turned out that it wasn't just any love white South Africans yearned for, but black love—black respect. The danger of isolating themselves was that they became lonely without the black gaze.

In that provincial capital, Carel said, he once received a strange visit from three young black men from a township. They introduced themselves as Rastafarians and said they "came to tell me that they loved Verwoerd. They claimed they believed Verwoerd actually understood Africa." Even to Carel, who always defended his grandfather, that sounded absurd, and he started to laugh. But the men went further. They told Carel they believed Verwoerd had secretly been a Rastafarian prophet. "They said he visited Haile Selassie in Ethiopia."

At the time, Carel dismissed the men. But he couldn't stop thinking about the encounter. Privately—he felt embarrassed publicly entertaining the idea—he did some research, investigating whether Verwoerd might really have gone to Ethiopia. And, years afterward, something inarticulable pushed him to drive out to the township where the men said they lived.

"I drove all over, but I couldn't find them," Carel said. Yet he found what he was looking for in another way. To his surprise, it turned out he was something of a celebrity in the township, thanks to Orania's notoriety. I never heard Carel tell any story with such pleasure as he recounted his visit to the black township where "people, when I stopped at the vegetable stalls, called me by my name."

23

Malaika

WHEN MALAIKA ENTERED HIGH SCHOOL, she began to write—first on Facebook and then in local newspapers. Foreign universities and international development organizations invited her to speak at conferences. They often gave her what she considered outrageous per diem stipends. "Say you're four days in Ethiopia—they'd give you $60 for supper," she said.

Her immediate instinct was to squirrel the money away for Dipuo. Malaika smuggled extra plates of food out of the buffet lunches and stowed them in her hotel room to eat for dinner, saving cash. She remembered the sensory relish she felt when she got back from her first trip abroad, stood at the currency exchange window in the Johannesburg airport, and traded fistfuls of dollars for South African currency. A triumphant sentence popped into her head: "I, Malaika from Soweto, can manage to save money!"

She bought Dipuo antique furniture, the kind Godfrey used to bring home. But she had a dream of her own, too. By 2013, Malaika had put together nearly a thousand dollars to fund a trip through nine other countries in sub-Saharan Africa.

She'd loved reading African thinkers like Andimba Toivo ya Toivo, a Namibian freedom fighter, and Samora Machel, Mozambique's first black president. She wanted to see the lands that had yielded such people for herself. She also was a little afraid, to be honest. Her budget only accommodated travel by bus or minibus taxi. "Oh! That was a horrible experience," she said of her first long-haul minibus taxi ride to Maputo, the capital of Mozambique. "The taxi was a coffin on wheels. It was squeaking the whole way." On a larger bus from Zimbabwe to Zambia, "people had lots of weird animals. There were cages full of chickens strapped to the roof."

Yet she felt a sense of freedom she had never quite felt in South Africa. The people in the countries she visited didn't seem to sculpt their thoughts in reaction to white people as much as South Africans did. "When I got to Mozambique, on the first day, I met this guy, Nicholas. He was Congolese," she remembered. He had ridden with her in the "coffin on wheels." She smiled naughtily. "I think he was a drug dealer."

But when he invited her to stay with him in a luxurious hotel room he had rented by the beach, she agreed. "I was so trusting. It was weird, actually."

Nicholas turned out to be a gentleman and showed her around Maputo. It looked nothing like she had imagined. While she was preparing for her trip, some of her friends had said, "Oh my God, you're going to *Africa*?" and wrinkled their noses.

Many black South Africans integrated the white claim that South Africa was different from "Africa"—higher than the rest of the continent; perhaps not even part of it. Black South Africans often call immigrants from other African countries "Africans," as if they, South Africans, aren't. When Malaika returned from her tour, her friends would ask, "So, are there *roads* there, in Africa?"

Malaika found herself posting pictures of Lilongwe, the Malawian capital, to Facebook as proof African people could do competent and cutting-edge things like build good roads and run great restaurants. "People would be like, 'Huh? Lilongwe looks like a normal city!'"

The year before she traveled, South Africans in townships

across the country had looted and burned African immigrants' homes and stores. The looters accused the "foreigners" of stealing their jobs. They chanted, "Drive the foreigners away!" By the time the unrest died down, several dozen African immigrants had been killed and tens of thousands were left homeless.

Newspapers referred to the event as an eruption of "xenophobia." Malaika thought that was bullshit. French expats were also foreign, but they weren't pejoratively called "foreigners" and *their* homes weren't burned. She preferred to refer to the phenomenon as "Afrophobia."

Black South Africans were historically unused to the visible presence of immigrants from other African countries. Black people from other countries were rarely let into white-run South Africa, and they didn't perceive it as an alluring destination. That changed, though, after apartheid's end. Suddenly, the continent's most developed economy was open for African business. ANC leaders felt pressure not to limit immigration from other African countries lest they look as prejudiced as their predecessors. Immigrants, legal and illegal, streamed in from the Democratic Republic of Congo, from Nigeria, from Somalia. When, in 2000, the dictator Robert Mugabe plunged Zimbabwe into a catastrophic economic crisis, millions of desperate Zimbabweans flooded over the border.

Most black South Africans I met said they believed South Africans had a duty to help their African "brothers." But, in practice, many resented the implication that—because they achieved their liberation last and endured the presence and capital investment of white people the most—they had an obligation to rescue every other victim of colonialism on the African continent, even people whose own liberation movements had fucked up. More aggravating were white South Africans' constant intimations they preferred black "foreigners."

White South Africans often claimed that, if only black South Africans acted as cordial as African immigrants did, they'd never say one bad word about black people. In 2009, the head of an NGO that tracks African migration told me white South Africans had developed an unarticulated but rigid preference for "African" employees over black South Africans. "People who work in a [South African] garden, you can just assume they're Zimbabwean," the analyst said. "Ghanaians work in security."

When I asked white South Africans about this preference, many just shrugged and claimed "African" people were "friendlier." They said they didn't know why. Black South Africans, they said, bitched about their working conditions while "Africans" were grateful and diligent.

It wasn't hard to understand this phenomenon. Many African immigrants don't have papers and fear taking their employers to the government-run labor dispute board. Even if they've immigrated legally, they have far more to lose by being disobedient. So many risked so much to get to South Africa. I met a Congolese taxi driver who swam across a literally crocodile-infested river. A Nigerian coming by land has to cross seven national borders; an Ivorian, ten.

African immigrants to South Africa are a self-selected group, unusually tolerant of risk. For so long, black South Africans wanted to see *themselves* this way—as fighters. And now here were these other black people, apparently more capable of accessing jobs—and exuding a boastful swagger. Reflecting on black South Africans' complaints about the national unemployment rate, Zimbabweans sometimes proudly announce, "I knocked on a few doors and got a job. It's not that hard!"

In fact, some African immigrants envied black South Africans. When a South African woman I knew flew back from a conference in Zambia, she was seated next to a Zambian economist. As their plane drifted down over Johannesburg, the economist remarked wistfully, "I wish *we* had had apartheid."

The South African started laughing. She presumed the economist was kidding.

She wasn't. "Look at those roads!" the Zambian woman exclaimed, pointing at the tangle of highways. "Look at those buildings! Honestly—you don't know how much some of us wish *we*'d had that."

Embedded in the comment, though, was also a reprimand. If *Zambians* inherited such a highly developed country, the economist implied, they would have done something great with it.

A black journalist I knew interviewed a veteran of Umkhonto we Sizwe who trained in Zambia. At one point, members of the Zambian military came to drill with the black South Africans. One Zambian soldier, with barely veiled contempt, turned to the South African and asked, "Man, what are you guys doing? As far as I can tell, in South Africa, you are five black people to every one white person. And yet here you are, endlessly preparing for war in *our* country. You talk constantly about taking back your land. But you could take back your country. You must ask yourself: What are you afraid of? Why are you weak? Are you sure you want to be free? The numbers don't lie. It's five to one. Any day you wanted, you could take your country back."

Defensively, the veteran tried to explain that South Africa wasn't like Zambia. It had been far more comprehensively colonized, and the tendrils of the white police and military penetrated everywhere. But the Zambian's comment burrowed into his head. He still dwelled on it, twenty years later. *What* was *wrong with us?* he would think. Because the Zambian's math seemed unassailable.

Another time, on a shuttle bus to a soccer game, I overheard a Nigerian and a black South African arguing about which of their peoples had dealt more successfully with the legacy of white domination. "South Africans," the Nigerian woman was saying contemptuously. "They have the worst attitude. They don't know how to get on the right side of employers."

"You guys are drug dealers," the South African woman spat back. "You come and cannibalize our country. You only have an opening here because of what we *made* for you. Because of our struggle, our suffering. And yet you embarrass yourselves, bowing and scraping before white people! You're willing to participate in a rigged system for scraps."

"Could you even find Nigeria on a map?" the Nigerian woman retorted. "You don't believe you're a part of Africa, because you are still racist against your own kind." She pulled up a map of Africa on her phone. "*You're* the ones who are hung up on your relationship to white people. Nigeria is only poor because *we* fought the whites so hard they all had to leave." It went on like this for twenty minutes, the two women fighting over who were the better Africans, until the driver had to pull the bus to the curb and physically separate them.

Malaika also got involved with a new Black Consciousness movement led by a charismatic twenty-seven-year-old writer, Andile Mngxitama. He had a different mien from older black South African leaders, a defiantly crude swagger that said: white people are *lucky* to listen to my ideas. In essays and speeches, Mngxitama declared that black South Africans who treated white people kindly were like antebellum American "house Negroes."

"On the plantation," he wrote, "the house Negro was given leftover food, and he loved the master, and he spoke like the master. . . . When the house of the master was on fire . . . even when [he] could hear the agony and cries of the field Negroes being beaten, [he] still did not accept that the whole institution of slavery was based on violence. [He] loved the house of the master so much [he] wanted to save it." Mngxitama exhorted young black South Africans to be like "field Negroes." When the master was sick," he wrote, "*they* prayed to their Black God that the master must die."

Dipuo disliked Mngxitama's coarse language. But this kind of rhetoric, harsh as it was, felt thrilling to Malaika. Mngxitama wanted to bring pan-African thinking to South African young people—writers like Frantz Fanon and Frank B. Wilderson, a black American scholar who argues that most black people still suffer from internalized antiblack racism. Malaika was taken with Fanon's argument that a fundamental neuroticism lingered in black people. She saw this in her own relatives—even in Dipuo, sometimes, if she was to be honest.

Malaika believed most black South Africans didn't really hate other black people. She thought their antipathy was a product of poor education. Exposure to Mngxitama's ideas would make them realize black people were not their enemies. After the wave of lootings, Mngxitama launched a campaign he called *Singamakwerekwere Sonke*, or "We are all foreigners," expressing the sense that all black people were still alienated in a world dominated by whiteness. Malaika helped plan his Johannesburg march, throwing herself into generating enthusiasm on social media.

But on the day of the march, only fifteen people showed up. Disappointed, she and Mngxitama carried their stacks of anti-Afrophobia pamphlets to a minibus taxi depot nearby. There, though, things got worse. "The only reason you want us not to kill foreigners is because *you* are being fucked by Nigerians," one passenger told Malaika with a leer.

Suddenly, three minibus taxi drivers with guns shoved her and Mngxitama into a room in the back of the depot and locked the door. They confiscated the pamphlets and "accused us of wanting to turn the country into a haven for 'foreigners,'" Malaika remembered. She left the scene "engulfed by sadness."

She'd actually witnessed an assault on an immigrant. Walking home to Meadowlands through a normally empty Soweto field one day, she noticed a group of men shouting in a corner. Curious, she approached. She saw a man lying on the ground and another man bent over him.

With a sick feeling, Malaika realized the man bending over wasn't helping the prone man but was kicking him in the stomach. Just then, another man rushed up carrying a jug of gasoline. He poured it over the prone man's body.

Horrified, all Malaika could do was turn away.

When she got home, she told her uncle Ali what she saw. Ali confirmed he'd heard a rumor that, indeed, a group of Sowetan men had burned a Zimbabwean immigrant to death that day. But the "foreigner" had been stealing, Ali insisted. He defended the Zimbabwean's killers. "People here are very poor," he said, as if Malaika had become a foreigner in Soweto, too, and didn't realize it.

Oddly, pan-Africanism could also be considered a white tendency. An elitist thing, a utopian theory dreamed up by academics in ivory towers. "They have nothing," Ali said of the Sowetans who burned the Zimbabwean man. When "foreigners" come, he said, "what are they supposed to do?"

"We could not have defeated white domination," Malaika cried, "only to find ourselves killing each other!"

"When you get older," her uncle just said darkly, "you'll understand."

24

Dipuo

As Malaika grew older, sometimes it was impossible for Dipuo not to feel awe for her strength. When Malaika was born, she took her mother's placenta out with her. Her child had seized its own crown of glory—unaware, yet, that she had to ask anybody's permission.

And yet "Malaika also became a very vocal child," Dipuo said. "Talkative. I took out my frustrations on her," yelling at her to shut up. "And then I couldn't even say 'I'm sorry.'" She felt afraid of having to talk to Malaika about sex. "I didn't have a history of passionate moments with any man. I didn't know where to start."

With growing terror, she wondered if she was carrying forward the legacy of her own mother's behavior, taking out her personal disappointments on her daughter. "When I started associating with [boys]," Malaika remembered, Dipuo "started being a private investigator. She would listen in on conversations I had with them, and if she had even the smallest suspicion that one was asking me out, especially an older one, she would confront them and threaten to beat them up." One night, Malaika returned home late after a thrilling, platonic meeting with Mngxitama. Dipuo found his phone number, called him, and told him if he so much as looked at her daughter again she would burn his corpse.

Occasionally, too, she hit Malaika. "And then, when I was alone, I would think, 'Oh my God! I have hurt my daughter.' And I would wonder, 'What is this anger? Where does it come from? And when will it end?'"

And she had recurring nightmares. In one, she revisited a real episode from her time in the People's Committee. One evening, she, Gadifele, and some others went to the house of a young woman they heard was a "spy." Dipuo pulled the woman out of her bed onto her front lawn and pelted her with stones until she fell, bleeding, onto her knees.

The girl later died. Dipuo would wake up from the nightmare paralyzed, unable to move her arms or legs, wanting to scream. But nothing came out of her mouth.

Dipuo also said she'd learned Richard Maponya, the businessman whose shop she helped burn, had *not* been a spy. He'd been working for her—for the ANC in secret. Dipuo felt tortured by guilt that she'd injured a man who'd actually been her ally. "He could not even defend himself at the time," she told me sadly, lest the police get word of his anti-apartheid activities.

At the Truth and Reconciliation hearings, a black woman gave chilling testimony about a "necklacing," a brutal attack sometimes made on suspected "spies." In a necklacing, assailants wrestled a car tire over their target's head, poured gasoline into its rim, and lit the tire on fire. The witness recalled that her husband was necklaced without knowing why. After stepping out of his house one evening, a group of young black men pushed him to the ground and forced a tire over his head.

But as the unknown attackers emptied a jug of gasoline into the tire, it looked to the man's wife as if her husband *decided* not to resist. As if he decided to send the message: well, comrades, you have deemed me unworthy to live, and since I respect black men, I must accept your judgment. The woman saw her husband go limp and say in a clear voice, "Do what you want to do to me."

I heard little about necklacings when I moved to South Africa, given how prominent they were in the country's narrative before apartheid ended. Between 1983 and 1989, the South African government executed a thousand of its citizens—almost all black—at a gallows in Pretoria. Less than half of that number were killed by extrajudicial necklacings during the same time frame. But Jan-Ad Stemmet, the South African historian, told me the press "covered the necklacings with special gusto." South Africa's state-run TV channel "actually aired graphic footage of a necklacing at eight o'clock," Stemmet said. "Now, take into consideration that South Africa had one of the most stringent media censorship systems on earth, and you'll understand that the government would only have played up the necklacings if it served them. The government pointed to the necklacings with the argument: 'If that's what they do to each other, just imagine what they're going to do to whites.'"

At the time, something in the way white people talked about necklacings kind of made Dipuo want to participate in one. Every time a white person claimed black people were innately violent, Dipuo took a little pleasure in showing she didn't care what they thought.

It reminded me of something an American man once told me. He grew up in the shipbuilding city of Mobile, Alabama, but he moved to Illinois to get a master's degree. There, for the first time, he experienced the contempt Northerners had for the South. Other students mocked his accent and asked him where his corny country records were.

He'd never liked country music, but they wouldn't accept that. If he suggested they go to an Italian restaurant, they'd counter by claiming he probably *really* would prefer to fry up some roadkill in a popcorn machine.

"Fuck it," he eventually thought. "And *fuck you*." If he couldn't change their minds about Southerners, at least he wouldn't let them catch him feeling ashamed of what they insisted was his heritage. He bought his first pair of cowboy boots and some Glen Campbell records. Only in the North did he begin to become the kind of Southerner that Northerners detested.

Dipuo didn't say how the woman she stoned in Soweto ultimately died. But when I asked her whether she ever participated in a necklacing, she just looked down and was silent.

I also asked Dipuo if she sought to give testimony to the TRC, which was supposed to be a healing experience. At first, she said "ordinary people" weren't invited to testify. That wasn't true. Not everybody testified in person, but anybody could submit their stories to the TRC's files. But then she admitted the block was more internal. How do you say, after fighting so hard for liberation, that you are still wounded? And how do you admit you're haunted not only by what white people did to you, but by what *you did*?

In the early '90s, there was one black voice who acknowledged the true depth of black pain and ambivalence. Chris Hani was the head of the South African Communist Party and a leader in Umkhonto we Sizwe. He was a generation younger than Mandela, closer to Dipuo's age. In an era when black leaders went around mimicking Mandela's polished, genial manner, Hani wore rough military clothes and rejected Mandela's forgiving attitude. In the delicate years right before the end of white rule, he'd say things like, "I don't mince my words when I am speaking about [the white] regime. I hate it intensely." He questioned giving amnesty to apartheid officials and sympathized with what drove young black people to violence, imbuing it with a kind of rationality and dignity. "Why *should* they be cool as icebergs," he tartly asked a foreign reporter who inquired about the necklacings, "when they are being killed every day?"

Dipuo remembered Hani's attitude as "these people"—white

people—"must go. They must go back to Europe!" She let out a warm, nostalgic laugh. But in the early '90s, "nobody could say Mandela was wrong," she said. So she and Gadifele nursed their affection for Chris Hani in secret. "On the one hand, we wanted peace. But we really loved Chris Hani."

One April afternoon in 1993, Gadifele was wrapping up at the horse-racing track where she worked when her manager made an unusual request. Would she keep the jockeys running races?

"How many more?" she asked, confused.

"Run them indefinitely," he said grimly.

After an hour, the news made its way to her. Hani had been shot and killed by a white assassin.

When she went to the People's House, Gadifele was surprised to turn on the radio and find "even the white DJs were crying." "Please, please, calm down," they begged. She realized they were terrified. Black leaders were afraid, too. Deep down, so many people assumed Hani's attitude represented black South Africans' true, vengeful feelings. Oliver Tambo confessed to a reporter that he worried "our young people are driven by hate." Gadifele also realized her manager, a black man, wanted to keep running the horse races indefinitely because he was afraid black spectators would start to riot when they went home and heard the news.

In the People's House, Gadifele and Dipuo held hands in silence. "Can you imagine everything going quiet in an entire country?" Gadifele asked me. And then Mandela's voice came over the radio, speaking live.

"Our pain and anger is real," he stated evenly. "Yet we must not permit ourselves to be provoked."

Dipuo remembered realizing: "This is a trap." White leaders, she thought, must have arranged Hani's assassination to get black people to riot and generate an excuse to scuttle the democratic transition. (A government investigation proved her instinct part true, linking Hani's death to a conservative white parliamentarian.)

Mandela, though, saw through it. A white man killed Hani. But Mandela spoke pointedly to *black* people in his speech.

"If we riot now," Dipuo thought, "we'll be called 'warlords.' *We'll* be called the unreasonable ones." The white world, Mandela's speech made clear to her, "is watching us now. Going forward, the pressure will be more on us than it is on them."

It was a dark thought. Was this what getting power was going to feel like? Like being surveilled?

Black South Africans did not riot en masse. But more than a decade later, Dipuo still longed for a chance to reveal she was with Hani in her heart, not as forgiving as Mandela, or as perfect. So did others. In the mid-2010s, a lawyer recounted a conversation she had with a journalist who advocated urgently for black rights in ways that could be perplexing. The journalist defended a politician, for instance, who was on trial for rape on the grounds that *any* rape accusation against a black man was inherently racist.

The lawyer wondered if the journalist's obsessive advocacy was an effort to make up for hidden shame. She brought up a rumor: that the journalist's ex-husband had collaborated with the apartheid regime. The journalist begged her to believe that she hadn't known—that she was innocent. Yet the way the journalist looked at her, the lawyer wrote later, made her feel strongly that underneath this ostensible denial lay a plea for her to understand that she *had* known. To reveal herself to be tainted—and thus, paradoxically, to be free.

In 2008, the ANC removed Thabo Mbeki from the presidency, and somebody took over who spoke powerfully to these longings. Jacob Zuma was imprisoned with Mandela on Robben Island, but in the 2000s, he started to take a markedly less conciliatory and less Western-friendly tack. Unlike Mbeki, he didn't ever assert controversial views under the cover of anonymous documents.

He talked openly about how unjust it was that white people still held so much economic and moral power. And he didn't seem burdened by bitterness or by the longing to appeal to white elites. At his rallies, he danced exuberantly in leopard-skin pelts and encouraged his supporters to sing a bellicose anti-apartheid song called "Bring Me My Machine Gun."

Before he became president, Zuma was also put on trial for rape. He was acquitted, but the charges were credible. Afterward, he admitted to sleeping with the victim—and then brashly claimed that, in African tradition, women feel insulted if a man doesn't provide them with sex, and that he'd protected himself from HIV by taking a shower.

Some black elites were appalled. "He is not ashamed at all," a top journalist wrote—in horror. They felt his gestures toward African authenticity were tacky and shallow and his flouting of the conventional norms for world leaders was embarrassing. Westerners were having a field day mocking Zuma's outfits and sounding the alarm about his rhetoric. The journalist recalled sitting in on a Harvard seminar whose attendees burst into guffaws at the mere mention of Zuma's name. Yet "he is not ashamed . . . that the world is pointing at us and laughing."

But that was exactly why my friend S'thembile, who was born in the early '90s and grew up in a formerly white neighborhood, told me some of her "posh" friends secretly liked Zuma—even though he seemed to be calling for a degree of economic transformation that might threaten their own families' position. What was wrong with a black man who wasn't ashamed?

Regarding the corruption allegations that swirled around Zuma, S'thembile said her friends *"liked* it that he broke the law." How many black South Africans rose without breaking some laws? If not after apartheid ended, then beforehand?

Even if you *had* become "well off," she said, Zuma implied it was legitimate to still feel out of place because you were black.

"You have an identity of your own," she heard him saying. "You don't have to live in their world."

An entrepreneur in one of Johannesburg's townships explained it to me further. "There are people who will never benefit here if things are done 'right,'" he said. He mentioned Rosa Parks, who broke a law by refusing to give up her seat to a white passenger on her Alabama bus. "Zuma, technically—he is often wrong. But even if he got into power the wrong way, he could do right."

The run-up to Zuma's presidency coincided with what ought to have been an exuberant moment in Dipuo's own life. After Godfrey died and Matshediso started her *sangoma* training, Dipuo realized she could no longer pay the rent on the brick house she'd optimistically named Tlhomedi, "Our Home." She had to move her family back into a shack. The new shack's roof leaked worse than their old one did. During thunderstorms, Malaika got almost as wet inside as she would have on the street. She stopped inviting friends over, because having to ask them to help her bail the shack out with buckets was too embarrassing.

And then, as foreign interest in South Africa waned, Dipuo's Western-funded NGO had laid her off. Out of work, she'd begun to suffer from debilitating headaches. She had to sign up for a humiliating "feeding scheme" that had her stand in line for a single loaf of bread and two liters of sweetened milk per day.

But a few months before Zuma's inauguration, she landed a job as the personal assistant to the CEO of a giant advertising agency. Some of her friends were jealous. The CEO promised she'd contribute creatively.

It soon became clear, though, she was far less than a creative partner. The firm referred proudly to its new black hires as "previously disadvantaged," as if, by hiring them, they had transfigured them to not disadvantaged overnight.

Yet Dipuo couldn't escape the feeling the executives didn't want her there. It was frustrating that she couldn't explain this clearly to her friends. There were no formal discriminatory policies, no outright laws, that disempowered her. But her white colleagues didn't meet her eyes in the hallways. Or if they did, they looked confused or annoyed, as if they didn't understand why she had materialized.

They asked her for coffee, forgetting she wasn't a maid. And they requested she cut her dreadlocks, alleging it was a "norm" for professional women to wear their hair in sleek bobs. At a couple of early meetings, Dipuo raised her hand to suggest an idea.

She'd been the head of a People's Committee before she was seventeen. She was used to leadership. It never occurred to her she didn't have valuable contributions. But nobody called on her. "My bosses expected blacks to do administrative jobs," Dipuo told me sadly. "But they didn't think black people could be creative. They didn't think black people could be geniuses."

Three years into Zuma's presidency, inspired by his rhetoric, thousands of miners went on an unprecedent strike. Cloaked in traditional blankets, they occupied a rocky hill in a mining area called Marikana to demand a raise from their employer, the platinum giant Lonmin. They sang protest songs and waved knives and knobkerries, wooden batons given to boys as a symbol of power.

One of the protesters was a mine surveyor named Doctor. As a child in the late '80s, his ambition was to become a pro soccer player like the striker "Doc" Khumalo, after whom he nicknamed himself. Doctor always felt sure he would achieve his dream. The singular focus of the anti-apartheid struggle made it seem as though, once apartheid fell, anything would become possible.

But he couldn't get a tryout for Khumalo's team, and he kept running out of money. At one point he landed a contract working for a garbage collection company; on his fridge, where most people display family pictures, he hung a set of photographs of himself grinning with his white supervisors at a soccer game, his arms slung chummily around their shoulders. In 2008, though, his contract ended, and he went to work on the mines.

There he observed how black and white people still lived in different worlds. Low-skilled black workers who got hurt underground got smaller settlements than their injured white colleagues. His own salary stagnated and he discovered that sending his daughter to a well-reputed school instead of the local, bad one would cost him more than half his monthly wage.

By 2012, Doctor's story was typical. A third of working South Africans still got by on less than $2 a day while only half of South Africans under twenty-four could find a job at all. Black households' average income was still just a sixth of that of white ones.

Doctor loved Zuma—and trusted him. But as president, Zuma didn't behave like Doctor expected. He seemed to retreat into haughty silence—he gave fewer rallies—and a kind of stereotypically white lifestyle. Journalists investigated a mansion he constructed with government funds. A crony of Zuma's declared that its massive swimming pool was only a "fire pool" for firefighters to use in case of emergency.

That claim insulted Doctor's intelligence. But he was most disturbed by the mine strike at Marikana. Instead of championing the miners, Zuma sent his police to roll a length of barbed wire around the miners' hill. They doused the miners in tear gas. When the striking miners spilled off the hill, they got trapped in the barbed wire enclosure and the police opened fire with semiautomatics, killing three dozen. Medical examiners later showed some were shot at close range in the back of the head.

The event, dubbed the "Marikana massacre," left many in South Africa deeply unsettled. Episodes like this were supposed to happen *under* apartheid, not after. But in a particularly shocking twist, Zuma's government arrested 270 of the surviving miners and charged them with causing the murder of their fallen comrades—the exact convoluted legal reasoning the apartheid regime used to entrap anti-apartheid activists.

Doctor didn't feel sure whether the presidency—the title, the building—changed Zuma, or whether there had always been something scammy and manipulative about his claims to respect the working poor and African traditions. But somehow, he had become the worst kind of black diamond himself. When Zuma bothered to show up at Marikana to console the surviving miners, he came in a finely tailored suit and a fleet of bodyguards held umbrellas to shade him from the sun.

In truth, there had always been an unresolved tension in the ANC's fight against the world white South Africans created. Was the goal of the liberation struggle to radically dismantle this world—or just to move more freely within it? Over the course of twenty years, the tension seemed to be quietly resolving toward the latter aim. For a black South African to become a mining magnate was, in one sense, considered a manifestation of post-apartheid justice. Kuseni Dlamini, who served until 2011 as the first black CEO of Anglo American South Africa—another huge mining conglomerate—explained to me the allure of joining the top ranks of institutions from which you had so long been barred, even if your former self might have judged these institutions rotten to the core.

Returning to South Africa in the early 2000s from Oxford, he had two options: go back to the homeland where he'd been born to teach college or accept a job at Anglo American. The choice was obvious. The homeland would have felt disappointingly "familiar," he said, whereas "in South Africa, historically, Anglo American had always been a very, very big deal." For him, personally, getting to run a mine seemed to be the ultimate transfiguration, a "transcending of the dark period of the '80s"—if not, of course, for most of the mine's languishing black employees.

A great disconnect had opened between the black elite and the black poor, not only in their incomes but in their sense of self. Fifteen years after apartheid ended, many black leaders substantially occupied former white identities. The former mine-union leader whose 1980s strikes crippled the apartheid economy became a 9 percent shareholder in Lonmin, the mine where the Marikana massacre occurred, and a director of its board. The media revealed he sent emails to Lonmin's management describing the striking miners as "plainly dastardly criminal" and suggesting the police take action against them. He also took up a hobby particularly associated with white South Africans: game ranching. He was pictured in tabloids at big-game auctions wearing a colonial-style safari shirt embroidered with the name of his ranch and throwing down world-record multimillion-dollar bids for a single buffalo.

The totality of the transfiguration could be breathtaking. A few months after the Marikana strike, I attended a "Poverty and Inequality" conference cohosted by the South African government. Participants got treated to a gala dinner with tables of meats, cheeses, and glitter-covered cupcakes. On the final morning, a top ANC official, Kgalema Motlanthe, spoke.

Motlanthe also came of age organizing for the mineworkers union. After giving a short, uncontroversial talk to a crowd of professors and students, he fielded a question from me about how he interpreted the Marikana massacre. He didn't mention economic inequality. Instead, he ascribed the unrest at South Africa's mines and in its poor neighborhoods to a sort of black-magic-inspired primitive conspiracy. The idea, he claimed, would only "germinate among a handful" of power-hungry renegades. In order to persuade the other miners to abandon faith in their accustomed leaders, these mutineers would "procure the services of a *muti* person"—a witch doctor.

It was eerily reminiscent of the way apartheid-era leaders used to speak of their problematic "natives." White leaders also denied widespread unhappiness and ascribed the behaviors of the black poor to uncivilized traditions. But Motlanthe barreled on. The way to address the miners' discontent, he concluded, was "to separate them from the *muti* person and to break that spell. Then you can deal with them."

When I visited Doctor's small house, one of his friends, Abey, wandered in to watch TV. A government executive was defending the police's response at Marikana. The men clustered around Doctor's crackling TV set, then tsk-tsked in disgust. "Julius Malema will become president," Abey proclaimed.

Malema, a thirty-one-year-old politician, was Abey's next hope. He rose through the ranks of the ANC's influential young person's wing by calling attention to the way a disproportionate amount of South Africa's wealth still lay in white people's hands. Around the time of the Marikana massacre, he began to criticize Zuma for selling out. In fiery speeches at the mines, Malema blamed ANC leaders and the black diamonds for perpetuating the misery of the black poor. "They have been stealing this gold from you," he shouted.

Abey wore a Che Guevara–style beret just like Malema's atop his drawn face. Thirty-one years old, he, like Doctor, had nurtured an ambitious childhood dream—to be a sound engineer—but he had never been able to find a steady job and now "my dream is gone."

The men fell silent. "But Malema is a crook also," Doctor finally said.

When I requested an interview with him a few months after the massacre, Malema chose a five-star boutique Johannesburg hotel, explaining that the hotel was "very private, very private," and he had enemies—higher-ups in politics who were "using state institutions to try to bring me down." One of these institutions was the South African tax department, which had slapped him with a $1.8 million outstanding tax bill. (He never paid it.)

The reason, he alleged, was that his rhetoric frightened the ANC old guard. "The gap is widening and it's worrisome," Malema mused as we waited for the brioche-encrusted rack of lamb he'd ordered. "The poor will have nothing to eat but the rich." Establishment black leaders chose to cash out after the democratic transition, he said, rather than remain true to their principles. "They speak in forked tongues. The leadership is conflicted between wanting to lead the ANC and to be in business at the same time."

The problem was that, as he rose in prominence, Malema became enmeshed in "business," too. When not riling up workers in his Che beret, he wore Gucci and a $5,000 Breitling watch. He made headlines for attending a party where sushi was consumed off the bodies of scantily clad women. Much more serious allegations of corruption follow him. In late 2012, prosecutors brought money-laundering charges against him. Three years later, the charges were dropped, but Malema wasn't exonerated. A judge ruled the prosecutors just waited too long before bringing him to trial.

In Doctor's house, Abey's scowl deepened. "We wonder: Who can we believe? Who can we trust? Because the very same people we are complaining *to* turn out to be the people we are complaining *about*." This reversal, I thought, would always happen as long as the basic structure of South Africa's economy remained intact. The South African mining economy and the broader apartheid economy that was built on it were designed to produce a rigid two-class system in which a mass of poor served a small, wealthy elite. The advent of black rule somewhat diminished the correlation between class and race, but it did virtually nothing to narrow the great divide between haves and have-nots. Success in South Africa was still associated with personal enrichment and a shift of sympathy away from the poor to the fellow wealthy. The country was stuck in an eternal cycle in which the heroes of today, as they move up in society, became the oppressors of tomorrow.

South Africa has one of the highest rates of economic inequality in the world, a relic of apartheid. *During* apartheid, the unspoken presumption was that the people that system oppressed would never want to maintain anything of it. But inequality has actually increased since apartheid's end. One friend of mine, a journalist named Mukelwa, recalled interviewing the widow of an anti-apartheid activist. "We were in it to change it," the woman had said bitterly. "Now look at Blade." Blade Nzimande was a high-rolling government official who was photographed in a new-model BMW. A newspaper cartoonist caricatured him piloting it over the dead body of Karl Marx.

But when the miners started protesting at Marikana, Mukelwa said that "even someone like me"—barely upper-class—"thought, 'Oh my God, why can't these people behave? What's going to happen to the value of our currency?'" The daughter of a poor single mother, "I used to buy my groceries once a month." Now she stops after work at a fancy grocery and forks out half of her maid's daily wage for a bottle of fresh-squeezed orange juice.

"If we were honest, we would realize we are doing this all wrong," she went on. "We buy into this Western thing of obsessing over products made by companies that plan obsolescence, to keep us wanting and wanting and wanting." And yet: in that fancy grocery store, "I feel feelings I never felt growing up. I can finally think about other things besides just finding a meal. I can *live*. So, now I find that I, too, want things to stay the same."

While she was in high school, Malaika had a traumatizing encounter on the way home from a community library. She didn't want to tell the full story, but she did recount her mother's reaction to

250

it. She had mostly kept her vow never to cry again after Godfrey died, and that was the only time I ever saw her tear up.

The two women fought, but they also called each other "sisters." As soon as they got smartphones, their camera rolls filled up with selfies of them lying together in Malaika's bed, their legs entwined, beaming up at the lens.

But Dipuo went silent after the event. It seemed to Malaika that the moment she most needed Dipuo was the moment Dipuo couldn't bear to look at her—as if the fact that she'd been hurt had made her mother ashamed of her.

Dipuo told me she had resolved not to "pressure" her daughter. She would only ask about it if Malaika brought it up. That was the vision: that black children would, in effect, get to choose what pain they would allow to impact their lives. After apartheid, they would get to choose not only where they wanted to live and which kinds of jobs they would go after but the nature of reality itself. They could decide whether things like poverty or trauma had any power over them.

If Malaika didn't mention the trauma, Dipuo said, was it her right to tell her daughter it had been a trauma? Maybe Malaika decided it was not to be included in her story.

It was a hopeful theory. But it was terribly burdensome in practice. Malaika so badly wanted to be reassured she hadn't somehow brought on her own suffering. "Nine years," Malaika said to me. And she began to weep. "My mother didn't bring it up with me for nine whole years."

By herself, though, Dipuo had wept, too, for her daughter. It broke her in two to know she hadn't been able to shield Malaika from degrees of pain she had hoped black women wouldn't ever have to experience after apartheid ended. Amid all her own post-apartheid disappointments, the one hope she clung to was that what she had fought for in the '80s—at such a profound cost to herself—wouldn't be in vain for her daughter.

But Godfrey's death, her layoff from the NGO, the humiliating "feeding scheme," and—somehow worst of all—the disappointment that turned out to attend finally penetrating a wealthy company were too much. One afternoon, Malaika came home from school and Dipuo wasn't there. She didn't come home at night, either. Matshediso told her Dipuo was in a hospital somewhere, very sick, and that Malaika had to pray, because her mother had something very bad and might never recover.

Dipuo had been hospitalized for a nervous breakdown. "I don't think anyone knew how hard things were for her," Tshepiso told me. "She never wanted us to worry. She always wanted to appear strong for us."

Sowetans had a word for this kind of feminine strength: *imbokodo*. It meant "rock." Ostensibly, it was used as a compliment. But *imbokodo* also means a grinding stone, the specific kind of whetstone people in villages used to make cornmeal. *You are supposed to be unbreakable*, was the message the adjective sent.

Dipuo became so ill she couldn't read or, at times, recognize her own name. Matshediso had to take a minibus taxi to the hospital every day to help her daughter put on her underwear.

For two weeks, Malaika didn't know why Dipuo had vanished. Godfrey had left and never returned, and now her mother was gone, too. She began to have fits of rage that terrified her, slapping teachers at school and punching a classroom window, breaking the glass. Some friends whispered she must be "possessed" by an African "demon."

Malaika's teachers insisted she see a therapist. In the woman's office, she broke down and truly sobbed for the first time since Godfrey died. For Never-Never. For her mother, whose pain felt like her own but which she could neither fully understand nor heal. For her brother, Lumumba.

Five years earlier, Dipuo had a short relationship that produced a baby boy. She chose a traditional first name for the child: "Morena," meaning "Lord," like in the hymn Soweto's bus preachers sang.

> *Morena . . . onkise qhobosheaneng.*
> *Onthuse ke tshabele teng.*
> *Ha ke le qhobosheaneng le hao ha dina ho mphilela.*

> God, take me to your refuge.
> Help me to run there.
> When I get to your refuge, they won't be able to find me.

But just like Malaika chose what she wanted to call herself, she chose to call her brother "Lumumba," after Patrice Lumumba, the Democratic Republic of the Congo's first black prime minister. In 1961, Lumumba was assassinated during a coup backed by the Belgian and American governments, which believed he was a communist and wanted to demonstrate their enduring influence in Africa. Malaika especially loved a speech Lumumba gave right before he died. Black "independence has been transformed into a cage where we are regarded from the outside," he'd said. But "history will one day have its say. And it will not be the history that Brussels, Paris, Washington, or the United Nations will teach."

25

Christo

FOR A DECADE, THE DORMITORY VERSCHOOR assigned Christo thrived. Reitz became a model on campus; only two Reitz boys didn't complete their undergraduate degrees. The boys won the yearly campus singing contests and the float-building prizes. They showed such skill in inter-dorm rugby competitions that, in 2007, a professional league in Argentina invited them to play. Floating down with his boys in a jetliner over Buenos Aires's umbrella-dotted beaches, Christo told me he "finally felt we had made it." So recently the Afrikaners were pariahs, but now his boys were going overseas as models of manhood.

Back home, though, the wind was changing direction again. In the mid-2000s, UFS appointed a new president. He had an economics PhD from Harvard and did stints at the World Bank. He also felt uneasy with the campus's segregated dorms. It had never been written into any formal campus policy, yet in the years since Verschoor divided the dorms by race, segregation had become permanent. Students chose their dorms and, if they were unhappy, they could move early on in their freshman year. Out of the twenty-odd dormitories, some years there weren't any whose inhabitants weren't exclusively white or exclusively black.

The new president yearned to put his university on the global map. "I wanted to prepare the students for tackling the problems of the world," he recalled to me. "The problems of Africa! Tackling poverty, and wealth, and marginalization. I wanted to prepare them for a workplace where not only would they survive a diversity of backgrounds, they'd be enriched by it."

Would-be foreign professors and donors, however, recoiled when they visited the campus. The new president worried his friends thought he was cool with racial segregation or that he'd taken the job because he secretly liked it. The words of "certain black Johannesburg businessmen," he muttered. "They really hurt."

So in 2006, he decided he was going to aggressively desegregate the dormitories. He read books on the desegregation of American college campuses, from which he gathered it would be useful to be as firm and sweeping as possible—to create tabulae rasae in which neither "black" nor "white" culture dominated. He instructed Verschoor and Ramahlele, UFS's first black dorm father, to go to the dormitories and inform the students they wouldn't be able to practice any of their "traditions" anymore. Not the hazing, not the special outfits, not the veneration of the animal mascots. And the dorms could no longer be monoracial. They would have to admit freshmen from a mix of racial backgrounds.

These changes were implemented in February 2008. One morning a week or two later, Billyboy was disrupted again at home. This time it was by a 5 a.m. call from the university's spokesperson. "There's a video," she hissed, "that's going to destroy this university."

Ramahlele threw on his clothes and raced to the administration building. He and the university president huddled around a computer and watched a six-minute film someone had uploaded to YouTube the night before. It had been filmed by four white male UFS students, and in a few hours it had already attracted tens of thousands of views.

The film presented itself as a parody of what might happen during the campus reintegration. "Once upon a time," one of the students narrated, the Afrikaners "lived peacefully here. And then, one day, the 'less advantaged' discovered the word 'integration' in the dictionary." To the theme music from *Chariots of Fire*, the filmmakers went on to depict how they might treat their black dorm-mates. They had five janitors who worked in their dorm—four black women and a black man—pose as actors, subjecting them to rugby, dancing, and beer-drinking contests. Finally, they forced the janitors, who were old enough to be their grandparents, to get on their knees and drink a brown liquid out of a pot.

Halfway through, one of the students paused to explain the nickname he used for one of the maids. "What does *sefebe* mean?" he taunted the woman.

"A whore," she answered.

The video makers were from Reitz—Christo's dorm.

The video's release created a national uproar unlike almost any other after apartheid. South Africa's major political parties all condemned the video as an "atrocity." Radio hosts lamented they hadn't even *known* dormitories at a prominent post-apartheid campus were still segregated. Hundreds of black students occupied the UFS quad in protest, and the administration had to shut the university down for three days.

Watching the video, Ramahlele wept. Under apartheid, "I was in prison a number of times," he told me. "Yet I never felt so traumatized or so angry." He thought back to the way, during meetings to brainstorm new names for the dormitories, one white dorm father had agreed that his dorm, named for Hendrik Verwoerd, should be rechristened. But the man then said he was only willing to accept—to *accept*, as if he still had the right to dictate terms—the name "House Hennie."

"Hennie" was just the common Afrikaans nickname for Hendrik. From "House Hendrik Verwoerd" to the sly, wink-wink

"House Hennie"? Ramahlele started to laugh—until he realized the man was serious. The white administrator really thought that would be enough—enough for black people to get, enough for white people to give.

"There are white people who have been playing a game with us all along," Ramahlele thought darkly. And then a darker thought came to him. That he had been *right* as a child.

Right about the idea he, as an adult, persuaded himself was simplistic: that change would only happen in South Africa if black people got rid of white people. In the '90s, he decided this idea was primitive. Now, he wondered if his adult belief in racial reconciliation wasn't the naive hope, and his boyhood notion that there would be no freedom without driving white people away was the deeper truth.

In the meeting, he had a sudden, unbidden vision of himself setting the whole UFS campus on fire. "Let it burn!" he thought. The vision felt like a relief. And then, just as suddenly, he felt the onset of a piercing headache. At an urgent care facility, a doctor told him his blood pressure was dangerously high.

It never returned to its regular level. Ramahlele found it stunning that the destruction of an idealistic fantasy—one he'd never even dared articulate to himself out loud—could sicken him physically. But "that is the price I paid," he told me bitterly, "for hope."

I first went to Bloemfontein to visit its notorious campus. As soon as I got there, I heard chatter about a man named Christo. Administrators said that if I wanted to understand what had happened, I had to understand him. Christo's "is the one story that lies at the heart" of the UFS strife, the university president told me. People even suggested Christo had instigated the original 1990s race riots. If not for him, they said, there never might have been any problems.

At the same time, they told me it wasn't really worth trying to find him. They claimed he was cagey and never talked to reporters. When I located his law office's number and called it, I was so startled to hear him say "Hello?" that I hung up. It felt like getting through to a devil on the first try.

The janitors sued the four filmmakers with *crimen injuria,* or "injuring the dignity of another person." This crime, unique to South African jurisprudence, can theoretically refer to any kind of injury to dignity. But the charge was created to prosecute people who commit racist acts. It's also rarely leveled, since the burden of proof for explicit racist intent is high. The "Reitz Four" video case became the highest profile *crimen injuria* trial to date in South Africa.

Christo agreed to serve as the boys' lawyer. But he also retained another attorney for them. In the Bloemfontein courtroom—the city's largest, but still small and packed with spectators—Christo let that attorney talk. He sat with the accused in the dock. His close-cropped military-style haircut made him look like a fifth defendant, exposing the pink, youthful skin at the back of his neck.

The argument he made on behalf of the video makers when he first received me in his office was that he *was* a defendant, too. He'd laid photocopies of news articles across his desk: "My Ordeal at the Hands of Racists," read one headline. Another article described how one of the boys' family members had been expelled from their church. "They did a bad thing, but they suffered," Christo said.

After half an hour, though, Christo cleared the articles off his desk and pulled out the manila envelope with the pictures of his army buddies. He dumped out its full contents onto the desktop. There were dot matrix printouts, classified briefings from his time in the 32 Battalion; the overhead projector sheets on which he'd written out his military alias "Charles James Dalton"; blurry photographs of him wearing blackface; the shots of Nicolene, the girl he liked in high school; and pictures of his family farm, with the cattle and the camel thorn trees. This was the boys' story, he told me. His story.

I couldn't ever figure out, over years of conversation, whether Christo meant the Reitz boys reminded him of himself—many of them came from still-unintegrated rural areas and, like he had in 1992, encountered a radically different moral environment when they arrived at college—or whether that, by understanding who he'd been, I would understand what he'd created. Certainly, he eerily replicated the exact situation he had sought to forestall. He wanted the boys in his dorm never to feel the shame he felt when he was charged in court as a "terrorist." Now, almost twenty years later, he sat with his young men in yet another defendant's dock.

Their other attorney advised the video makers to plead guilty to the charge of injuring the janitors' dignity. But he also asked to provide the judge context to mitigate the boys' sentence. This context parsed the difference between two forms of motivation in South African law: *dolus directus*, or "direct intent," and *dolus eventualis*, which is less damning. *Dolus directus*, as Christo explained it, "is if you shoot at something, you aim at it and you hit it, and it dies. *Dolus eventualis* is if you aim at a stone, the bullet ricochets, and somebody dies."

In *dolus directus*, the motivation and the outcome are married. The intent is to hurt, and that is indeed the result. *Dolus eventualis* requires the intervention of a third entity between the injurer and the injured: a stone; time. The bullet leaves the gun, seconds pass. It knocks a rock. Or: the world the bullet enters shifts *after* the shooter aims.

Christo was arguing that the way the Reitz boys treated the janitors was not necessarily wrong in and of itself. It became wrong as history slid forward, as the world began to abandon its tolerance for asymmetrical, paternalistic relationships between white and black people. It struck me that many Afrikaners saw apartheid and their history as a sin of *dolus eventualis*, not *dolus directus*. Their exceptionalism, their culture, their mission to make a place for themselves in southern Africa hadn't inherently been wrong until it collided with a growing black population and until the standards of acceptability when it came to race relations shifted.

But when Christo's ancestor set out on a ship from Amsterdam, he already carried with him the seeds of a cultural idea that would bear strange fruit all over—in Europe, in Asia, in Oceania, in North and South America, as well as in Africa. Its wide-crowned trees are still blooming, appearing to give pleasure and shelter, but beneath the soil their roots are still sucking up water and choking everything. I thought of what my friend Cobie said when I asked him, once, what constituted the essence of Afrikaner identity. His answer was one word: "pride."

The Afrikaners "come from very good genes," he went on. "It was the adventurers and the best people out of Germany, Holland, and other European countries who came to South Africa. The Afrikaners have always felt superior, and with good reason."

Could Afrikaners change? I asked him.

"Only a little," he judged. "Otherwise, we're no longer Afrikaners."

After the video went viral, the UFS administrators closed Reitz. They sealed the dorm off like a hazardous waste site with a razor-wire-topped chain link fence. Christo was angry about that. How different, he asked me, were his boys' sentiments from what many other South Africans said around the dinner table? The Bloemfontein newspaper condemned the boys in a harsh editorial. That appeared to be an easy way for the editor to distance himself publicly from racist sentiments while probably still harboring them.

It's true that, if you spend enough time with even self-professed liberal South Africans, you'll hear them mutter about litter or broken stoplights—and that it never used to be this way. Wasn't that the same idea, Christo asked, that his boys expressed in their video? Wasn't it possible white administrators and white reporters condemned his boys precisely because they knew how much their inner monologues, at times, resembled what his boys said out loud? How much daylight was there, really, between them and their condemners?

At other times, Christo agreed Reitz ought to close. When he decided to defend the video makers, his law firm feared they'd lose other clients, and he ended up resigning. He had to start his own small firm, something he'd never wanted to do. He said he was searching for something else to which to devote himself. Should he play the trumpet? he asked me listlessly. Go back to school for a degree in political science? If he ever ran a dorm again, he said he would advise the students not to learn from their ancestors but to paper their dorm room walls with inspirational quotes by the American football legend Vince Lombardi. He reckoned those were so banal they could never be attacked.

Only one of the four video makers agreed to talk to me. Danie took an offer to work in a new "Diversity Office" the university created after the video scandal. Sitting in that office under a motivational poster with a picture of a cheetah, Danie told me his colleagues—black women—were subjecting him to subtle tutelage on the way he spoke, even how he dressed. His standard uniform growing up on a farm had been khaki shorts and a rugby jersey. They told him that outfit was basically racist. Gamely, he said he'd "learned a lot" and that he wanted to show me "who I really am." But his upper lip was twitching, as if he were under stress.

"From when we were born," he explained, "this is how it was: about 90 percent of the population was black." But even after the end of legalized segregation, he and his friends in a farming community "never had anything to do with them"—black people. "We would never connect. We didn't know their culture, actually." At weekend barbecues, his elders told him "all bad stories" about black South Africans' intentions toward white people.

He loved to play rugby and hoped to qualify for a youth national team. But by the time he tried out, the team had established racial quotas. He didn't make the cut. That felt unfair. Did he have to be personally responsible for ending racism nationwide? Why did a rugby team have to be integrated, anyway? Couldn't rugby be something Afrikaner boys particularly liked? He said he thought black people "had" soccer.

Of course, it wasn't clear if he'd have made the team anyway. But by the time he got to university, he was feeling a tremendous, free-floating anxiety. His parents were "privileged in the past to live out their traditions," he acknowledged. But now he reckoned white men "were going to be at the receiving end of a very malicious circle." When he watched Jacob Zuma and Julius Malema on TV, the men looked very angry to him.

"Am I just supposed to ride this thing until the bottom falls out?" he wondered. Other white boys on campus were saying they were going to have to "pay for what their grandfathers did." And if they didn't, then their children would. Danie touched his heart. "What happens is, you get a sort of hatred," he said.

"It was never my, nor any of our intentions, to hurt the janitors. We were just scared of the unfamiliar." Privately, he admitted he felt he treated them *better* than many self-described "progressive" white students did. One janitor "took about half my clothes" home in a black plastic bag every year. He'd felt intimate with them. "I thought we had a joking relationship," he said. "I thought they enjoyed the filming experience. It's not often they get a video made of them." The janitor whom the video makers called *sefebe*—whore—called the white students *gat*, or "asshole" in Afrikaans, Danie claimed; he thought it was an inside joke. "We cared for them." He backtracked. "From *our point of view*," he amended, "we cared for them."

Danie's efforts to rehabilitate himself meant he kept having to admit he was stupid. He kept interrupting himself, undercutting his account of his past with admissions he'd been completely blinkered. That was the only option other than to admit he'd been knowingly malevolent. "I imagined that, if [the janitors] were feeling bad, they would have told me," he said. Then he grimaced. "Which I guess was stupid."

It made me think of a white journalist I knew who remained politically progressive after apartheid. Yet a certain kind of comment on the articles he published online made him feel enraged. They weren't the rudest ones. They were comments by black South Africans alleging he was *missing something*—that there was something about his society he would *never* understand. "No matter what they want, I am not going to be a good white," the journalist told me bitterly.

"What's a 'good white'?" I asked.

"Someone who admits he's an idiot and goes around begging to be black," he said. The journalist admitted that the warm welcome he might get from AfriForum types and white right-wingers made the prospect of joining their ranks feel alluring, even if he didn't think their depiction of South Africa's reality made any sense.

Fundamentally, Danie's overall plea was he had been a fool. I saw that was what the *dolus eventualis* defense amounted to, and it was hard to sustain. Of all the flaws human beings can admit to, being a fool might be the hardest.

The one thing Danie was firm on was his love of Christo. He denied any element of Christo's leadership led him astray. *Vasbyt,*

Danie said, was especially life-changing. After he completed the obstacle course, Christo awarded him a medal for special bravery. He blushed as he remembered the moment. "Dippies," he murmured reverently, using Christo's army nickname. "We all would have gone to war for him."

PART
3

26

Dipuo

IN THE MONTHS AFTER I met her, Dipuo and I got together often. I noticed she was losing weight. Without vanity, just a marveling pleasure, she'd twirl in my full-length mirror, adjusting the long scarves she wore and touching her slender hips. She enjoyed looking at her body because she'd been working on it.

When Dipuo got out of the psychiatric ward, she decided to embark on a concentrated drive to better herself. "I remember telling Malaika, 'You know, I made so many mistakes,'" she told me. "I said, 'I love you. I'm sorry. I have issues. It affected who I was as a mother.'"

While she lay in the hospital, the ad agency had terminated her. This was illegal, and Dipuo wanted to fight them in court. But the corporation threatened her with costly counter-actions until she gave up her case. Not long after, Malaika was diagnosed with a serious heart murmur.

"For three years, Malaika was on expensive medication," Dipuo told me. "I was faced with the choice to save my daughter's life or preserve mine." She had trouble finding a job thanks to her poor credit rating. "I lost everything. I lost any social life I had. All I have," she joked grimly, "is the money for my coffin."

But then she brightened. Healthwise, "I won a victory, because Malaika is cured." She looked forward to Malaika getting married. "Let's say Malaika and Chiratidzo"—Malaika's college boyfriend—"will be married. When they are having their first child, Malaika will come back home to my house."

That was the custom where Matshediso, her mother, grew up. After giving birth, young mothers returned to their mothers' homes—or their mothers came to them—for a few months to apprentice in parenthood. Dipuo hated living with her mother after Malaika was born. But she was determined to do this duty well for her daughter. "I must help her become a good mother," she said.

To do that, though, she felt she had to find some inner peace. Since she was young, she'd always been searching for a father. First in Oliver Tambo, that disembodied voice over the radio; then in Mandela, and then in Chris Hani. Hani was dead now. So many of her other heroes had disappointed her. Perhaps looking for help outside was the wrong way.

She'd long disliked the idea of psychotherapy. Could the fecund, deep, and layered understories of our lives really be demystified by sitting for an hour a week with somebody you paid to listen to you in a capitalist transaction? But after she got out of the hospital, she saw how therapy helped Malaika, so she went.

The only one she could afford was a student in training and a white man. He'd glance at his clipboard after she'd describe stoning a young woman to death, look up, and murmur blandly, "So how did that make you feel?" as if such a stark experience of trauma and horror was on par with the pain a white woman might have experienced as a teen after her sister got the bigger ice cream cone.

"Maybe I had my own prejudices," she mused. "Truth be told, I hadn't gone to white doctors. I felt it was my duty to give black people a chance. Whatever white people can do, black people can do." But the therapist also didn't give her much feedback. "People like him were part of our problems," she found herself thinking in the sessions. "And now I have to sit and wait here for him to give me my solution?"

But she didn't give up. Of all the adults I met in South Africa, Dipuo was the one who became most straightforwardly dedicated, after apartheid, to doing inner work to heal the wounds her country's past wrought on her.

White people tended to shy away from discussing the wounds apartheid inflicted on them. To talk about them seemed to constitute an admission of perversity or weakness—you're saying *you* were traumatized by a system designed to benefit you?—or, conversely, threatened to reveal a truly staggering, frightening well of pain and shame. I went to two white therapists after armed men mugged me at a Johannesburg intersection. For a few weeks afterward, I found myself nervous in the presence of groups of young black men on the street. My neighborhood had its fair share of white criminals, and I worried my reaction was irrational and racially biased.

And I assumed in South Africa—with its centuries of twisted race relations—white people went to therapists all the time for help wrestling with racially biased impulses. Apparently they didn't. The therapists said they knew of no psychologist specializing in working through racism—and seemed very alarmed that I felt any concern about it. "You shouldn't feel bad," one kept saying urgently. "Yours is a *normal* human reaction." My protestations that I didn't feel ashamed of my feelings, but I really wanted help resolving them, fell on deaf ears. And I realized many white South Africans have *so much* guilt about racism that tamping down shame in the moment it appears—not dealing with the source of it—was the therapeutic priority.

Older white South Africans I met sometimes told me they

were unable to remember their childhoods. They'd say they had no memories from before the age of ten or twelve, and then add, "Isn't that true of everybody?" I rarely had the heart to tell them most people have memories from much earlier, because I thought they might subconsciously have suppressed their memories as a form of self-protection.

For many of them, any childhood memory is tainted. They know incontrovertibly, now, that the freedom they had to ride around their sparsely populated, pretty neighborhoods on bicycles was a function of inhumane laws that barred black people from entering these neighborhoods. They know any idyllic beach vacation they took with their families was a thrill their government blocked their black countrymen from enjoying at the point of a gun. In the mid-2000s, a white South African band released a song about this kind of guilt called "Heaven in the Countryside." The music video spliced home-video-style images of white kids playing in the surf with footage of white soldiers goose-stepping through black townships. It made visual the recognition that every single ordinary pleasure of white South African life is now associated with a price tag of repression and violence. The Afrikaner poet Danie Marais has written about the memory of his first kiss—and how troubled he feels when he remembers it happened under apartheid. "It seems unlikely, almost perverse, that one's own personal experiences of beauty and innocence could have happened in such a time and place."

It surprised me, then, how dedicated Dipuo became to healing *her* apartheid trauma, because it seemed like she might have the most reason to blame her pain on others and wait on them for reparation. But she was intensely proactive. She studied Zen Buddhism and meditation. She saved money to pay for an arduous, multiweek self-improvement course that encouraged participants to recalibrate their lives according to a "vision that works to transform personal effectiveness to generate a lasting sense of happiness, connection, and fulfillment."

Eventually she found something that stuck: organic eating. By the time we met, Dipuo no longer consumed dairy products, meat, white bread, or processed foods. Once a week, she trekked far from Soweto to source mangoes, avocados, and coconuts—her staples—from a Mozambican vendor who himself sourced the fruit from small farmers he trusted not to use pesticides. To drink, she collected rainwater in a tank.

"I wanted to go through transformation," she explained. "Spiritual growth, you know? Trying to forgive people and to forgive myself. I thought I would clean myself. This is how our ancestors did it." South Africans have some of the highest obesity rates in Africa, she noted, and "this thing that was not ever originally ours—fast food and refined sugar—is killing people in Soweto."

Malaika found Dipuo's embrace of organic eating irritating. When the three of us stopped to eat at restaurants, Dipuo would order gluten-free dishes and mineral water. "I cannot handle the fluoride in tap water," she would say plaintively, and out would come the harsh jigger of Malaika's laugh.

"You are a snob."

Organic eating seemed like another white tendency—something black people knew about forever, but which white people claimed they discovered and then converted into a vehicle for self-enrichment. She unabashedly preferred Chicken Licken, a fast-food chain.

But Dipuo was dedicated. One afternoon after she and Malaika spoke to me in my cottage, she slipped out while I was washing the coffee cups. She found my landlord, Kathy, a landscape designer, and engaged her in a conversation about vegetable cultivation. Then she requested from Kathy a gift of a small edible plant, something she could tend.

It represented the hope she had time to figure out how to make life flourish and bear fruit—and her determination to model, including for her neighbors in Soweto, how to grow your sustenance yourself. It symbolized her conviction she could finalize her grief and move on.

Kathy gave her a horseradish seedling in a terra-cotta pot. Dipuo brought it back to my cottage to show it to me and Malaika. Horseradish, Kathy said, was a "purifying herb" that "forces tears," which is what Dipuo wanted. Kathy told her to talk to the plant to encourage it to grow.

When Dipuo related that, Malaika burst out laughing again. But Dipuo was taking the advice seriously. In front of us, she spoke softly to the plant and touched one of its tender leaves.

"What did Kathy tell you to say?" I asked.

Dipuo tilted her face down toward the seedling and smiled. "You're beautiful," she murmured. "You've been given a good inheritance. You've been planted and seeded well. But now it is up to me to tend to you, beautiful. Believe in me. Believe in me."

27

Malaika

AFTER SHE GRADUATED HIGH SCHOOL, Malaika set off for the still white-dominated university she'd dreamed of attending, one of the best-rated ones in the country. But she only lasted a couple of weeks. Her first day on the quad, she noticed how black students hurried with their books clutched to their chests and their faces cast down, as if they felt surprised and sorry they existed.

She scurried that way her first few months at Melpark Primary. But she had been a child. It awed Malaika to see black adults acting so fearful. At a get-to-know-you party, a white student designated as a "welcomer" insisted on speaking to her in Afrikaans. When Malaika forcefully requested that the girl speak English, a group of older black students begged her not to make a scene. They whispered that it was still the Afrikaners' campus. All they had to do was survive so they could get diplomas. *Our time will come*, they said. *But later.*

Unwilling to stay, Malaika returned to Soweto and then picked up work traveling the country with a book fair. In Cape Town, she met a different kind of black student. At a book launch, this man made a scene, shouting that the organizers were prejudiced for not allowing a waiter to eat the fancy hors d'oeuvres. Flustered, the organizers not only gave the waiter a plate of food but waived the man's own entrance fee.

Malaika was impressed. In some ways, Chumani Maxwele grew up in even more straitened circumstances. The son of a miner and a little older than her, he'd been raised in a dusty village. In 1994, when he was barely ten, he'd been startled in the middle of a soccer game with his friends by an unfamiliar noise coming from above—something between a rumble and a drone.

He let the ball dribble away and tilted his head up to the sky. Chumani had heard rumors that the ANC was flying planes around the country: the planes were dropping campaign leaflets decorated in the ANC's black, yellow, and gold. Legend in his village had it that planes, a rare sighting, were flown by influential people, even people to be feared.

Up until then, power was something he only ever glimpsed on TV. In his village nurse's house, he watched tanks manned by white men in battle gear rolling into crowds of black protesters. But now black people had their own planes. That implied a promise: the promise of transformation, of the freedom to change your circumstances and be something different from what history had prescribed for your kind.

Several years later, Chumani moved to a township outside Cape Town. But it turned out to be a bitter place. Almost half the residents were unemployed. "In a one-kilometer stretch of road, you'd pass a thousand people," Chumani told me when I met him. "For me, that was shocking."

He discovered people loitered on the streets because there was hardly room to stand up in their claustrophobic shacks. Families defecated in plastic boxes collected once a week by the municipality. In the winter, a bluster of whipping wind and sideways-slanting rain, the township flooded, and sometimes the shacks dissolved wholesale, their tarp roofs and sides disintegrating like sandcastles in a heavy wave.

In 2006 Chumani landed a job at an upscale supermarket. On their first day, he and the other salesmen—all black people—were given uniforms: a pressed shirt, a tie, and patent leather shoes. His colleagues seemed proud. They were businesspeople now, real office worker types!

But Chumani could see he was not in an office. He just looked the part. The vast majority of the supermarket's customers were white. He was on his feet attending to the needs of white people, not too different from what his father had done.

He had heard the ANC's planes, he realized, but he had never flown on one, literally and figuratively. Freedom was an illusion. A promise heard but not experienced.

And so, one morning in early 2015, Chumani traveled to the township, picked up one of the buckets of feces on the curbside, and brought it back to the University of Cape Town (UCT), a formerly white college, where he'd just enrolled for a degree. There, he took the bucket to a bronze statue of the colonial administrator Cecil John Rhodes, which held pride of place on campus downhill from the convocation hall. "Where are *our* heroes and ancestors?" he shouted to a gathering, curious crowd.

Then he opened the bucket and hurled its contents into Rhodes's face.

Chumani's "poo protest," as it came to be known, inspired other black students. Mase Ramaru, a UCT senior, recalled to me how she'd taken a class with a rare black lecturer and overheard white students complain in whispers about his "black accent." They claimed it made him hard to understand. "It becomes less about his ability and more about the color of his skin, and that he's not articulating himself the way people want him to articulate himself," she said.

Thousands of students gathered by the Rhodes statue to

demand its removal. For five weeks, they tagged it with graffiti and covered it with garbage bags. Saying it represented how the university still celebrated white culture—its curriculum was Eurocentric, its governing council was mostly white, and its financial support for black students was weak—they occupied the administration buildings, holding lectures on apartheid history and beating drums.

The movement spread to other campuses, including Malaika's. A few years after leaving the Afrikaner-dominated university, Malaika started at another formerly white college on South Africa's southern coast. She became passionately involved in the protests. Students boycotted their classes, like black youth did in the 1976 Soweto student uprising. The media aired images strangely reminiscent of apartheid: a young black man being arrested and violently handcuffed; a young black woman, her head wrapped in a colorful cloth, pacing in the enormous crowd, raising her fist and yelling a freedom cry: *"Amandla! Awethu!"* ("Power! To us!")

One surprising thing was that many of the protesters hailed from upwardly mobile black families. The young man shown on TV getting arrested was Kgotsi Chikane—the son of Mbeki's former chief of staff. On the face of it, Kgotsi could have been a poster child for post-apartheid promise. His family moved out of Soweto to the formerly white suburbs and he attended a private high school that cost $4,800 a year—30 percent more than the average black South African household's whole yearly income.

At university, though, Kgotsi had begun to feel aware of his race. In his dormitory's cafeteria, the students sorted themselves into white tables and black tables. His white friends celebrated the fact that he was their "black friend," saying he "grounded" them.

Kgotsi's first reaction to Chumani's poo protest was ambivalent. He hadn't grown up in a place where people crapped in buckets. But then he became embroiled in a Twitter battle with a white student. The student claimed the protest "was actually disrespectful to the black poor, because a black janitor would have to clean up the poo," Kgotsi remembered. "I said, 'Why are you suddenly so exercised about the plight of the black poor, only now, when *your* symbol is attacked?'" He realized there was still an "us"—black—and a "them"—white, and that black people like himself, however empowered they might appear, still had to endure being tutored by white people on what constituted good behavior.

Kgotsi found himself leading a demonstration. Beforehand, he chained his wrists together, his hands pressed into a gesture of supplication intentionally reminiscent of photographs of African American slaves. Paradoxically, adopting this pose of entrapment felt like the *real* liberation. "People started taking pictures," he recalled. "And then I realized . . . black students weren't taking pictures. The white students were taking pictures," as white people had stared at the entrapped black body for centuries.

White students joined the marches. UCT's head, a white professor, released a statement calling for the Rhodes statue's removal. But many older leaders of color dismissed them. UCT's few black administrators, including an older Black Consciousness movement leader, refused to lend their public support; one leading black education professor told me he felt the protests were "crude."

The apparent unwillingness of black leaders to support the students' awakening baffled Kgotsi—and amplified his anger. In mid-April 2015, some fifty students broke into a UCT council meeting. They climbed through a window and surrounded the conference table, singing struggle songs. The white members of the council just sat there. But the council's head, a black anti-apartheid activist who'd been imprisoned with Mandela on Robben Island, stood up and grandly gestured for the students to leave.

They climbed up onto the table and crawled toward him.

"Who made you the policeman of black rage? A black man?" one student spat, his eyes filling with tears. "You are disgusting! Don't you have your own children?"

Mase Ramaru, the UCT senior, told me she began her "own education" in black thinkers like Steve Biko. She had not learned them in public school. "I studied the Cold War for six years. I studied the American Revolution in detail. But the specifically South African history began with the democratic era."

The omissions had mystified her. Was there something somebody hadn't wanted her to know?

Malaika also realized that, growing up, her education seemed almost intentionally whitewashed. "There is a history of Africa we did not learn about," she told me. "A history not of diseased people or suffering people. We didn't learn about African civilizations. We didn't know about Lumumba or Toivo ya Toivo," the Namibian freedom fighter. "We didn't know names like that!"

It turned out these lacunae in black students' educations were intentional. The state school curriculum black students described as infuriatingly "blank" regarding South African history was designed that way deliberately. In the mid-'90s, the government's curriculum redesign committees eliminated history as a standalone subject, folding it into "human and social sciences." "Everybody wanted to turn their faces away from the past," Rob Siebörger, an education professor who participated in the curriculum redesign, told me. Many major episodes in South African history just weren't addressed.

Forgetting was a part of the deal the ANC made when it took power from white people, Xolela Mangcu, a sociologist, told me. "The ANC denied issues of identity," generally stressing the forging of a new "rainbow nation" over a narrative of black liberation. One theory went the ANC could not afford to scare white people. But Mangcu thought there was also a powerful emotional component to the denial. What had black people fought for over so many years if not their children's release from a suffering black identity?

When I flew to Cape Town to visit UCT, the cab driver who picked me up, a black man from a nearby township, spontaneously told me a potent story. His son was fourteen, he said; he was fifty. Recently, his son had come to him to ask him what he, the father, experienced under apartheid. The question made the older man feel angry. "I don't want you to know about the past," he had informed his son. "You are free of all that!"

"We thought our kids should be grateful and shut up," Dipuo told me. Dipuo let Malaika read her historical pamphlets about the liberation struggle. But she also sought to conceal from her big aspects of her own youth and its pain. At the end of our visit to Gadifele's house, I asked Malaika if she'd known the place where she'd often played with Gadifele's children had been a landmark in Soweto's anti-apartheid movement.

"No," Malaika said quietly. "I never knew the extent to which my mother and Gadifele contributed to the struggle."

"You knew my brother Kgadi was in exile," Gadifele interrupted.

"No, I didn't," Malaika countered.

Gadifele paused. It had been important for her to believe Malaika was *connected* to black history—but also, paradoxically, to imagine Malaika could be unaware of it. Gadifele's brother Direlo's death could be redeemed so long as what black people struggled for had become real for Malaika. "Other kids," Gadifele said, turning to me and smiling proudly. "They drink alcohol. They take drugs. But Malaika has a beautiful life. This is what we fought for."

Malaika said nothing.

Mangcu, the sociologist, told me he, too, felt the instinct to shield young people from history. He supported the student protests. But he also had a young daughter who attended a "posh," predominantly white school—the dream of so many black parents. "All her friends are white children. I try to avoid a conversation about black history with her. I'm afraid of how she'll process it. How she'll relate to her friends. So I haven't had the courage to do it."

Mangcu, though, reckoned the historylessness black parents believed would be a blessing for their offspring was backfiring. Students like Chumani, Kgotsi, and Malaika had little context for the persistence of race in their daily experience. Initially, they would interpret these experiences personally. Why is my family poor? Why did somebody ask me to be her "black friend"?

When they discovered black history and identity, the lateness of the discovery made them angry. "We think we're trying to protect our kids," Mangcu said. "But our children are starting to deal with what we haven't dealt with."

He gave me an example from his own family. "My nephew went to all these posh schools. He started to see, over time, how differently his white friends were treated. He became very, very angry. This happens a lot. Sometimes people even drop out of society."

At twenty-nine, his nephew committed suicide. Mangcu couldn't help blaming a society that hadn't given him a sense of who he was.

After Chumani's "poo protest," the UCT administrators voted to remove the statue of Rhodes, the colonial leader. They trussed it up in rope and hoisted it away by crane, leaving a bare plinth behind. The night before, thousands of students gathered to sing struggle songs and snap pictures of the crane on their smartphones.

When the statue finally rose off of its base, a sustained cry went up from the crowd. "It was a joy, because something you envisaged happening did happen," Chumani told me.

Counter to the administration's expectations, though, the plinth continued to be a touchstone. Months later, when I visited, black students were still massing around it. They held up their fists in the gesture the black American athletes Tommie Smith and John Carlos made at the 1968 Olympics. *Nithi sixole kanjani amabhulu*, they sang, *abulala uChris Hani?*

I didn't fully catch the words, so I asked a student, a boy in Converse sneakers, what they were. "They mean, 'How can we forgive those Afrikaners who killed Chris Hani?'" He broke into a part-sheepish, part-proud smile, as if to acknowledge the incompatibility of the lyrics with the experience of reconciliation his generation was supposed to be having.

Malaika reckoned the student protests tapped into an "incredible amount of nostalgia" for a particular kind of black dignity and resilience forged under oppression. For centuries, as in many other parts of the world, white people in South Africa denied black people a positive history. They were accorded no cultural achievements remotely commensurate with those of the West; they were considered primitive beings in need of tutelage. It took enormous courage to remain human against that attempt at erasure, and that courage—the courage of resistance—became a foundation of the black South African character.

The struggle songs the students sang didn't merely capture the longings of a particular moment in time. They had formed the basis for an entire culture. Like spirituals sung by black slaves in the American South, many of the songs pair tormented lyrics with a mysterious harmonic serenity, capturing the capacity of black South Africans to retain some normality and honor in the face of brutality. This itself was a massive achievement, perhaps even as great as liberation. And it established a powerful identity that could not, it turned out, so happily be abandoned for a tabula rasa.

As black people gained some power in a society such as South Africa's, what would happen to this identity of resistance? Implicit in the criticism made by some elders is that it remained a trap, a negative, aggressive attitude that had to be outgrown. "The master's tools"—bellicosity, race consciousness—"can't take down the master's house," the top education professor told me. He worried the reemergence of an older black identity had dangerous practical implications for a multiracial society.

But Malaika told me she felt a fuller public conversation about the past had to happen—both for South Africa to face the unfinished business of rooting out racism and to loosen the psychological hold of the past on its children. "When we go on the street, we [young people still] sing songs from apartheid," she reflected. "Our language in protest is still reminiscent of apartheid language. If we weren't still learning about our identity and history, wouldn't we have composed new songs?"

On her campus, Malaika found herself lashing out at white students as well as the black students who chose them as allies. At a meeting, a fellow black activist proposed that sympathetic white people could serve as black students' "human shields" at the protests. The underlying assumption was black police officers still felt more hesitant to shoot white children than black ones.

The embittering thing, Malaika told me, was that she "was surely right." Posing white students in front of black ones as human shields *would* be tactically effective. But hearing it said out loud felt so offensive Malaika spat curses at her. "I got so angry," she told me, that "I was willing to be expelled. White student activists protest with us and tell us that their struggle is our struggle. They'll even claim to disown their families. But they can always go back."

She realized, with sadness, that she had always paid more attention to the generosity directed toward her by white people. It stood out because it was unexpected. But when she thought about it, a truer accounting suggested black people mostly facilitated her life journey. People like her friends Daniel, Diana, and Kabelo, who pushed her to rally through her mother's illness to finish high school. A black mentor who paid her first-year college fees. Another black friend who helped her settle a major debt.

And then there was Mike Maile.

Malaika met Mike early in her time at university. Mike and his brother were anti-apartheid activists in a township in the '80s; after 1994, both entered politics. Mike grew wealthy and moved to a formerly white suburb.

He saw her essays and sent her a Facebook message. He liked her radical way of thinking, he said. Then he invited her to his house. "Gosh," Malaika remembered. "It's very beautiful. It has a cigar cabinet and a bar. It's got a beautiful pool. It's got security guards and cameras everywhere. . . . It's the biggest house on the street."

Mike had his own children, but he began to treat Malaika as one of them. He gave her money and invited her to eat dinner with his family. "When you've never had a father and this man comes, it's overwhelming," she said. She began to call Mike her "father" in public.

She *had* a father. But not the kind of father she'd learned, at Melpark Primary, you were supposed to have. Not the kind of father who helps you with your homework and challenges you to be a better version of yourself. Sometimes, Mike would ask Malaika to stand in his cigar room and deliver his "big politician friends," as she called them, lectures on philosophy and politics. "He'd call them up and say, 'Come over and listen to my clever child.'"

Who the fuck is this girl? Mike's friends would ask him irritably after the lectures. Some of Malaika's speeches exhorted them to hew much closer to early Black Consciousness thinkers' revolutionary, pro-poor stances. *Who the hell is she to judge us?*

But Mike would scold them back. "My daughter has an independent mind. I'm not trying to raise a stooge here. This is an intelligent child."

Dipuo was with us when Malaika recounted this story, and she laughed in appreciation. "He just loved the idea of you cutting his big-shot friends down to size!" There was something delightful for Dipuo, too, in how eager Mike—a bona fide black diamond, someone who might roll up his car windows in distaste if he saw her walking in his neighborhood—was for the company of *her* daughter.

"We had a falling out once," Malaika remembered. "It was over one of my men." Mike thought one of her boyfriends wasn't good enough for her. Intent on expressing her own preferences, she stormed out of his house. "Then he sent me money. It made me very angry. I felt like he was buying me. For him, money is a solution to many things. Almost as if it resolves everything."

"He does it to assert his power," Dipuo reflected. "He thinks, 'I can give a person money and they'll shut up.'"

One New Year's Eve, Mike told his family—including Malaika, who was visiting—"Nobody leaves this house." They'd be having a family celebration, he said. Then he went out to buy party supplies.

Irritated by Mike's big-man swagger, Malaika called a taxicab to take her somewhere else. When Mike reached her on her cell phone, "He was like, '*What? What?*' I'd never heard him so angry. 'You *defied* me!' Then he hung up."

After an hour, though, her phone pinged with a notification. Money was streaming into her bank account. "Even if you're not going to listen to me," Mike texted her, "at least I can know you're not in need."

He helped pay for her heart medication and for her college tuition. If Malaika ever joked to Mike she might have to prostitute herself to achieve her dreams, *ping*: a bank deposit alert would show up on her phone. "If I said I wanted to open a restaurant, he would have bought me a restaurant," she told me.

For however much Malaika needed Mike, he needed her, too—maybe more so. Malaika surmised that supporting her might be a form of unadvertised penance for his own post-apartheid shortcuts. For it was alleged Mike grew wealthy not only while he was in government, but because of his government connections. He headed a government IT department that awarded contracts to a firm linked to one of his own investment companies. (After investigators discovered the department paid millions of dollars to employees who didn't exist, Mike resigned.)

I asked Malaika if Mike's business deals bothered her. "We all," including his own kids, "knew he profited from corruption," Malaika said. "It was obvious. He grew up poor. Very poor. Now his cigars come straight from Cuba. They bring his wines up into the house in cases."

But, she went on defensively, "he employs disabled people. He can be so generous. One day, he just found a database of disabled people with qualifications online. He bused them into his office and told them, 'This is *your* office now.' By the time I met him, he'd already made a lot of his money. And I did talk to him. I'd say, 'You are corrupt.' But I wouldn't say it made me have sleepless nights. No," she concluded, firmly. "He is a great dad."

After she transferred to Melpark Primary, Malaika had started to notice people in Soweto respected her more—in certain ways. But they also started to say she had white tendencies. "There's a lot about you that's very white now," they would suggest, with smirks. "Like your taste in music." Thanks to her exploration of the CD selection at Bounty Hunters, she fell in love with Elton John, whose music Sowetans considered a bafflingly alien taste.

When we drove around Soweto, we visited a couple of her old friends. "I was seeing those people for the first time in many years," she told me later. "I look at the people I grew up with, that I played with, and I don't—-I don't relate to them anymore." Her voice went halting, suddenly full of grief. "And because we don't relate to each other, our conversations tend to be stuck in the past. How we used to do things. We have very little to talk about in the present or about the future. They don't ask me questions like, 'What is your collegiate research about?' Some of them didn't even finish high school."

She doesn't ask them about their lives, either. "I feel uncomfortable talking to them about their conditions. I don't even want to ask people, 'What are you doing now?'"

She mentioned a friend we visited who had a baby. The woman received us in a shack where a TV was playing a South African soap opera about the lives of the newly rich. A black lawyer was arguing with a finely dressed executive about the traditional expectation, in black communities, that people should share their wealth with their families. "I went to law school!" the lawyer was shouting. Now his extended relatives were shaking him down for cash. To make it in the world—the white world—you had to leave those old traditions behind, he declared, or even abandon people you used to love. "With all the degrees I've acquired," he griped, "I'm not going to let anybody else get rich off *my* sweat."

Malaika had barked with contemptuous laughter. Talk about white tendencies! Her friend, though, hadn't laughed. She *longed* for that kind of life. Malaika could laugh. She could ostentatiously reject white values precisely because she had the option to acquire them.

At Melpark Primary, Malaika once criticized Tshepiso for lying to their schoolmates. Tshepiso had started telling people Dipuo was *her* mother, too, and not her sister. She felt embarrassed by how poor her own mother—Malaika's grandmother—looked and that she still worked in "the kitchens."

Malaika tried to school Tshepiso on the importance, for black people, of not feeling ashamed of your circumstances. Tshepiso spat back a retort Malaika never forgot. "For you, it's easy," she said. "You'll have alternatives. You know you are not going to stay this way. Some of us don't have that kind of luxury. I may remain in this place"—Soweto—"forever."

After being teased for her white tendencies, it felt good to visit Soweto in the company of a phenomenally successful black man like Mike Maile. In the abstract, South Africans might complain about the black diamonds. But in the flesh, they provoked a more uncomplicated awe. Mike owned a white BMW with a fawn-colored leather interior. "When he fetched me with it in the township, everybody was like *'What the fuck!?'* and wanting to take pictures of it."

When we spoke about Mike, Malaika's college graduation was approaching. "Mike asked me, 'What clothes do you need? What hair do you want?' He wants to buy flight tickets for my mother and my grandmother so they can see the first person in their family graduate." He also sponsored driving lessons so Malaika could treat Dipuo to the ultimate South African experience of status and freedom—driving your own automobile, instead of taking the minibus taxis. With Mike's support, "I'm getting my first car," Malaika told me. When she told Dipuo, her mother got "so emotional she even cried. 'Now you'll have something that's yours and yours alone,' she said."

The conversation tapered off and we sat in silence for a minute. "Mike Maile," Malaika murmured dreamily. "The first time I went on 'vacation,' it was with him."

Mike rented a house on the beach. He paid for Malaika's little brother to come, too. Malaika realized Lumumba would never have to struggle with the knowledge—when his white friends bragged about their vacations—that he had never left Johannesburg. Every morning she would get up, walk out the door onto the sand, and feel that blanket of blue water climbing very cold over her feet.

28

Christo

IN THE BLOEMFONTEIN COURTROOM, the Reitz boys' arguments were delivered by an interpreter—an elderly black man who accessorized his khaki pants and collared shirt with a neon-yellow-and-blue-plaid blazer. In the hall, the interpreter told me his name was Ernest Motsi. The following week, he said proudly, he would be "with the Bloemfontein court for twenty-two years."

He told me it was a point of "pride" to translate Afrikaner plaintiffs' and defendants' words into English. He tried to imbue them with "dignity"—to reveal, in what would otherwise be bland legalistic proceedings, the underlying human emotion and heart-felt drama. When somebody's argument purported to reveal a secret, he'd drop his voice to a dramatic whisper. When it detailed an accusation, he'd snarl.

It was remarkable to watch Motsi, a black man, inhabit the white boys' personae and afford their feelings a kind of dignity. As the trial got under way, the judge asked one boy if he understood the charges against him. Staring down, the boy muttered something in Afrikaans. "Yes!" Motsi shouted with determination. "I understand, and I am guilty as charged!" Motsi nearly brought himself to tears as he translated the boys' mitigating evidence—a story of post-apartheid discomfort and shame. "The university told Reitz it had to integrate," Motsi translated. "These students had no say in the new identity being constructed." He kept a straight face as he described the students' grief over several imperiled traditions: "Dancing in our student bar. Boat races with beer."

It was a will on the part of black people to afford white people dignity I saw so often. Many black South Africans still have very little power. But one power they do have is that of understanding. It could form a paradox in South African life, because this perceptiveness often showed up as an excessive solicitousness of white people—even an attitude of submission.

But I began to feel white South Africans envied black people's fuller knowledge of the universe they shared. Once, I took an Uber to a majority-white neighborhood in Johannesburg to buy a bookshelf from someone who'd advertised it online. My driver was a young black man named Themba, and he was slow and deliberate. At one point, a white teen in a pickup truck began to tailgate us aggressively. As Themba rolled up to a stop sign, the white driver squealed past, nearly clipping Themba's mirror, and screamed "Fuck you!"

I was livid. Themba and I had been talking about his upbringing on a white-owned farm, which was full of hardships—fuller, I presumed, than that of any white young man who could afford a new-model pickup truck. But Themba wasn't angry. He just looked thoughtful.

"It's because of his parents," he said. "That man's parents grew up in a country in which whites were special. They can't adjust. And they pass that message down to their children. So, I can't blame that guy. It's because of how he was raised. We love our parents, no? We love our parents. How could he go against what his parents taught him?"

When I visited Gadifele's house, I told her and Dipuo that I'd gotten to know a white man who patrolled Katlehong around the same time Gadifele's brother Direlo died there. Christo, I said, was the kind of soldier who barged into their houses at night and demanded they rat out their parents and siblings. I told them how disoriented Christo became after 1994, even though his murder charge got dropped and he was given a material chance to start over.

I thought they'd mock him. Instead, they fell quiet for a minute.

"I mean, this country is beautiful," Dipuo finally said. "Yes, the whites wanted to be spiteful, and to make sure they damaged things so the ANC inherited a country that had fallen apart. But to just give up a country they believed they had made beautiful? To give up their power? To give up such beauty? To give up everything they had worked for? I don't think it would have been easy. Some of us are still not very warm toward white people," she said frankly. "That is black people's truth. It's nothing personal. But I'm trying to imagine things more, now, from a humane point of view—I'm a human being as well. I am warming up to the idea that it must not have been easy for them."

"They were in concentration camps," Gadifele cut in, referring to the Afrikaners' predicament after the Anglo-Boer War. "They replicated them in the townships. They replicated their own pain. But first, they were in concentration camps, watched by policemen and not given food. So, I sympathize with them. Because they, too, have gone through their own pain. And young guys in the military—nineteen, twenty. The things they were made to do in the early '90s were ruthless."

"I'm imagining your friend had to go through counseling," Dipuo said. "Having been forced to witness all that killing and to kill."

Gadifele said, "Your friend must be a torn-up man."

"A twenty-one-year-old," Dipuo said, "is really just a child."

It was sad how little comfort white South Africans permitted themselves to take from black people's post-apartheid empathy. All the time, they told me it wasn't worth applying for small business rescue funds from the new black-led government or asking for help from black policemen or even their black neighbors. They insisted black people had no interest in white people.

The irony was that black South Africans had far more interest in white lives, even in white people's suffering, than vice versa. But something extremely powerful stood between white people and the hope that black people could comprehend them, and that thing was pride.

I don't mean "pride" in the sense of the clichéd term "white pride." I mean that there are few forms of unqualified pride—the conviction that you are a good person, one who's positively contributed to society—available, now, to white South Africans. One of its few remaining available forms is appearing to survive a huge difference between who you believe yourself to be and who you're understood to be by the world. It depends, in other words, on *that gulf remaining wide*. It relies on feeling a sense of victimhood and on insisting some part of you can't be shown—and, thus, on hiding yourself.

Over the course of our years of conversations, after Christo told me about so much of his past, at times I felt his attitude toward me shift. Ultimately, he told me he was willing for his full story to be written. But at times, he'd stop returning phone calls or get skittish about what I would put into print. "I've realized," he'd worry, "that you shouldn't print" this or that detail. He'd say that if I told his whole story, prosecutors in the new government would take him to court and throw him in jail.

I talked to a few high-level prosecutors, and they agreed this would almost certainly never happen. New evidence would have to be uncovered. And to reconsider all the thousands of closed or unresolved cases from the chaotic early '90s would open an insane

Pandora's box. Sometimes I thought what Christo was really saying was that he wanted me to *write* that I couldn't write his story.
I got the sense he was torn between a desire to air everything and
a knowledge that a vital part of his identity depended on him *not*
being able to tell the truth about what he had felt or done. Depended on it being too dangerous.

Despite everything, despite all their disadvantages, black people had one noticeable freedom in South Africa white people did
not have: the freedom from feeling they had to hide. White people almost never walked on the street. This aversion to walking
wasn't necessarily attached to real data that walking was dangerous. Deep down, I think even the most ostentatiously fearful ones
knew that. Not infrequently, my friend Cobie admitted he felt
jealous that I went to townships like Meadowlands. *He* wanted to
sit on a corner with a woman like Dipuo, he said, and chat, and
hear what her life was like, and watch Malaika play in the street.

"I can take you," I said.

"No," he said sadly. "I can't go."

"It's totally safe during the day," I offered.

He looked at me and said flatly, "I know."

It was too important for him not to go. Too important for
his sense of himself to sustain the premise that if he went to a
township, he would be attacked. "When Thabo Mbeki became
president," Cobie told me, "I was terrified, because I knew he was
going to chase the whites away."

"But he didn't," I pointed out.

Cobie was unmoved. "He didn't do what he wanted to do."

The white South Africans I interviewed always wanted to speak in
the safety of their homes or offices while black people wanted to
walk around, to go into shops and restaurants. Malaika, Dipuo,
Elliot, and other black South Africans would go with me to

white-dominated malls, though they acknowledged they some-times felt uncomfortable. I frequently asked Christo to show me Reitz, but he always put me off. One morning, we finally went in his pickup truck.

It was a hot and windy day, and he drove recklessly—a kind of driving I had only seen in Soweto among the boys who spun the wheels of the cars they suspected, deep down, were the best life would ever afford them. Once we got on the campus, we jumped out and sidled up to Reitz. Through the razor wire, Christo pointed to a cement wall. "Here is where we do the historical lectures," he said.

I noticed he was speaking in the present tense. "And here"—he pointed to a patch of faded grass—"is the place where the stu-dents drink tea on Friday mornings." The bungalows had been painted pink, but the summer winds had airbrushed them with dust. During his tenure, Christo had his boys plant the quad up with luxurious stands of lilies and tall, orange birds-of-paradise flowers. But the flowers had gone wild and their ragged foliage gathered trash so that, instead of blossoms, the yard bloomed po-tato chip bags and Styrofoam French fry cartons. In the middle of it all, a pay phone stood, its receiver dangling off the hook.

Christo's own cell phone rang and rang; the ringtone was an army tune. He ignored it. His voice dropped, like he was a recon-naissance officer again probing the site of a mystery. "Now here is where we do [barbecues]," he whispered, creeping farther along the fence. "Every bungalow has its own garden. We do a kind of competition with the gardens. At the end of the year, the winning garden gets a case of beer."

I noticed a metal door in the fence was hanging open. "Hey," I called out. "It looks like we can go in."

Christo blanched. He pivoted and started practically running back to his truck. "We should finish in my office," he called back. "I don't think we're allowed to go in."

I'd actually done a little research ahead of time. The razor wire fence was a symbolic gesture, a barrier against vandalism. Reitz wasn't officially locked. Despite its forlornness, sometimes the university housed exchange students in it.

I explained that to Christo. But he just shook his head. "They will arrest me," he said, "if I go in."

29

Dipuo

IN EARLY 2017, DIPUO ASKED me to meet her for breakfast in one of Johannesburg's wealthiest neighborhoods, at a café on the ground floor of a skyscraper with mirrored windows. Normally, she didn't want to eat out in a place like that. Too pretentious, too expensive.

She was smiling when I walked in. But the smile dissolved into a brittle, pursed-lipped expression as she perused the menu. She ordered eggs, potatoes, and bottled juice—things she normally proudly avoided. "Do you have brown toast?" she asked the waitress halfheartedly.

"Only white," the waitress offered. "But it's homemade ciabatta."

"Fuck it," Dipuo said, loudly enough that other patrons turned to look.

Without prelude, Dipuo told me she went to a clinic a few days before and was diagnosed with stomach cancer. The doctor suspected it had been developing for a very long time. Indeed, he suggested her aversion to tap water and fatty, processed foods—which she had thought were signs her body wasn't supposed to be consuming them; that they were white imports imposed on black people—had been the effect of the tumors beginning to invade her stomach lining. In other words, she told me, she had

296

misinterpreted the signs or projected her own wishful conclusions onto them. She'd gotten a sense of resolution out of the feeling that, no matter how much she didn't understand what was happening around her or couldn't control it, *she knew her own body*.

But the doctor informed her she didn't. What she'd thought was a resolution had just been a papering over of the real, deeper problem, another bare and gestural fix.

The whole time I'd known Dipuo, I'd been perplexed by why her comrades called her "Stalin" in the '80s. She seemed mellow. That breakfast was the first time I saw a flash of "Stalin." As she recounted the meeting with the doctor and the upending of a decade's worth of attempts to resolve her disappointments, her tone was matter-of-fact, almost harsh, as if she wasn't going to let it break her, this new problem. As if she was ready to battle through it like she'd always done.

But that only lasted a few minutes. It was too much. When Malaika recently visited her from college, Dipuo confessed in a whisper, they'd slept in the same room, and she'd crept into the adjacent bathroom every night to vomit, gagging and silencing herself so as not to wake and frighten her daughter. Dipuo hoped the vomiting was triggered by the intensity of recounting her old memories to me. That it was, in a sense, her final purge. But now this.

She'd always associated cancer with white people. With their pale skin, with their "stress," and with the technologies they were obsessed with, like strange dietary supplements and microwaves. The matriarchs in her family had never gotten cancer. When she mentioned her diagnosis to a couple of friends in Soweto, they speculated it must have arisen from a "recessive gene" passed down from her father's family with the white ancestor.

Briefly, this theory had felt like a relief. This disease was not *her* problem, on the deepest level. It was not her heritage. It had been introduced into her life, like so much of her suffering, by white people.

But even as she voiced the idea she dropped her head, smiled a sad smile, and then rolled her eyes, as if to acknowledge the explanation felt a little too scripted and convenient. Privately, she had a different theory. It was a much darker one. But it had felt intuitively right as soon as she thought of it.

"He was married to my mother's relative," she said softly. Her eggs and toast arrived, but she just pushed them around her plate listlessly with her fork. "I spent holidays at their house."

When she was fourteen, an older relative in Soweto snuck into her bedroom and raped her. "I was a virgin," she said. She felt so ashamed she "literally ran away from home and onto the streets." In that year, 1985, so much unrest was gathering in the townships that her absence from home and school wasn't that noticeable. "There were no exams written that year in Soweto," she said. But even as she took to roaming the neighborhood at night—a huge behavioral change—"I never told anyone. Not even Godfrey."

That was her sense of how these things were handled. She often heard rumors in Meadowlands about sexual abusers. But the gossips tended to put their hands over their mouths as soon as they began to speak. "Our boyfriends, our husbands, our children's stepfathers," Dipuo went on, "were abusers. And yet we didn't talk about these things, because often, those people were the sole providers for the family."

That was one reason. There were others. South Africa still has one of the highest estimated rates of sexual assault in the world. In 2009, one in four South African men in a government-run survey openly admitted they had committed sexual assault. This phenomenon existed in the '80s, too, driven by factors like a migrant labor system that kept men from their families and housed them in testosterone-soaked mine dormitories where, to ease the humiliation of their powerlessness, they egged each other on to make violent personal conquests. White South Africans pointed to the rape problem as a justification for apartheid. If the country was integrated, they said, black South Africans would rape *their* wives and *their* children.

The idea was so offensive and tired that it seemed to demand black South Africans insist no sexual violence existed at all. In the late '90s, during the HIV epidemic, some activists—including South Africans of color—urged the government to tackle rape more openly. In response, an ANC cabinet minister flippantly said on live TV that he'd "been standing here for more than twenty-six seconds and I haven't seen anyone raped!" The comment suggested that to allege South Africa had *any* rape problem was tantamount to the crudest racism—to claiming all black men, even professional cameramen or top-level politicians, raped people indiscriminately in the middle of televised broadcasts.

I'd asked Dipuo before about South Africa's high incidence of sexual assault. Normally, she was up for answering any question, even a potentially offensive one. This was the only question she rebuffed. "Why do you ask about that?" she had snapped. "In Europe, men rape. In America, men rape. We don't have any special problem."

The rape was the first thing that came to her mind, though, when her doctor told her she had cancer. She suspected the anger and guilt she could never express about it had grown in her like a cancer until it *became* a cancer. Now, she said, she'd even begun to distrust what she'd told herself about her motives for her activism against white rule. She'd begun to wonder whether they had been noble—or the opposite, a projection, a displaced reaction to the rage she felt toward her own community for failing to protect her. "I realize, now, I was actually an extremely violent person," Dipuo told me.

She said she became "violent" immediately after she was raped. "Before that," as she recalled it now, "I was okay in the world. I couldn't be bothered" with activism and social justice. Was her subsequent flaming anger really driven by righteous fury over black people's suffering? Or was it subconsciously more self-involved? Had the anti-apartheid struggle offered her a convenient excuse to take out on other people a more personal humiliation she couldn't name?

At the café, Dipuo told me that, in the People's Committee, she was especially ruthless with alleged rapists. "If there was ever a schoolgirl who came to say, 'This boy forced me into sex,' I unleashed the worst ever form of punishment." Years later, she said she had learned one accuser "had been lying. She had consented to sex and wanted out. But the damage was done." She said she'd also learned the young woman who featured in her recurring nightmares—the alleged "spy" she helped pelt to death with stones—"had been innocent."

Actually, that girl's innocence was never confirmed. There were only rumors to that effect. But Dipuo stated it as if it were a fact. She was responsible for a blameless woman's murder, she stated. And then she began to cry. "I was the leader. I was the prosecutor. I was the judge."

By the time we finished eating, Dipuo seemed a little refreshed— resolute, as if she'd made a necessary and valuable confession. It stunned me that the confession was that she was a monster. But it reminded me of the afternoon I went to take a look at Rand Mine.

Dipuo wasn't around. I'd planned to walk to the top myself to see where Malaika was conceived and where Christo shot the homeless man. When I got to the base, though, around three o'clock on a Wednesday, two men were standing at the trailhead with their arms crossed.

I asked them if I could climb up. They chuckled, as if it was a funny idea that they had any authority over the hill. "We stand here all day because there's nothing else to do in Meadowlands," one said laconically.

He said his name was Lucky and offered to take me to the top. The climb was a steep scramble, but the summit was, indeed, mystical, a stark counterpoint to the densely settled township just seventy feet below. At the edge of a shimmering pond, a child squatted and pushed a lily pad around with a stick like children push toy sailboats around the pools at Versailles.

Lucky was born in 1970, the same year as Dipuo. When he was a kid, his friends also called the mine dump "Six Feet Under." The name referred to a legend that, thanks to the shafts hidden just beneath its surface, a boy could take a wrong step, puncture the thin dirt shell, and vanish into his grave.

That didn't diminish Rand Mine's appeal. It only increased it. The bravest boys, Lucky said—the ones who thought they were going to make it in life—hauled their bicycles to the top and roared down the north slope, which was bare like a sand dune and leveled at the bottom into a wide and glittering beach.

The mine was shuttered now. But Lucky told me "foreigners"— Malawian and Zambian immigrants—crept through its abandoned shafts at night, chipping out its last slivers of gold to sell on the black market. Superficially, he made the observation as a complaint. The foreigners' actions made the dump unstable, Lucky said, and every now and then it shuddered and exhaled clouds of particulate that swept through Meadowlands, making people cough.

But then he admitted he also admired such people. Somehow, they seemed to have the freedom of mind to harvest whatever they could from what white people had left behind. It never occurred to him to crawl beneath the dump like that. Freedom, for him, had always meant something bigger; something disconnected to any aspect of his former enslavement. He'd always hoped, somehow, he would soar from the top of Rand Mine and alight on the sky-scrapers he could just see from its summit. But he was still waiting for something—for instructions or some kind of permission.

Lucky pointed toward Johannesburg's downtown. The

haze was thick that afternoon, and it flattened the buildings' three-dimensionality so the city skyline looked like a gray construction-paper cutout. Lucky wrinkled his nose. That flattening effect, he said, was due to black people: to the way Sowetans still used coal fires. Then he put his hands on my shoulders and rotated me around 180 degrees. "It's so bare," he said of the township, acidly. "People are cutting down trees since we got our freedom." Sowetans, he claimed, were cutting down the few trees the apartheid government planted in their neighborhoods "because—I don't even know why. Stupid reasons. Just for a bonfire to hang out on the street."

Back at the base, we met up with Lucky's companion, who introduced himself as Sonnyboy. Sonnyboy said that, twenty years after apartheid's end, he'd concluded the white regime had actually checked certain bad impulses native to black people. "Under apartheid," he mused, "we were restricted." Back then, he assumed that was a bad thing. But then he gestured at the pungent piles of trash on the street. That kind of litter hadn't been there when he was a boy. Everyone had been so poor, and so afraid of the white people's laws and police, that they "didn't produce much trash, so there was less dumping. And we couldn't get drugs."

"*They* took care of things," Lucky agreed, meaning white people. "They managed things." He claimed the mine owners planted saplings atop the slag heap for black people's protection, to keep the dust from blowing into the township. It was only when white people's "management" ended, he said, that "our children started getting sick and dying."

I mentioned it was white people who put a toxic mine dump near black children's homes in the first place. But Lucky just grimaced and sucked air through his teeth, as if to say, *Forget about all that*. To trace the problem back so far wasn't factually wrong. But in his view, doing so had become impractical, or even constituted clinging to an albatross. The more practical thing, now, was to hold black people accountable for their circumstances.

Once, I showed Dipuo an in-flight magazine I picked up on a domestic airline. The writers were all white, and some of the articles were so racially tone-deaf they read like parodies. One profiled a white woman named Dorothy who herded black, homeless men she literally called "funny-looking chaps with teeth missing" into a theater troupe that performed for coins at white-patronized pizza parlors. The article's writer presented the troupe as a gift of dignity to black people. "A couple of years ago, Bongani Dlamini . . . was a homeless drug user," it read. "In the past, Dlamini allowed his self-pity about being an orphan to fuel resentment. But through Dorothy's breathing exercises [and] emotional-release work, his self-respect returned." The magazine quoted Dlamini gushing, "Shakespeare is very interesting! And Mama Dorothy always explains the things that are difficult!"

I expected Dipuo to be irritated. But instead she just chuckled dully and suggested we move on. How many times could you get angry about that kind of thing just to see it reappear?

In a poor township north of Johannesburg, I listened to two thirty-something black men—an entrepreneur and a somewhat better-off journalist—debate the township's high unemployment rate. The journalist pointed to the legacy of white racism. His children went to formerly white schools, he said, but he bet he couldn't get a job at one of those schools because "we've always been doubted by white people."

The entrepreneur chortled derisively. "If you were to say, 'Let's go out and look for a job,' fifty percent of our people won't do it," he countered. He felt any explanation for black people's contemporary privation other than their own bad habits was a dodge. After all, black people now held the reins of government, no? Along the main road into the township, woodworkers displayed cupboards for sale. "Those cupboards—you will see they are made by someone more enterprising from Zimbabwe."

The journalist let out a heavy sigh.

"No, everyone knows black South Africans are a mess!" the entrepreneur shouted. "I'm progressive. I'm doing a 'joint venture' with another black company for the 'empowerment of the locals.' But our own people must be blamed."

"I can't afford anything at Sandton," the journalist yelled back, referring to an upscale mall nearby. "I can't buy a Häagen-Dazs ice cream cone with my whole daily salary. Why do you think that is?"

"It's the narrow-mindedness among us blacks," the entrepreneur said immediately. "What if I say I appreciate white people? Why is *that* wrong? I think it's smart." He said he liked it when the American president at the time, Donald Trump, dismissed African countries as "shitholes." The comment generated righteous indignation among South African intellectuals. But "when that guy was saying this thing of 'shitholes,' I said to my friends, 'Guys, think deeper. Let us have *deeper* views. Isn't it a shithole, South Africa?' When that American president asked, 'Why am I giving you aid money and you are not improving your shitholes?' Well, that was a very good question! Our leaders, they whine, 'This thing and that thing, we can't do them—they are above us.' But that white man, Donald Trump, could have done them!"

The journalist burst into contemptuous laughter.

"Why is he laughing at you?" I asked the entrepreneur.

"I don't know," he said irritably. "People like that man"—he gestured at the black journalist—"don't understand the truly deep things. We are all supposed to be signing on to the view that white people are shit. Well, some of us *like* white people. We're not as dumb as you"—he gestured at both me and the journalist—"think we are."

It interested me that, to prove he wasn't as dumb as a white person or a black elite might think, the entrepreneur felt pressed to state a stereotypically white view that black people are lazy. But I also saw how such an opinion could afford him a sense of superior wisdom, even power. There is power inherent in knowing a secret. For everyone, everywhere, the conviction that you know something others haven't yet recognized can be immensely satisfying. In his all-black township milieu, the entrepreneur's secret—his iconoclastic, counterintuitive knowledge—was that *black* people, not white people, were to blame for most of South Africa's problems.

Sometimes even Dipuo said things like this. Once, she estimated for me that, in the late '90s, 80 percent of Meadowlands residents had HIV. She derisively blamed their own behavior. It was thanks to their innate carelessness, she said. Actually, she hugely overestimated HIV's prevalence. Epidemiologists reckon no more than a fifth of people living in Soweto at that time were HIV positive.

As the years went on, to claim that problems in South Africa had become uncoupled from white people or from the legacy of white rule became an oddly sophisticated view, especially among the poor. Nearly every year, foreign reporters produced dispatches from black villages in which the residents declared they wished white people would return to power. "My life was better during apartheid," *Time* magazine quoted a fifty-three-year-old black man in a 2009 contribution to the genre.

One black farmer I knew worked for the apartheid police. Back then, he'd hated white people so much it took all his self-control not to turn his service gun on his white colleagues. Far from central oversight, the white commanders at his station didn't assign him to do rounds. Instead, they gave him a unicycle and made him ride it around the station yard for their entertainment. They heckled him and tossed pebbles to throw him off balance. As he wobbled around, he felt gripped by a hate he hadn't even known a human being could feel. "I gritted my teeth and said to myself, 'It will not last forever.'"

After apartheid, he decided to become a farmer because that was what white people were proudest of doing. "I don't even like animals," he confessed. But his police commanders bragged about white people's farming prowess. To succeed as a farmer would be sweet revenge.

Over time, though, he came to feel the most contempt for other black farmers. They were an embarrassment, he told me. When they struggled with their irrigation pivots, they seemed to prove what he'd been hell-bent on disproving: that black people could not compete with white people. Fifteen years after apartheid's end, he said he'd retired his hatred for white people. "Multimillionaire white guys have been my leaders, in terms of mentorship." We were speaking on his farm, and he gestured backward to a herd of sheep. "In fact, I have decided, now, to say 'thank you' to apartheid. It is because of apartheid that I am where I am today."

For him, looking down on other black people became a way of distinguishing himself as savvy. And a way, oddly, of showing he had *not* been broken by his tormentors—that they hadn't succeeded in provoking him to primitive racial resentment. I saw how, for him, agreeing with white people could feel queerly like a way of seizing power back from them after they did so much to inspire his hatred. How admiring them could feel like achieving independence *from* them.

And also, if black people were to blame for what was missing in contemporary South African life, then in theory they could fix it. Another black small businessman told me he thought my belief that black and white people were equally competent was pretentious and theoretical. "Go and research it and you'll see. We are not disciplined. If blacks could be disciplined and say, 'This is the law,' what we could do!" His tone turned fierce. "I tell my friends, the day God makes *me* president, I'll bring more whites into the government. I'll force my ministers to work for whites! And within five years, I tell you, I will have transformed this country."

Black people had power, in other words—just not a power they were choosing to exercise. Otherwise, they were waiting—waiting for white people to give them what they were owed. A Holocaust survivor wrote that self-blame, strangely, can be a "defensive *omnipotent* fantasy." It was a strange paradox, but at a certain point after racial segregation ended, concluding that white people had been right to distrust you became a way to feel free.

Dipuo didn't seem very angry with her rapist. In fact, she sought to defend him—to humanize him. She learned, much later, that he assaulted several other victims. "I heard, among other reasons, that he was small, as a man," she said, almost compassionately. "His penis was so small, and he was a sexual predator to younger women because he felt that they could accommodate him."

She could easily have attributed the assaults to apartheid and its depredations. Even black men who weren't housed in the restive mine dormitories were made to feel helpless to prevent the cruelties the police and the white government inflicted on their friends, their wives, and their children. Many turned that impulse for revenge—too dangerous to exert directly—inward, subconsciously allying themselves with their oppressors and taking out their hatred on their loved ones as if, by degrading them, they could retrieve a sense of agency and neutralize the shame they felt for failing to defend them.

But Dipuo rejected this potential cause. Her mother, she told me, once described to her the courtship rituals in the rural villages where her relatives lived. Looking back, it seemed to Dipuo that there were seeds of distortion there, before white people came into the picture. Wasn't it more courageous and practical to take responsibility for that? When a man wanted a wife, Dipuo said, he would go to a river where young women were washing laundry, grab a girl's arm, and twist it hard enough to make her cry. The disturbing thing was that, if a woman cried out in pain, that was taken as a coy sign that she *liked* the man. If her face remained impassive, that was a no.

Dipuo usually defended black communities at every opportunity. But that morning in the café, she challenged me. A culture in which the wail of a woman was interpreted as assent—wasn't that wrong? Wasn't it time to acknowledge there were things wrong with black South Africans, in a vacuum? The thought gave her a kind of inner stillness—to finally hand over to white people, in some realms, the sense of moral superiority they'd been fighting over for so long. To say to some invisible referee: *Fine. We've been beaten.* To walk off the field, go home, and deal with her and her community's wounds alone.

30

Christo

CHRISTO EVENTUALLY *DID* DECIDE TO run another dormitory. When the UFS administrators closed Reitz, they left some of the students who hadn't been involved in the video without accommodation. So Christo rented an empty residence hall on the grounds of a nearby high school and began to reconstitute Reitz as a private residence funded by alumni donations. The first year, forty boys lived there. The next year there were eighty, and the year after that, a hundred and twenty. Christo went around the country to recruit them at high school rugby tournaments.

By 2017, the new dorm had enough standout rugby players that the A-team flew to Greece to play against professional squads. The players stayed in an Athenian beachfront hotel with a fabulous rooftop bar. And Christo moved the dormitory into one of Bloemfontein's most elegant structures, a new six-story building downtown.

I visited one blustery morning. The first thing I noticed were the lush stands of birds-of-paradise flowers. The next was a camouflage netting covering a patio out back. "That's the actual netting [Christo] used in the army!" a freshman named Piet called out.

Christo had asked Piet to show me around. Piet's father ran a farm in South Africa's southeast. Piet said he hoped to buy other farms nearby and create an agricultural empire. The contrast between these adult ambitions and his childish look—he was like a boy out of a Victorian painting, with plump, ruddy cheeks and long, curly eyelashes—was endearing. "They're bringing back the old things!" he said eagerly as he raced through the halls.

Piet told me the chairs from the old Reitz dining hall had been brought over. He said it made him feel "special" to sit in them. Sometimes, Piet even accidentally called the new dorm "Reitz," though Christo had given it a different name. "Why bother with a new name?" I asked.

"Reitz is the past. This is the future," he said blandly, sounding tutored.

"What's the difference between the past and the future?"

"No, nothing," he chirped breezily. The photographs that once lined the Reitz corridors—of its white dorm presidents, its rugby players, and its namesake, an Anglo-Boer War general—hung along the new dorm's main hall. "As you can see, the pictures are all the same."

In his room, Piet demonstrated the inspection he had to pass every morning. It was like the one Christo had to pass in the army. Shirts hung shoulder-to-shoulder in the closet, a perfect crease ironed down both arms. On the bed, toiletries laid out in a specific order: shaver, shaving cream, toothpaste, toothbrush, soap. There was a *vasbyt* every year, Piet said, conducted on a nearby farm. It ended with the same sunset view and the same cup of beer.

The new dorm's official motto was "Unity in Diversity." "Though we all speak Afrikaans," one of Piet's friends said by way of explanation, "the boys who come from the Cape speak more like the yellow ones."

By *the yellow ones*, he meant colored South Africans. Piet turned to introduce me to another friend. "This one we call Bushman"—a controversial term for southern Africa's earliest inhabitants. "Because he's dark." He paused. "And ugly." The other boys dissolved into giggles as the swarthy boy shoved at their shoulders.

310

It shocked me how overt it had become, the racial pride. Older men, like Monte, who'd been in the original Reitz were always circumspect about that. In the new dorm, showing me the lean-to with the camo netting, one boy remarked, "Did you know that, before 1652, there was not one single building in the entire continent of Africa?"

"What about the Pyramids?" I blurted out.

He paused. "I guess that's what we call in Afrikaans *'n uitsondering op die reël*," he allowed: an exception to the rule.

The stranger thing, though, was the way Christo's adversaries were letting him flourish. Verschoor and other UFS administrators closed Reitz not because anything was wrong with the property but as a symbolic act to communicate that the university would never again let a monoracial culture flourish there. After I visited Christo's new dorm, I mentioned to Verschoor that Reitz had *not* shut down but was being reconstituted around the corner.

He acknowledged he'd heard about that. But he didn't ask me anything further. Verschoor had tools at his disposal to diminish the new dorm's appeal: he could have completely prohibited it from participating in the university's inter-dorm rugby tournaments, for instance. But he didn't.

As Christo sought to re-establish his influence on campus, progressive administrators tended to treat his dormitories as an already settled fact, somehow too powerful to oppose. In 2014, when Christo's boys won the inter-dorm rugby league, the UFS administration let them represent the university at the national collegiate tournament.

Many UFS administrators insisted to me they were powerless to stop Christo. Even when his new dorm was barely more than an idea, they claimed his projects were already so popular they could not be quashed. He could be fought, but never defeated. At times, this so contradicted Christo's real, fragile position in Bloemfontein that I had to conclude they subconsciously *wanted* him in the picture. If the resurgence of segregationist attitudes in South Africa was inevitable—if the presence of a figure like Christo, and a powerful one, was inevitable—that would excuse some of their own failures to move integration forward rapidly.

The existence of public reactionaries may have given them something of a cover—as Christo surmised—for their own internal ambivalence. They couldn't race ahead too fast, they always said. Christo was in their way. Their claims made me think of certain progressive Americans I knew who insisted on reactionaries' almost unbeatable power. Ostensibly, revanchists were their enemies. But really, they were also their companions. I sometimes wondered: Who would these people be without their antagonists? What would *they* look like to the rest of society if those people vanished? Wouldn't some of *their* moral imperfections, their entitlements, be exposed?

One of the first books I read in South Africa was written by a white former anti-apartheid activist. She confessed she missed apartheid: it rendered every choice you made, as a white person, meaningful and potentially heroic—from the race of the people you dated to the books you read. Another anti-apartheid white journalist lamented that there was "no [clear] moral place" for a white person to "stand any longer" without apartheid's extreme manifestation of evil.

Believing a grotesque enemy still exists within your own community could be clarifying. I think some of that motive drove European and American foreign correspondents to Orania, the all-white town. It had negligible news value. But it gave them something to recoil from morally—and, thus, to feel more secure about where they stood on the spectrum of white people's behavior.

Foreign white people were always situating themselves on the white-people spectrum by locating unreconstructed Afrikaners at the reassuringly bad end of it. That put them in the pretty-good middle. Often, American acquaintances of mine brought up news stories about South Africa: in particular, ones that implied the country was failing solely because of white intransigence. I remember receiving multiple copies by e-mail of a story in a U.K. tabloid that claimed tens of thousands of Afrikaners were teaching five-year-old children how to kill black people at a secret shooting range.

I didn't think the "tens of thousands" part was remotely true. I wasn't even sure what Andre—the farmer I met who confessed that he feared his son was more racist than he was—said was necessarily true, either. Andre's worry had sold itself as sincere concern. And, to Andre, I believe it felt that way. But like so much of what I heard in South Africa—such an unexpectedly wide range of opinions and emotions—it ultimately absolved the speaker. If Andre's son became racist no matter what Andre taught him, then that proved this instinct lies deep in human nature and can't be eradicated. And so it wouldn't be Andre's fault that he hadn't eradicated it in himself when he was young—nor, perhaps, that he hadn't fully done so even now.

Fixating on extremists makes holding the fort—as morally ambiguous as your day-to-day life might be—a quietly heroic act. To be white in South Africa still recruits a person into constant unsubtle and subtle acts of cruelty and racial bias, whether it's underpaying your maid—even if you triple your neighbors' pay rate, it's still a pittance—or cruising past the half-dozen beggars you see on a ten-minute drive to the grocery store. There is little practical way to help all of these people, or the tens of thousands whose shacks you see from many office buildings. There isn't a way to dismantle systemic racism with your own hands. And so it was worth it for some people to keep Christo around—even to inflate his power. To believe that vicious varieties of white supremacy are reemerging paradoxically afforded progressive white South Africans a sense of comfort about where they ethically stood.

In the twentieth century, white South Africans had a term for dissolute aspects of the white colonial lifestyle: "white mischief." White mischief meant doing things that, in Western society, would have been unacceptable and getting away with them. It incorporated a sense that Africa was for the wild ones, the people too hot for Europe to handle. The actor Richard E. Grant, who grew up in Swaziland—heavily influenced by white-ruled South Africa— sought to define "white mischief" by recounting a time when he was ten and his mother had sex with his father's best friend in the front of a car while Grant sat in the back.

A formerly anti-apartheid friend in her forties told me that doing "white mischief," in her youth, felt like a way of courting self-ruin. Coming of age in Johannesburg, she knew "people were getting shot and dying" in the townships. Treating your own life as casually as the white government treated black bodies—driving rickety Beetles way too fast or doing drugs—felt like a protest.

But in retrospect, it felt like so much of what constituted white protest under apartheid was a dodge. After the TRC publicized exactly what black South Africans battled under apartheid, she felt embarrassed to recall what she and her friends had considered resistance—things like having a warm exchange with a black maid or taking a day off her university classes to join an anti-apartheid march.

My friend's sense of embarrassment made her shy away from politics or public life, as did the slow-dawning recognition of just how much more black people knew about their shared universe. Put simply, in post-apartheid South Africa she felt stupid all the time. She once thought of herself as daring, albeit in miniature. Now she didn't even know whether it was nice or insulting to ask her housekeeper to teach her daughter some isiZulu or whether giving the security guard a leftover pizza was generous or patronizing.

She could ask. But—she said apologetically—these kinds of situations occurred every day. She felt constantly disoriented, like a child who moves to a school in a new country and faces the choice between raising his hand every minute to ask for a translation, bothering everyone, or retreating to the back of the class, going silent, and learning nothing. Sometimes she admitted it felt like her black colleagues and neighbors didn't *want* white people to learn. That their standard for a "good white" was someone who magically already knew everything white people were prevented from learning as children. "I am asked too often to take time to explain my feelings," a black colleague once complained in a meeting. "I don't exist to give white people TED Talks." That struck her as totally reasonable. And yet, how *would* she learn?

Not infrequently, white South Africans who identified as progressive confessed they felt they wanted to withdraw from public life because they weren't permitted to *say* the truth about what they saw. Sometimes they imposed this constraint on themselves. To make any negative observation about the black-led country felt unhelpful or retro coming from a white person. Speaking up might imply black South Africans couldn't understand things without white input.

But it was hard not to feel as though realities that black people were allowed to point out—plain facts, like that sexual assault was a problem—couldn't be noticed by white people. It was possible to be criticized harshly for voicing either a pessimistic *or* an optimistic view of the country—in the latter case, to be condemned for neglecting to acknowledge enduring tragedies. The window you had to exist in, intellectually, could appear so narrow as not to exist.

At a party I went to, two voluble white women—who declared

themselves radical, anti-Western socialists—started to debate me about America. As Africans, they wanted me to know American greatness was a sham and American-style consumerism was a pox on Africa. As we spoke, the party's lone black guest—a young woman—crouched silently in front of the fire, pushing embers around with a poker.

Suddenly, she spoke. "I have been to America," she said.

Her sister, she said, moved there when she was fourteen. She followed and enrolled in high school in California. The two white women misunderstood America, she said, completely without rancor. There was racism, yes. But she found it much less racist than South Africa and exciting—a land of opportunity.

She said nothing else. But the party went silent. The white women's lips were pressed into a half-gracious, half-bitter twist. They had been shamed, and they wanted to argue. But their stated values—always to forefront historically marginalized voices—meant they had to take the black guest's word for it. Shortly afterward, they left.

That happened on a wider scale. Like cattle slowly wending their way back to a pen at dusk, after apartheid, white South Africans started to converge with each other in their tastes, even in their beliefs. White people who lived in illegally integrated "communes" in the '80s traded their arty, junked cars for SUVs and retreated behind electric-wire-topped walls, peering through their gates to fret about a broken streetlight or an unfamiliar black male walking on the road. Before I got to South Africa, I assumed progressive white South Africans, in particular, would be seizing the opportunity to acquaint themselves with black culture—taking African dance classes, learning black languages. Vanishingly few did. My friend who told me about "white mischief" said it seemed like posturing, now, to walk the streets toting a boom box blasting Kwaito or to live in a commune to send a message about capitalism. The white progressives who could afford to doubled down on having recessed lighting, black nannies, and steel-fortified doors.

The post-apartheid economy initially grew so briskly that, for some white people, life could become a kind of closed white-to-white loop, featuring small businesses that bypassed the government's affirmative action legislation, which targeted medium and big corporations. Some of the old apartheid-era rebels retreated into niche projects like micro-consultancies, two-man architecture firms, or enterprises so edgy they only had to serve a few high-end customers. Others moved into gated compounds, places they might have felt were wrong under apartheid.

These compounds can resemble old photographs come to life. White kids bicycle in the street while white men lope along fragrant, flower-lined fairways trailed by black caddies. One resident of such a compound actually bragged to me that his estate outlawed nonresidents from walking on its streets without written permission—just like the apartheid pass laws did.

Most of these compounds' residents wouldn't consider themselves revanchists. Yet they almost never expressed reservations about this self-sequestration. Brazenly, billboards from real estate companies popped up on major avenues, encouraging something called "semigration." A play on "emigration," the pitch made explicit that the goal of moving to such a compound is to feel you've left Africa behind without actually leaving.

You could get a dizzy feeling in white society—an uncertainty as to which people were problematic and which were willing, if not enthusiastic, to accept serious material integration. Poor white people I met could be far more open to interacting with black people than rich progressives. The latter often gamely talked up economic redistribution while underpaying their black gardeners. Poorer white people tended to voice more racist views. Yet, since they didn't have the cash to self-segregate, sometimes they had more ordinary, even affable interactions with black people.

When I went to Bloemfontein, I once stayed with a friend's father in a lower-middle-class, integrating neighborhood. My friend had warned me his father was a racist. Indeed, he used racially derogatory terms around me more than once. But he'd also befriended his black neighbor. During the week I stayed, I often saw the two men standing at the fence that split their backyards, chatting. My friend's father worked as a plumber and fixed his neighbor's toilets for free. When his neighbor's daughter got engaged, he threw her an engagement party, hosting a hundred strangers from the nearby township. In accordance with local black tradition, he slaughtered a cow on his patio.

I had another friend—a very rich, self-identified white progressive—who had a black man move in next door to him. His new neighbor owned a single chicken. The progressive got so stressed out by its crowing that he dug up an obscure noise ordinance to call the police on his black neighbor.

When I told Dipuo that story, she let out a dark and knowing laugh. It felt taboo, but sometimes she thought she preferred openly racist white people to self-identified liberal ones. "At least with the racists," she told me, "you know where you stand."

In the beginning, I wondered why the people who moved to the semigration compounds didn't just leave. Left-wing white South Africans seemed to exist on the knife-edge of unbearable frustration. "I can't take it anymore," they would wail after their car got stolen or their tire went flat after driving over a pothole. Once, the forty-something inheritor of a chain of office supply businesses— he already owned dozens of vintage cars—burst into a yoga class I was attending in an apoplectic fury.

It was his birthday, he said, and he'd brought a cake into work. But when he went to have lunch, he found his black employees had eaten it all, not saving him a single slice. He was finished, he declared. Didn't they know etiquette? Didn't they see him as a person, too? He was emigrating the next year, he announced.

I saw him at the same yoga class years later, voicing the same, terminal complaints.

Psychologists suggest that people don't persist in what they say are unbearable states of suffering unless some part of them has become subconsciously convinced these states serve them. Indeed, there was something valuable for white people to live on that knife-edge of frustration. For fear can feel, to the person who experiences it, like a variety of knowledge. Telling the particulars of what's driving you to despair invites another white speaker to tell his tale, and then, for both of you to conclude you know something about South African society others don't—that it is endangered or on the verge of collapse.

Often this sense of secret knowledge was pitted against foreign white people, whose judgment white South Africans hated. "Don't be surprised," one acquaintance wrote grimly on Facebook—in a message to potential tourists—"when you have your fancy-pants [South African] holiday . . . disturbed [by the] brutal, ugly flowering of [our] burgeoning civil war." On my Johannesburg street, a neighboring house became subject to competing claims over its ownership. It was frustrating: men would pull up in cars and yell at each other on the sidewalk. But I didn't think it was dangerous until a white neighbor phoned me.

"I want to let you know," she whispered, "those guys are aggressive. You need to be staying inside at all times with your door locked." Even the black street security guard, she told me, "fears for his life."

I had actually recently chatted with that security guard. Laconically, he told me he found the conflict over the house equal parts irritating and amusing, but he said he wasn't afraid. "He's afraid to *tell* anyone he fears for his life," my neighbor claimed. "But it's a fact." It became clear she wouldn't let me off the phone until I validated that she, a white woman, had the deepest read on the motives of the black men arguing over the house, and even of the black security guard. That she understood Africa, and Africans, perhaps even better than Africans did.

If white progressives recognized any good in their country, they'd also have to acknowledge that they—who frequently lived more comfortably than they could on the same salary anywhere else on earth—were making out like bandits. To survive a street plagued by gangsters is more honorable than to live in a peaceful neighborhood that doesn't look all that different than it did under apartheid. I was reminded of a passage in a book on East Africa in which the author visited one of Kenya's few remaining white citizens. The white Kenyan assured him that what looked like a calm landscape was rife with danger. "This isn't New York, okay?" he hissed. "If something happens, you can't call the police."

"Why do you stay here?" the writer asked, baffled.

"I love this place!" the Kenyan hollered incongruously. "And fuck," he added. "I'll shoot somebody . . . I swear I will."

The superficially appalling prospect that the man might have to kill somebody in self-defense was actually what made living in post-colonial Africa bearable. Many white South Africans, too, need to believe they live in a dysfunctional country. The Kenyan's vision of himself as locked in a mano a mano struggle with forces of darkness was a happier state of affairs than facing the more banal reality that he lived off the remnants of his colonial ancestors' money and might still be treated by black people with more residual respect than he really deserved.

Say it too often, though—that your country is a hellhole or that white supremacists are bound to gain the upper hand—and you start to believe it. Like a self-fulfilling prophecy, white progressives' claims helped bring about aspects of the outcome they dreaded, putting them into a never-ceasing downward spiral of anguish. When I visited Christo's new dorm, I asked some students a question: Do you think your grandchildren will still live in South Africa?

"Definitely," one boy said.

"My family will never go farther than the borders of Botswana or Zimbabwe," another said. "If you love South Africa like we do, you couldn't leave."

"I'll never leave this country," a third said.

"The liberals will think of it," the first boy added.

I found that to be true. Far more liberal white South Africans leave the integrated South Africa than you might expect, and far more people who dislike the new regime stay on than you might imagine. Partly, this is about expectations. If you hoped post-apartheid South Africa would be a cross between the Princeton economics department and the cool of Bob Marley, you are doomed to be disappointed. If you predicted apocalypse, at least you can wake up every morning and observe that it hasn't happened yet. But in the process of arguing that the country was becoming more and more disappointing, the "liberals," as Christo's student put it, often managed to convince themselves that was the truth. They found themselves researching the visa requirements for emigrating to Australia, like the cynical right-wingers they'd always hated.

PART
4

31

Elliot

I LIKED ELLIOT'S COMPANY AND regularly drove to his farm from
Johannesburg. The road there took me past a commanding hill on
which stood a monument the Afrikaners built to their nineteenth-
century pioneers. In the 1930s, a hundred thousand Afrikaners
had camped at the base of the hill to watch the designers break the
ground for it; its designers promised it would stand for a thousand
years.

It's tomblike and near-windowless, but inside, two wrought-
iron staircases lead up to a vaulted roof. Around the outside of the
roof there's a balcony, and I used to climb it and look out toward
Johannesburg. During midday, the haze hangs low and blue, and
I could imagine I was on a boat—a cruise ship or a tanker on the
ocean. I would cling to the rail and watch the gray gulls dip and
play around the turrets. I fantasized that perhaps the builders put
the monument so high on a ridge to imagine they were still on the
ships that brought them to Africa, still sailing toward a supposedly
perfect promise. I think we all sometimes wish we were on that
kind of ship. The troubles we face now would be waves, but there
would be a dry land, somewhere, on which we could land.

But the land we live on is an ocean. Beneath it are buried the
shipwrecks of explorers' ideas and old, inherited dreams. They
create the currents and whirlpools we perceive to be natural.

Ten years after I moved to South Africa, I spent five weeks in London. I ate at a bar in a formerly immigrant, newly hipster part of the city, where a young white sommelier with a bun told me we were on what was recently "the most dangerous street in London!" He sounded excited to live in a place that, for its longtime inhabitants, simply *was* life, and no symbol of courage.

I'd brought a manuscript to the bar with me. "What are you doing?" the sommelier asked, peering over my shoulder.

"Writing," I said.

"What about?"

"South Africa."

"Oh!" he said, looking more curious. "Does it have a good or a bad ending?"

People always asked me that. *Does the South African story have a good or bad ending? Is the moral of the story happy or sad?* Tourists asked where they could go to see "the truth" of the country's post-apartheid experiment. It seemed frustratingly difficult to locate. Driving on the highways offered a stark view of townships to their left and plush formerly white neighborhoods to their right. *Is that image—of enduring divisions—the one I should take away with me?* they would ask. Because other things looked surprisingly good—integrated and prosperous. These friends would recount taking a new high-speed rail connecting Johannesburg with its airport and watching young black men in trendy zip-up sweaters do business deals over iPhones.

The urgency in their questioning reminded me of when I was a child and I used to go into my backyard and sit in a wooded place near the property line. My mother had put an abstract statue there: a six-foot steel post with a corkscrew at the top. One side was silver and the other was painted black. The corkscrew part was semidetached and twirled in the wind. I'd watch as its two faces turned around and around from light to dark, ceaselessly. It felt as if the world around me looked like that: swiveling from light to dark, over and over again. From the triumphant conclusion of the Cold War to the tawdry, dispiriting public harassment of Monica Lewinsky and Anita Hill; from the miraculous rise of the stock market under President Clinton to the massacre at Columbine.

I was told my friends and I were history's happy inheritors, the forthcoming proof human beings had graduated finishing school and were committed to letting no more genocides occur—to happiness, freedom, and prosperity. But I already had the sense there were two realities, two versions of the world, competing with each other, and it wasn't ever clear which was the real one. There was the world in which a British princess could divorce her boring prince and become a globally respected crusader for justice and the world in which she died in a tunnel pursued by greedy paparazzi. There was the world in which the world was witnessing the end of history and there would be no more really significant conflict and the world in which an American blew up a government building in Oklahoma City, killing 168 people. There was the world in which a black man was elected the governor of a Southern state—my own—for the first time, and the world in which white policemen brutally beat Rodney King.

There was the world America led and the world in which Americans became convinced their own leaders were murderers. My parents, previously temperate Republicans, became convinced, in 1993, that then-president Clinton killed one of his own aides and that they might need to buy a gun. I remember the night that aide, Vince Foster, died by suicide in a park near our house outside Washington. My father came home from work and reported he'd seen Secret Service vehicles outside the park *before* the time of death the White House publicly announced.

My parents took a legal pad to sketch, at our dining room table, a timeline of events to prove the president had Vince Foster murdered. Now, in the age of online conspiracies, this may not seem so remarkable. But back then, to me, it did. How could we live in the most perfect world and our own president was a killer?

My schoolmates liked to come over to my house, I think, because the presence of these dual worlds—the twinned sense that we both lived after history and were still drowning in it—was more obvious. We'd jiggle open my front door and exit the twee suburban American sonic landscape of ice cream trucks and Rollerblades scraping across the pavement and enter a melancholy chamber filled with the chords of Brahms. My parents decorated in faded colors—dark wood floors, musty red kilim carpets, and yellowing, ninety-year-old Bolshevik posters.

A professor of Soviet politics, my father hated communism and worked to defeat it. Yet after its fall he had slipped into what seemed strangely like grief—a fog in which he stopped going to work to stay in his pajamas listening to records and reading Plato or carpet catalogues all day in a rocking chair. He began to collect items and art from the past, and our house came to feel like a museum—one that oddly sought to honor and preserve the memory of the war he had fought to end. In the fog, he lost his glasses constantly, which amazed me, as he was nearly blind.

It felt to me as if he didn't want to see: didn't want to witness the world he thought he *wanted*, the one he strove so hard to bring into being. The weirdest place he used to lose his glasses was in the refrigerator. I'd find them there, nestled behind just bought tomatoes and quarter-finished tubs of years-old olives.

He talked a lot about a story called Gyges' Ring. In this tale by Plato, a shepherd finds a ring allowing him to become invisible. Plato wonders: Would a man who believed he was good still be good if he knew nobody was watching? Plato suggests not. The story ends with Gyges, disguised as a royal messenger, seducing his queen and murdering his king. I thought my father fixated on this story because of his suspicion America was Gyges: the lowly shepherd turned head of a global royal court, only pretending to be good and noble; our true pursuit was naked self-interest, ego gratification, and plunder dressed up as magnanimity.

Until I was eight, I got treatments for a congenital gastrointestinal problem at a hospital in Baltimore. The treatments could be painful, and afterward, as a treat, my mother took me to the aquarium nearby. Its designer built pedestrian-tunnels through the tanks, and we'd wander through them surrounded on all sides by seals and whales. Some of them would turn toward us and thump their noses against the glass. The point was to make children feel we were trapped, thrillingly, in the animals' world. But of course, they were trapped in ours.

After, we'd stroll on a pier along a river that fed into the Atlantic. Popcorn buckets and the discarded plastic wristbands they gave kids at the Ferris wheel skittered along the wood in the wind. There was something I always found sad about the water lapping up against the pier's edge. It was dirty—thick with pale gray oil bubbles and trash.

There were supposed to be seals, but I never saw any. I had just emerged from what I'd been told was the real, natural world. But in reality, there were only seals, anymore, in the aquarium— the tribute we had made to what we had already ruined. The *real* world? We didn't want to look at it.

Over the course of a spring, my parents and I built a playhouse in my backyard. My father crouched in the long grass and hammered plywood while my mother brought me to a paint store to look over the sample chips. In the end, we painted it blue with an ivory trim. But as soon as Washington's August humidity made the paint job ripple, I never played in it anymore, because it wasn't perfect.

I hated when things broke down or decayed. In the spring, my mother and I planted seedlings in a corner of the yard. Snails always got to the mint and the tomatoes dropped unripe off the vine. I didn't want to do any research about how to fix it. I just didn't walk in the garden after that happened. It made me feel an extraordinary, hot kind of shame. I abandoned so many projects when they turned out imperfectly.

By the time I left my childhood bedroom, it had become a tomb for fledgling ambitions that all turned frightening as soon as they threatened to fall short of some ideal: there were binders of halfhearted paintings, boxes of third-place medals from geography bees and music competitions. I strove for success, but the medals only made me feel sad. I felt as if I had let my life down already.

At one point, I collected cacti: I had six on a table by my closet. One June, I forgot to water them before I went away to camp, and when I came back, their green bodies had gone gray and their prickles had softened and molted into my carpet. It took me ages, though, even to throw them away. I didn't see them when I walked into my room. Once I became aware I had failed them, my shame made a blind spot where they had been.

I remember my first high school boyfriend, who calculated the exact timing of the stoplights on the road between our respective houses so I'd know exactly when to leave his and by how much I had to break the speed limit in order to meet my curfew. This was our pleasure: to break superficial rules all while displaying, and thereby verifying to ourselves, the genius we were supposed to be incubating. We treated even teenage rebellion as practice for the future, for the neat adult accomplishments we were meant to achieve.

Joy and optimism, fear and pessimism, were the twin beams of the psychological houses in which we grew up. When I think back on it now, maybe fear was the load-carrying beam, more than joy. As much as we worried about oncoming terrors—kidnappers and jihadism and mad cow disease—what we feared the most, strangely, may have been a harder possibility: that this *was* utopia. That we were the ones we'd been waiting for.

One of the few things that never lost my interest was sink-holes. I loved to read about the limestone caverns beneath towns in Kentucky and New Mexico—and the ways they had been discovered. A boy would toss a ball, watch it disappear over a hill, and, when he went to fetch it, find it had just . . . vanished, as if into some parallel world equal to our own. There *had* to be a world parallel to our own, one in which all these contradictions were resolved. I would try to find it by descending on Rollerblades to the creek alone after dark, but I only found fireflies.

Just before I moved to South Africa, I heard a radio story about a sinkhole in a Pennsylvania town called Centralia. Like Johannes-burg, it had been a mining town. But the coal veins were depleted long before it became a city and most of the shafts were closed, leaving, essentially, an ordinary suburb on top of the mine. As decades went on, the inhabitants of Centralia more or less forgot they were living over the top of a shuttered mine—until some trash in the landfill caught fire and the flames lit a little tail of coal at the opening of one of the abandoned shafts. Soon, a fire raged for miles underneath the town, one so hot nobody could put it out.

But the really amazing thing is that people continued to build, even knowing they were building on fire. When outsiders delicately wondered what happened to the underground blaze, they would claim it was just up the road, under other houses. Were you going to change course—were you going to abandon everything you and your parents had created—just because it turned out the foundation was a problem? Most people don't do that. The town carried on building up until a boy playing in his backyard put his foot in the wrong place, broke through the thin shell of soil, and found himself surrounded by leaping flames.

After my friend Elliot realized he might never find a job in Johannesburg, he started spending his afternoons at a community
library. The library was built during apartheid, and walking in, he
passed a brass statue of an Afrikaner girl poring over a book. *Ken-
nis Bring Vooruitgang*, the plaque said. Knowledge brings progress.

The interior of the library had been superficially redecorated
with posters about black novelists and an ANC flag. But the vast
majority of the books on the shelves were still old titles in Afrikaans and English, mostly European history and DIY handbooks
like guides to home accounting or needlework. The message the
whole building sent was that the new narrative of South Africa
merely covered over the old reality like a thin tarp thrown over
soil, and the old, white body of knowledge was the substrate in
which you still had to plant yourself to succeed.

In the agriculture-and-animals aisle, Elliot had an idea. The
corridor contained few books of scientific substance, mostly gardening guides and pop animal-lover tomes like *The Horses in My
Life* and *Do Dogs Need Shrinks?* But it did have an intriguing set of
brochures—promotional materials for agricultural colleges.

These colleges are still frequented by Afrikaner men. The
pamphlets invariably showed a duo of hale and hearty white
boys standing by a prize bull at a cattle show. "It looks good," he
thought.

And then he thought he needn't narrow his ambitions just
because he hadn't made it in Johannesburg. He could become a
farmer. In fact, it struck him commercial farming was a greater
dream than acquiring some random office job. "It had been this
white thing," he told me.

That understanding made him feel defiant. "There is nothing
that has been designed for certain people," he told himself. "Our
blood is all the same. I want to prove to young black people: You
can be a farmer, as a black person."

Passion welled up in him as he contemplated the possibility of going back to school for agriculture. "There is not any way people can survive without agriculture," he thought. He imagined the children of the black diamonds, studying to enter professions, and what he would say to them. "Have a look. You can be a doctor. You can be a lawyer. But when you stand and prosecute a certain person who committed a crime, you need energy. Where does that energy come from? From agriculture. Let's talk about your gown—the robe you are going to wear to show you are a professional lawyer, and the briefcase and everything. They make those things from cotton and wool and leather. Those are products of agriculture. The tea you drink, the bread you eat, the margarine, the milk, everything is from agriculture. I would be able to say to them, 'You! Without me, you cannot survive.'"

He flashed me a mirthful grin. "God can live for many days without food. With only the spirit. But that's not for us."

Making it through college was a gigantic undertaking. The agriculture program he entered was math-heavy, and in his homeland high school. "I never got a real idea of mathematics, of 'solve for x.'" Unable to pay for a room in a campus dorm, he lived and studied by candlelight in a shed in a friend's backyard. After finishing the program, he undertook a research project, a sort of postdoc, in chicken farming at a company called Mike's Chicken.

Its owner's hard-work story—Bertus Kirstein grew it from a pair of sheds to a sprawling complex of fifty computer-operated broiler-chicken houses—inspired him. In Kirstein, a jovial, scientifically knowledgeable Afrikaner man, Elliot saw a vision of his future self. "I didn't have an idea of who I could be when I grew up," Elliot told me. "I had never seen that person. Now I saw it."

The way Kirstein talked about the business side of farming especially attracted Elliot. After his stint there, he applied for and received a land reform farm the government bought back from its white owner. Of that farm, he wanted people to marvel someday, "That one—it's a real business, indeed."

But things went wrong from the start. He never saw his farm until Michael Buys, the land reform official, left him at the gate. When he got inside, he saw it was a ruin. The previous white owner abandoned it months before the sale and the fields had grown over with prickly weeds. The workers' sheds were filled with trash—rusting cash registers, rotting egg cartons, moldy milk bottles—and their roofs had caved in.

The previous white owner had tried to make the farm appealing to tourists as a "safari park." The idea was ridiculous—the plot was small and near a city, and you could hear trucks downshifting on the highway and see fast-food restaurants' neon signs from the main house. When the white man sold the property to the government, though, he'd just abandoned all the exotic animals he'd put on it.

The profusion of wild beasts rampaging the farm taxed even the superior knowledge of animal taxonomy Elliot got in college. "There were so many kinds of antelopes. Impalas, waterbuck, kudus, springbok, and a certain animal I didn't even know with short horns and long hair." In his first weeks, Elliot cleared a small field to plant tomatoes while he figured out how to proceed, but wild boars trampled all his seedlings.

Worst of all, the previous owner left a $6,000 outstanding electricity bill, and the state-owned electric utility had cut the power supplying the farm's water pumps and lights. At night, sleeping on the floor inside the palatial farmhouse, Elliot would hear herds of creatures snuffling nearby. He'd go out onto the porch, but in the shadows of the overgrown trees, he could see nothing. So he'd turn on the flashlight on his cell phone and wave it in the darkness. A hundred moon-bright eyes would reflect back at him, and he'd feel more lost in a man-minifying forest than he ever felt in the homeland.

Over the next two years, Elliot cleared the roads, plowed the fields, and built new chicken sheds with his bare hands. I met Elliot just as he began to sell the first batch of chickens he was raising in them. From the moment he bounded out to the farm gate to greet me, grinning from ear to ear, he exuded so much pride. He wore polished brown leather shoes and a T-shirt branded with a logo of a chicken and the name of his farm, Mashabela, after his beloved grandmother. His cell phone twittered persistently. Incoming orders for birds, he'd apologize, swiveling away from me to punch out replies.

That afternoon I met him, though, was a high-water point ahead of what would become the most crushing period of disappointment of his entire life. It turned out the farm the government awarded him was completely inappropriate. It was just too small, with too little space for sheds; supermarkets wanted to sign contracts with suppliers who could provide them thousands of chickens at a time.

Elliot briefly switched to selling eggs, but egg-laying hens were hungrier. It can help a chicken farmer, financially, to grow feed on his property. But Elliot's plot was too small to plant corn, so he had to buy it all. There was no way even to balance his ledger books, much less make any money. After eight months he slid into debt, sold all his chickens, and gave up.

I happened to visit Elliot two days after he made the choice to abandon hope. He was sitting in a plastic chair outside the shed, slumped, his shirt askew and dirtied. "What are you doing?" I asked, startled. He usually looked so neatly dressed.

"Right now, I'm doing nothing, as you can see," he retorted tartly.

For a few minutes, he didn't elaborate. It was midday, and the sun was broiling. Long stains stretched from the armpits of his shirt and trickles of sweat ran into his eyes, but he showed no sign of wanting to move. His eyes followed the slow course of a pair of birds fluttering in the distance and his hands turned his cell phone over and over again in slow motion. The phone was silent. It was as if all the brilliant energy in him had consumed itself and the last embers were quivering in the wick at the bottom of the candle before smoking out.

It had been an article of faith for him that, with hard work and determination, he could become a success. His belief in that was almost American, divorced as it was from an attention to the way outside circumstances and the sweep of history play with our dreams like pieces of glass in a tremendous surf, spitting them up to glitter in the sun or swallowing them into the deep.

In truth, succeeding as a commercial farmer had always been impossible. Most smaller farms that succeeded under apartheid did so *because* economic sanctions protected them from competition. When markets opened up after South Africa's transition to democracy, farms that had once been economically viable suddenly weren't for lack of economy of scale. White farmers are now failing in huge numbers. Since the end of apartheid, the number of commercial farmers has dwindled from 120,000 to about 30,000, a loss that mostly represents white attrition. Between 1994 and 2009, when Elliot got his farm, three white owners failed to make any profit on it.

Not long before he gave up chicken farming, Elliot and I visited Mike's Chicken, the farm after which he'd proportioned his own dreams. We were received by Kirstein, his mentor, in the spacious office that had impressed Elliot. I could see why it had made an impact. It was huge, air-conditioned, and sparsely furnished, glowing with polished wood and steel accessories. The desk was the size of a dinner table and on the walls hung a set of oil paintings depicting strutting roosters. The whole scene telegraphed ease, arrival, power.

Kirstein looked like a don in *The Godfather*, broad and Italianate with a round face and dark eyes hooded by bushy eyebrows. He introduced himself, pressing his bulky frame against the desk's burnished edge to clasp my hand. Then he made small talk with Elliot. Elliot had worn his snowiest-white dress shirt and his shiniest black shoes, and he eagerly engaged his mentor: "What is the diet you're using right now?" he queried, pulling out a notebook.

"Sixty-five percent maize, plus sunflower," said Kirstein.

"And you enrich with bone meal?"

"I always say, 'If you give the bird what it wants, it'll give you what you want,'" Kirstein chuckled. But he looked strange when he said it, his mouth half-twisting into a grimace. In fact, he seemed distracted, his face tilted toward the ceiling while his eyes scanned its surface absently, as if he'd just absorbed some kind of shock.

Then he confessed he had. In a rush of words, he admitted that, that very morning, he'd sold his business to the government. "The Brazilians get two crops [of maize] a year," he said. "And their farmers get subsidies." Meanwhile, input costs were going up. He imported feed during the off season, but "with the drought in America, feed prices went through the roof. Last year was the worst, the worst ever."

Massive corporate farms could easily ride out such fluctuations, but not mid-sized ones. "Under apartheid, South Africa was a closed system," he reflected. "But to survive the ups and downs of being on the global market, you have to be integrated. You have to be huge."

The previous year, Mike's Chicken lost a whopping $2 million. "The business no longer makes any sense," said Kirstein. "Everyone thinks farming is glamorous. But it's not like that. I've been selling at a loss. When my truck goes out, I'm sending a check with it." In the end, he simply had to clear his debt.

But he seemed resigned to the change. "Sometimes you've got

to think about how practical it really is," he said, rubbing his eyes and shrugging. "It's the way of the world. That's basically what it is."

Elliot was morbidly silent as we got into my car to drive away. During the hour-long drive back to his farm, he stared out the passenger side window, his red phone in his lap. Finally he spoke. "We blacks saw businesses we thought had no challenges," he said. "But we were lying to ourselves."

It occurred to me that the black owner who took over Kirstein's farm probably also would not be made to understand its perils, and, when he subsequently accrued his own pile of debt, he would also blame himself.

Both black and white South Africans sounded surprised when I described white farmers' failure. The stubborn narrative remains that the white-built agricultural sector was a jewel black people are in the process of destroying. In 2010, the chief of staff to the minister of rural development wondered bitterly whether it wasn't true that black people just "can't farm." Land is "a liberation tool," he declared. Yet it seemed black people were "using it to add to their poverty."

This narrative operates in many other realms. Take the government itself. A story line has coalesced that the apartheid government, while unjust, was bureaucratically efficient and financially sound. In an operational sense, in other words, it was superior, even if it was morally evil. Even black-run newspapers carry stories about the black failure to live up to the apartheid regime's operational standards—of its inability to deliver textbooks to public schools; its incapacity to maintain parks or build public toilets; its nepotistic way of awarding government contracts; and its failure to provide reliable access to electricity.

People remember the apartheid era as one in which the lights were always on—at least in the white areas. Now there are frequent power outages. Books have been written about the black-led government's mystifying failure to steward the publicly owned power utility.

In fact, the new black-led government massively increased electricity provision. In 1994, half of South African households had access to electricity; now, only one out of ten households doesn't have access to power. This rapid expansion of services is unparalleled by any other contemporary nation, Western or not. In the last century, no other country on earth has so quickly provided new electric connections to such a large proportion of its people.

Yet the South African essayist Njabulo Ndebele has suggested the conviction the infrastructure and economy white South Africans created was functionally perfect has become *stronger* after apartheid's end. Perhaps that's because, without that illusion, there is nothing to hold the country up—no model, nothing to judge it by. But Ndebele reckoned this view of the past also kept South Africans "locked in a space of anguish."

Because the past was nowhere near as shining as is believed. Financial scandal repeatedly dogged the apartheid Parliament. Institutional nepotism was the modus operandi for the civil service. If a secret club called the "Afrikaner Brotherhood" became suspicious of you, you'd find it impossible to get a promotion. In the late 1980s, as apartheid wound down, officials began literally contracting with the Italian Mafia and pilfering from the government's coffers.

The apartheid government was almost bankrupt when it handed over the reins to black people. It was partly a relief for the last white leaders of South Africa to pass the buck. Instead of giving up a prize, you could also say F. W. de Klerk managed to sell a used car on the verge of a breakdown to a family that only realized, when they got in to drive it, that it was a lemon. But the family had no other car to buy, and they'd spent their last pennies on it, and it couldn't be returned. And thus, psychologically, it became necessary for them to convince themselves they'd gotten something of great value.

Such value has been built up for so long around white things in South Africa that I wondered how it would be possible for black people *not* to feel they were breaking them. This can breed tremendous resentment. I saw that in Elliot the afternoon I came upon him, leaden, in the chair outside his shed.

Searching for an explanation for his failure, he had that day uncharacteristically settled on his race. "It's because I'm not white," he told me when I sat down in another chair beside him under the sun. "Truly speaking. I don't lie to you."

All the notions of black inferiority fed to him from the beginning were incorporated into that conclusion, I sensed, but superficially it took on an angrier character. Toward the end, he tried to contract with a white slaughterhouse owner. The slaughterhouse owner said Elliot had too few chickens to make the arrangement worthwhile. Elliot spat with outrage when he described his belief that the slaughterhouse owner would not have treated him this way if he were white.

The anger we direct at others is, of course, often sublimated anger we feel toward ourselves. Nevertheless, "even if my life someday becomes a success," Elliot said bitterly, "as long as I live, that I will never forget."

Over the years I lived in South Africa, I sometimes felt I was looking at America in a funhouse mirror, at once recognizable and magnified so I could see its emergent features more clearly. There was the grief many progressives began to feel—a worry about being canceled, sneered at, or sidelined—just as their society came to look much more like what they argued for. There was the concern historically marginalized people felt that, in power, they might become like their oppressors, punitive and illiberal—and the secret, complicated wish they *could* be more like their old persecutors, commanding and seemingly shameless.

There was the brutal way historically powerful people goaded their perceived adversaries to resentment, and then held up that anger as proof those people hated them. There was the way people retreated into conspiracy theories, or brazenly insisted on things that weren't true to wield disruptive social influence when they reckoned wielding normal influence was beyond them. There was the assertion that no man should have to say sorry or have to endure wounds to his pride.

Whenever people asked me if the South African story had a good or bad ending, I always felt tempted to ask in reply: *Good or bad for whom?* Like in America, people observed that a certain unity of *feeling* existed in South Africa—grief, anger, and hidden shame. Everybody insisted they were playing a frantic defense. That claim often departed from reality. But then it created new realities.

While I lived in South Africa, American friends of mine of all political stripes bought guns. I suggested to some of them that the likeliest outcome of such purchases was that they'd end up shooting themselves, or somebody who didn't deserve it. That wasn't the point, they'd say. They were only *reacting* to an encroaching danger, not *acting*. It struck me that nobody in these societies felt like an actor, though everybody felt as if they were stuck in a deadly play.

Because everybody's behavior so often seemed to mirror each other's, some people suggested this meant South Africa was far more united than it appeared. If only black and white people could recognize each other's emotions, they'd say, so much could be different.

I didn't think so. Black and white people are angry or feel grief for entirely different *reasons*. And if the country succeeds by one marker, it will have to fail by another. There is simply no squaring this stubborn circle. One measure of success, for instance, is white people's self-reported optimism about the country. That number will only be high, practically speaking, if not too much has changed—if not enough change is delivered to black people. Another is how many high-ranked jobs black people get. If they get enough, that will mean some white people have to lose them.

The electric grid has been expanded, but it's also overtaxed. Far more people have electricity, but blackouts occur in more areas. The way white South Africans see it—literally, from inside their houses in formerly white neighborhoods—it looks like all the lights are going off in the country one by one. But, meanwhile, they have not come on for black South Africans as they expected. *All* South Africans anticipated getting electricity not long after 1994.

Every possible real outcome for this country, I realized, would feel like a loss.

In the mid-2010s, though, I saw a different kind of conversation emerge on Malaika's Facebook page, one less moored to South Africa's national debates about white influence and black worthiness. Her friends talked about gender, sex, and what jobs or relationships would simply make them happy. They aired generational struggles, like the way their elders patronized them. ("When old people ask you, right in the middle of a critical workplace discussion, to go and make tea. Ugh.") They talked about money, clothes, beauty ("Shopping for bras when you are fat but have nonexistent breasts is the stuff nightmares are made of"); food (grilled fish with Caesar salad and oxtail stew); self-development ("I need advice on where I can go for computer classes on weekends"); and what they dreamed of naming their children.

These Facebook threads ran thousands of comments long and were often funny. "Biko didn't die for this" turned into an ironic refrain. "Can you imagine dating a man who eats Kentucky Fried Chicken 'zinger' wings?" Malaika wrote. "The dignity of [such] males must be restored. Biko didn't die for this." Another night: "I had such a bad stomachache earlier. I was farting for hours. Biko didn't die for this." A few weeks later she reflected, "A walk around town under a starry night and a full moon. Steve Biko died for this."

By then, Malaika was writing political columns for a newspaper. But you didn't see newspaper articles in South Africa about bras or computer classes like you saw ones about whether the country had succeeded or failed. By necessity, she and her friends were tiptoeing into lives beyond that question. A country where people live isn't a story, one that ends. But I wondered if they kept these interests to themselves to hide them from the glare of post-apartheid discourse, which lit everything to black or white, right or wrong. Lest people ask: *So what does it mean that a black student after apartheid needs to pay for her own computer classes?* Lest it all enter some evidentiary file as proof that South Africans had or hadn't outgrown a defining past.

While I lived in South Africa, I found myself listening to an American folk song called "Boulder to Birmingham." It's an ode to the songwriter's deceased mentor.

I would walk all the way from Boulder to Birmingham
If I thought I could see your face.

Listeners in America in the '70s, when the song came out, would have known what the songwriter meant by "I would walk from Boulder to Birmingham." Boulder, Colorado, was a progressive enclave while Martin Luther King Jr. called Birmingham America's "most segregated city." The songwriter was saying she'd be willing to see social progress reversed in exchange for another look at her loved one's face.

Many folk songs, though, hide a subversive lyric in the bridge. This line can complicate the song's apparent message. It's the line you didn't want to include, the alternative truth that's hard to reveal. In love songs, it can evoke a note of doubt. In triumphant, *fuck-you* breakup songs, it can consist of the admission that if your ex-lover just picked up the phone and called, you would take her back.

In "Boulder to Birmingham," this subversive line is "The hardest part is knowing I'll survive." In other words: the artist *knows* she wouldn't give up her life or undo history to get her friend back. She knows—perhaps she already feels—she's begun to forget and move on.

I think I dwelled on the song because it resonated with the feeling I had that South Africans of all kinds also suffered from survivor's guilt. On a flight from Washington to Johannesburg, I loitered in the aisle with a black South African man who looked like he was in his early forties. He was wearing a tailored suit and his nametag from an international conference was still attached to its breast. He inquired what I did for a living.

"I'm a writer," I said. "And you?"

"I burn tires," he said, grinning.

We were drinking gin-and-tonics between economy and first class, from whence he'd come. Playing off his smile, I started to chuckle. "When did you last burn a tire?"

He turned serious. "No," he said, frowning. "I *do* burn tires. Burning tires is my reality."

I got the sense people felt afraid, sometimes, to acknowledge good developments in the country because it felt like dishonoring the past. That they wanted to pay tribute, respectfully, to all the suffering that went before by finding things still broken about the present. One white man I was friends with grew up under apartheid. Just after it ended, he became a photographer. One of his first newspaper assignments was to shoot "the new South Africa."

He snapped pictures of Nelson Mandela and new black-owned businesses. But the assignment that got him a promotion was a photograph of black and white kids on a university campus fighting each other with sticks. It was a familiar scene, but also, so much *had* transfigured so fast that his editors felt naive or Pollyannaish to believe in the transfiguration.

For white people, there was the shame of surviving even though they deserved a fuller reckoning. For black South Africans, there was also the shame of surviving—even of doing well, in some cases—despite how much of their parents' and grandparents' suffering went unacknowledged and how many black people the country's changes had still left behind.

32

Christo

CHRISTO NAMED HIS NEW DORMITORY "Heimat." Technically, it just means "homeland" in German. But the word is famous for the way Nazis used it to refer to their dream of an ethnically cleansed Aryan state. When Christo told me the new name, I frowned involuntarily.

That seemed to make him smile. "It only means 'home' in German," he said. "We're a 'culturally based'" dorm, he went on, making air quotes. "Like the Native American fraternities in the United States! If any black person wants to apply, we'll admit him, so long as he speaks Afrikaans and abides by our 'Heimat values.'" He smiled and raised his eyebrows, as if to recruit me into a shared secret—that ridiculous pretense might sometimes be the only way white people could operate in the new South Africa. "I really don't know why no black students have applied."

When I first met him, Christo avoided this kind of provocation. Back then, he seemed to have been flirting with the idea that something went awry with his Reitz project. When I began to write about him, I expected he might worry about how closely I associated him with the incendiary video.

Instead, he requested I scrub any feelings of ambivalence about his past. Earlier, poring over the projector sheets on which he'd fleshed out the alias "Charles James Dalton"—the one his superiors approved, but which never would have worked since he couldn't speak English—we caught each other's eyes and broke into helpless giggles. How strange, even nonsensical, his military orders could occasionally be!

But now he wanted to ensure the old military wasn't "made out as a second-ranked type of army when it was regarded as the best in Africa and one of the most efficient in the world." He said he was worried his fellow veterans could give him "flak" or find him disloyal.

By the time his dorm expanded, it was as if any ambiguity he'd felt about his past was like the irritating shard of sand that gets into an oyster. The oyster layers over and over it with shimmering nacre until the shard becomes the treasured pearl. He asked me to amend a remark he'd made on tape about the video makers—"they did a bad thing, but they suffered"—to "they did a *seemingly* bad thing." Without rancor, he said the UFS administrators had integrated their dorms simply because they thought "there should be no more such thing as an Afrikaner." And he said there was never anything wrong with Reitz in the first place. "One time," he said, "we asked a black rugby player to play on our side because we were short a player. And he said okay. So, as you can see, there were zero [race] problems."

The Heimat boys mimicked his self-assurance. The incendiary video "was very nice," Piet said. "A 'cultural evening.' We'll probably do the same things." He said the Heimat boys suffered from some "stigma" in the eyes of their fellow black students, "but it's only because we're hardcore."

He and his friends liked to roll to campus in a sherbet-orange Mercedes convertible, the boys in the backseat standing up like Roman centurions in a chariot. But when I pushed them, they admitted to deep anxieties. One—let's call him Tinus—grew up on a farm nearby Christo's.

Tinus was the person who drove me out to Christo's parents'

farm. In the car, he evinced a deep adoration for the South African landscape and the culture into which he'd been born. He waxed rhapsodic about his Afrikaner upbringing—barbecues with a bread called *stokbrood*, cooked on a stick over a fire, and ostriches, which were his favorite animal. He'd heard of an old Afrikaner farmer who was an "ostrich whisperer." The man would put his hand under ostriches' chins and they'd stop ruffling their feathers and bow in submission. "The ostriches go into a different state when he does that," Tinus said reverently. When he grew up, he said, he wanted to have that same magical intimacy with the land.

But he was unsure he'd inherit his father's farm at all. It was near a former homeland, and by night, some inhabitants took dogs and hunted small animals in the fields. He was perpetually afraid they were casing it out for a more comprehensive theft. The other truth, he added, was that these black villages didn't pose the greatest threat to his family's farm. Economics did.

White South Africans exited apartheid with a swaggering confidence in their capabilities. But it turned out living in a pariah nation artificially insulated them from being tested. Thanks to the bubble in which white people lived, apartheid South Africa was a place they could simultaneously believe that they were up-by-the-bootstraps *and* that they were already at the apogee of Western civilization—that South African wines were the world's best wines, South African fruit the best fruit, the South African army the superior army. For decades, high walls—the censorship of books, TV, and radio; the embargoes preventing an influx of foreign products—safeguarded this impression from disturbance so comprehensively it was as if white South Africans lived in a screened garden on whose walls landscapes were painted in such detail they mistook their garden for the whole world.

Many white South Africans who emigrate return, finding it unbearable to live in white-majority countries like New Zealand in which their skin color doesn't still confer so many material and psychological boons. Shortly after I got to South Africa, I met a man whose brother had made a big deal of moving his family to Australia. It broke his heart, he declared. But there was no more room for the white man in South Africa—no respect, no fairness. He said a move to Australia was the only way to secure his family a future.

A few years later I learned my friend's brother had quietly brought his family back, with no fanfare. When people asked, he said his wife had missed South Africa's "wide-open spaces." Of course, Australia has "wide-open spaces." My friend told me his brother actually struggled to find work in Australia. He'd gotten a supreme shock, finding himself just another white guy in a sea of white guys struggling to stay afloat in an ordinary white working class.

On Facebook, I once saw a progressive acquaintance celebrate her "journey" from "growing up poor" to running a successful business. Black South Africans lashed out: no white South African of a certain age, they said, "grew up poor." All of them, bar none, were born with silver spoons in their mouths.

But the thing was, compared to her neighbors, this woman *had* felt poor. In school, the other white kids—the only kids she ever interacted with—made fun of her clothes. There was little means, then, for her to understand the greater world she was in relation to, no more than a lower-class Nebraskan relates himself to a poor man in Bangladesh. But when her critics claimed her success didn't reveal her character any more than if she held out a hat under a fountain of money, she felt so wounded she deactivated her Facebook account.

A boy like Tinus never had the benefit-cum-disadvantage of these walls. Heimat sort of re-created for him, in miniature, the sensation of being in apartheid South Africa. But Tinus had a smartphone. He could see news stories about protests on the mines and at other colleges. Tinus told me he stayed up at night reading hundreds of comments on the articles on South African news websites.

Most of them were written by black South Africans, and he was desperate for some clue about his country. "All the stories [Christo] tells us are army stories," Tinus said. "Everything we do in Heimat is based on the army. I like that. To know that our history, it's not all bad. Yet I also feel that there's a lot of stuff happening now that we"—the Heimat boys—"can't even say why it's happening."

When I was getting ready to go visit Christo's parents, I planned to ask them about the shooting on Rand Mine. The first night, Johannes and Jaco, who was visiting, gave me a demonstration of their family band. In the living room, they pulled out their guitars and accordions and sang—first Afrikaans folk songs and then Bob Dylan. After an hour, Jaco got up to go to bed. On instinct, he flipped off the lights as he left, and Trudie and I sat for a minute in the dark.

It seemed as good a time as any. "Did Christo seem different to you," I asked, "after he shot the guy while he was in the army?"

There was a long pause. Then Trudie's voice emerged. "I don't know about that," she said.

"You didn't know," I asked, taken aback, "that when Christo was a freshman at UFS, he had to travel back and forth to Johannesburg to appear in court on a murder charge?"

"No," Trudie said flatly.

I couldn't see her face. Was it possible *I* was going to be the one to tell Trudie her son was once charged with murder? I wondered if she just didn't want to talk to me about it.

But then I remembered how, earlier in the day, Jaco said something odd as we walked in the field where Christo led the games of "white men versus terrorists." Jaco confessed he worried about

Christo when he came home on furlough from his military training. Christo looked "thin," he remembered. His older brother
had never been fat, but—like most rugby hookers—he had heft
in his thighs and shoulders. That cushion seemed to have been
seared away, leaving only sinews and bone. And the transformation wasn't only physical. Something seemed whittled down about
his personality—focused and tightly strung.

When they were kids, the brothers played pranks on each
other. One entailed creeping up on the other brother while he
was sleeping and clapping right by his ear. On one of Christo's
visits home, Jaco decided to play the prank. In the past, Christo
always shuddered, then woke up and slapped Jaco playfully
across the face, and they laughed and wrestled together until
they were tired again. But this time, Christo leapt out of his bed
and saluted. He stared forward for what felt like five seconds,
and Jaco felt frightened. "Christo!" he cried out, until the trance
was broken.

It was a trance Christo never seemed to fully come out of. He
was sensitive to noises, the way people are when they concentrate intensely, except he had that demeanor all the time. When
a dog barked in the middle of the night, Christo would shout in
his sleep. Other nights, Jaco would wake up and hear his brother
padding fitfully around the house.

"Before he would leave to go back," Jaco said, "he would
be especially quiet and still." It gave Jaco an uneasy impression
Christo didn't fully want to go back. But when he asked, Christo
would just say everything was fine.

So Jaco resorted to using his camera. He wanted to penetrate
his brother's newly opaque mindset by snapping furtive photographs and examining them later, like evidence. One photograph
that Jaco took of Christo hangs on Trudie's dining room wall. It's
one of only a couple of pictures she displays of Christo in his military uniform. His eyes have a faraway look.

"I was trying to understand him," Jaco told me. "What was behind that pensive look? But at least," he concluded with what sounded like real relief, "he never had to kill anybody." It didn't sound like a line he'd delivered for my benefit.

Haltingly, I told Trudie a little of what I knew about what happened on Rand Mine. Christo had encouraged me to go visit his parents, and I wondered vaguely if he might have hoped I'd discuss it with Trudie. If he felt, at the time, too anxious to do it himself and then, later, too embarrassed he'd felt bad.

But then Trudie spoke again. "I knew he"—Christo—"was going on missions," she said. "Or that he was sent off somewhere. Or that the group was 'moving out' from the base. He was once given a trophy for being the best rugby player on the base. But I never asked him about his work. He mostly told us jokes and funny stories—about *vasbyt* and other things. But I never asked what they were going to do or had done. I thought that if he wanted to tell me, he would have."

It struck me that Trudie's flat tone wasn't necessarily the tone of somebody lying. It might have been the tone of someone hearing information that's new but that doesn't surprise them. Trudie had kept the photo of a five-year-old Christo in his army costume in a special place—in her recipe book. She'd missed some of his childhood, outsourcing it to Elsie during her subsequent difficult pregnancies. His admission to an exclusive military unit suggested that, even without her full-time nurturing, her eldest son fulfilled some of his biggest dreams and got the life that he wanted.

Christo knew how important it was to his mother to believe she raised him well. But if he sought to conceal his real experience, it hadn't worked. She knew something had shifted.

Verschoor, Christo's dorm father, told me a story about Christo a couple of times because it had stuck in his mind. After Christo got into an especially bad fight with a black student, Verschoor called

Trudie at the farm. "We're experiencing, sometimes, that your son is responding to provocations in a rather aggressive way," he said delicately. He wanted her to help him discipline Christo, but he expected her to be defensive.

Instead, she started to cry. "Oh, professor," she wept. "He wasn't like this before. The army stole my child."

With his new dorm, Christo was willing to turn himself into a pariah—scorned by fellow white authority figures like Verschoor in order to offer his students the image of an unflappable figure. Of a man who hadn't been changed by his country's changes. He sensed the uncertainty in young men like Tinus, and he wanted to protect them. He wanted them to be able to feel proud of who they were, prouder than anybody had reassured him he could feel when he was at university.

But I didn't always get the sense his Heimat persona represented his whole self. When I visited him in his law office, he asked me to tell him stories about my liberal education and my travel to other African countries, as if he was hungry to hear about another kind of life. He revealed he had a fantasy life he sometimes imagined he was living. In that life, he got a PhD in political science overseas and ran a wine club. In real life, he became a symbol of Afrikaner identity. I noticed that in his fantasy life, he wasn't even necessarily an Afrikaner.

He acknowledged a few times that his childhood belief that life on the farm was wonderful for his nanny Elsie and her son Thomas might have been blinkered. He'd believed, when he was young, that Thomas and Elsie were part of his "family." Now he wondered if they loved him as much as he'd thought. If they *hadn't*—if they privately supported the ANC, for instance—they never could have told him, he realized. "If they had said that" and word got around—he gave me a sad little smile and made hand-cuffing gestures on his wrists.

On the afternoon we drove to see Reitz, on the way back, Christo detoured to pick up his son from school. After we parked, Christo's son walked to the truck with his arm slung around a black child. Christo greeted the two enthusiastically.

"That's such a good kid," he reflected later, referring to his son's black friend. He said happily that he liked that his son's school was racially integrated. "Those kids think differently. I don't think they'll be as burdened as we were."

But when it came to the boys in his dorm—men the same age he was when his life went awry atop Rand Mine—Christo didn't see them in the same detached light. He saw them as he was just before that terrible day—and he sought to intervene so that, for them, the world didn't flip on its axis, leaving them without ground beneath their feet. His boys thought they needed to see themselves in him. I thought he needed to see himself in them, just as much. Through their eyes, he could see himself as a man with an unblemished past.

Christo as he was in the army exists again in Heimat. Indeed, Christo as he always wanted to be—as a soldier in Angola—has now come into being there. "Have you noticed the way he smokes?" one Heimat student asked me. He explained that Christo's unusual thumb-and-forefinger grasp on a butt let him cover the burning end with his palm. It was a habit, the student felt sure, that came from when he had to stop terrorists from spotting him on the battle line at night in Angola.

33

Malaika

DRIVING THROUGH A FORMERLY WHITE neighborhood with me at dusk, Malaika lashed out at the drip-drip quality of white people's concessions. Everything still felt like a pitched battle, an exhausting one. Every curriculum change was a fight, every move to make a black person the head of a leading bank or university. "They"—white people—"did help bring me here," Malaika said, gesturing at the pretty houses we were passing. "But it's not enough."

In the formerly white neighborhoods, white people still called the police on their black neighbors for hosting parties. These complainants cited ordinances, as if South African law, now, was some kind of holy, neutral arbiter instead of an inherited system designed by now dead people to sanctify their own, sometimes arbitrary customs or prejudices. These same white people, Malaika noted, didn't utter a peep when their white neighbors broke noise ordinances by firing up their lawn mowers at seven on a Sunday morning.

I recalled to her how, in my twenties, I visited a German friend in Munich. We took a train out of the city to hike in a Bavarian village. The village was quaint, with rustic, hundred-year-old houses. But I had distant relatives who died in the Holocaust, and surveying the idyllic scene, I remember feeling an uncomfortable twinge of resentment. I knew ordinary Germans suffered during the Second World War. But the fact that the village's beauty seemed to have remained intact while, thirty miles away at Dachau, so many other people's dreams were extinguished seemed wrong. Where were its visible scars?

"I can relate to that," Malaika said quietly. "I don't love white people. I'm not going to lie. But," she went on, her voice strengthening, "I really, really do not want to see white people suffer or get beaten up. Because I've seen what that does to black people. I don't want white kids to suffer. I don't want white kids to be evicted from their houses. I don't want to see them carrying their small bags."

It was sad how hurt she sounded by the prospect of white children suffering. She could sympathize with their putative suffering precisely because it was what black people endured at the hands of white people. "That's exactly what white people did to us," she said. "They erased our humanity. So now, when black people are beginning to say that white people don't have any humanity, it scares me."

She worried this was happening already. A black friend at college had arrived speaking "English with a very nice accent." But several years in, "the extent to which she was radicalized" by her encounters with white students "scared even me. I have never seen black rage like that. She resents white people. She doesn't believe white people have the capacity for humanity. The thing that terrifies me—now I am going to quote from Alan Paton's *Cry, the Beloved Country*. He says, 'My biggest fear is that when white people have turned to loving, black people will have turned to hating.'

"But I'm frustrated, because I don't know what else can be done. Nobody likes to play the victim like white South Africans. A white South African can be sitting in a house like this one"—she gestured at a mansion we were passing, its garden lights illuminating sprays of pink bougainvillea. "He can work for an international consulting firm that gets [millions of dollars] in contracts from the government each year. And he will still complain about a government affirmative action program that really brings so few black people into a company like that. White South Africans love making us feel like we've wronged them. I know, deep down, there is no way that white people don't know what they did was savage. But for them to admit that is too heavy. Because admitting it means you have to say, 'How do I repair this damage?' They would have to fix things they are unwilling to fix. But the minute they say they are sorry—the minute they recognize [apartheid] was wrong—they would recognize that they must give back."

I wondered what would actually happen if white South Africans more fully acknowledged what happened in the past—and if black South Africans were allowed to more fully acknowledge their damage and pain. When I began to read contemporary white South African literature, I noticed a big theme was the apocalyptic destruction of the infrastructure of privilege—from the demise of houses, farms, gardens, and swimming pools to the breaking of gates and walls through neglect or revenge. Home invasions form the pivotal scenes in the most talked-about post-apartheid books by white authors, from memoirs like Kevin Bloom's *Ways of Staying* to novels like Eben Venter's *Trencherman* and J. M. Coetzee's *Disgrace*.

These are superficially presented as fearful scenarios. But I began to feel they were a fantasy, not only a fear. In these books, having boundaries violated often afforded their privileged protagonists a strange sense of relief. Many white South Africans' houses don't have a bell, discouraging visitors. Instead, they display ominous plaques depicting a skull or the name of the security company the owners have paid to answer their panic buttons with teams wielding guns.

Spend a little time with the inhabitants, though, and you'll sense how aware they are that such fortresses can't—or shouldn't—hold.

One white friend of mine mused to me that both he and his wife know "deep down" that white people in South Africa "got away with" hundreds of years of injustice.

His wife almost never admitted this, nor revealed any ambivalence about their four-bedroom house or self-isolating lifestyle, for fear of making herself "a target for retribution." Privately, my friend suspected "the opposite"—that keeping mum and apart inflamed black anger. His wife's view generally won out, as it seemed the more prudent. He told me, though, he wished the reckoning would just come, so everybody could get it over with.

I thought of the time a longtime boyfriend and I broke up. It was a bitter breakup, and afterward, I strove hard not to dwell on the hurt of it. I tried to dwell, rather, on the things I had done wrong, on the theory that taking personal responsibility was the best way to learn and move on.

Yet bits of the memories came up unbidden. They felt like a riptide and dipping my toes in threatened to drag me into a dangerous sea. When my new partner spoke—even when I spoke—I would hear my ex-lover's voice. I began to walk on eggshells, anxious I was replicating features of our broken affair everywhere else in my life. There were times I felt such bitterness I thought I knew the real meaning of the word *hate*.

And then, one night, I went into the kitchen for a glass of water and, for some reason, all the memories came flooding back. An actual physical pain brought me to my knees. The full acknowledgment of what had been done to me, and that I had suffered, was made clear to me, and I had pity for myself.

Pity. We use the word most often, now, as an epithet. Black South Africans aren't supposed to "wallow in self-pity," Dipuo told me once. But the word comes from the Latin *pius*, meaning faithful or compassionate. The linguist Michael Shapiro calls it one of the most important subspecies of love, the one that implies that to love is to keep faith with the truth. The truth that people hurt. The truth they can be injured. It suggests full attentiveness in the face of all the sides of a human life.

And I realized I hated my ex-lover, principally, for the way he had made me hate myself. At the end, I had begged him to take me back on my knees. How had I let those things happen to me? How could I have been so weak?

But acknowledging that weakness released some of it. I got up off the kitchen floor and it was as if the depth of my anger was gone. I could forgive the past. In the days afterward, I thought I understood what thoughts I still had that came out of that encounter. But I didn't think as much of the person anymore.

What would really happen in South Africa if all the defenses of white learning and infrastructure stopped? What would happen if that was replaced by shame? Is it true the next step would be a giving-up of material goods—or could that step alone change things? The Afrikaans word for reckoning is the same as the word for "bill," like the bill you get at a restaurant. There is the sense of a bill unpaid hanging over South Africa, a ledger off balance. Numbers in the red. Alert notifications coming from the bank that the society is overdrawn. People keep ignoring them, but they keep coming.

White people suffer because they know they deserve punishment and they didn't get it. Fear hangs over them like when you steal something from your parents as a child and you expect to be punished. But, oddly, they seem to be treating you with the same smiles. My mother did that—acted like she didn't know I had lied or did something I shouldn't have. The polite way she treated me put me incredibly on edge. I felt as if I were being fattened for the kill.

Black South Africans, meanwhile, are supposed to no longer acknowledge the damage done to them, as a sign of strength. Once, Malaika wondered to me why she and her friends fixated on heroes who were dead: people like Biko, Robert Sobukwe—another apartheid-era black South African activist murdered by the white regime—and Lumumba, the martyred Congolese fighter.

Was it because dead men and women couldn't disappoint them? Or because they could imagine that, if these people had lived, they would have somehow embodied an impossibly perfect, undamaged dignity, the kind her mother's generation was supposed to embody but couldn't?

But unhealed wounds leak at unplanned times and in unanticipated ways. While Zuma was president, a white artist painted a mocking portrait of him, depicting him naked. A black judge who didn't even like Zuma described being overwhelmed and unexpectedly brought to tears just *looking* at the painting, by the way the white artist seemed to take a black body and strip it, like the old white police had done. "I was forced to remember," the judge said, "that there is hurt, there is pain, there is anger, and there is even hatred in my heart."

A white farmer I knew, though, wondered to me whether it was tactically wise to move on. Under apartheid, he worked as a government spy. He had to read Biko for his job. A superior told him it was necessary to know black people's mindset.

Unexpectedly, he found Biko gripping, even touching. "If you want to say something radical, dress conservatively," Biko wrote. That felt perceptive. Other passages made my friend look forward to apartheid's end—to sharing a country with proud people who said things like, "I'm going to be me as I am. You can beat me or jail me or even kill me. But I'm not going to be what you want me to be."

After 1994, my friend got a master's degree in "African theology." Then he moved to the countryside and took over managing a palm tree farm. He loved farming and eventually purchased several farms of his own. He also took on a side gig representing local black communities in their land reform claims.

To win back a white-owned property, black South Africans had to prove their specific ancestors once occupied the land, and old gravesites could be evidence. With his degree, he was brought in as an expert witness on historical African burial practices.

At first he loved the work. Some black communities, he said, made a distinction between two categories of deceased people: the "living dead" and the "dead dead." The "living dead" weren't zombies. They were remembered by their descendants. He found that idea beautiful, that you never truly died so long as you weren't forgotten.

But he also felt troubled as to why, over the years, he was the one called in as the "expert." Didn't black South Africans take the time to educate themselves in their historical practices? Didn't black judges trust their own experts?

It could have reminded him of what Biko wrote—that the strongest tool of oppression will always be the "self-doubt in the minds of the oppressed." But he began to feel it was a tacit acknowledgment of what white South Africans often got pilloried for suggesting: that black people *needed* white people. He perceived that black South Africans still relied heavily on white people's practical work while complaining about their influence.

Also, he felt a strengthening pull from his own memories. It was as if his younger self was appealing to him, begging him not to forget and relegate him to the "dead dead." He dwelled on visceral—even joyful—memories of his intelligence work under apartheid. The longer he went without talking about it—like Christo, he was advised to keep that work quiet—the more he found he wanted to do so. A lot of it had felt thrilling, like the time he said he hid between racks of women's dresses in a London department store while tracking an ANC exile. He confused his target by getting the store manager to embed cryptic Black Consciousness terms in her messages over the intercom.

That had called on a kind of ingenuity he liked to think he

still had. And now that he had a farm, he sympathized with white farmers set to lose their land. He found himself tempted to do a bait-and-switch, handing the advantage to white farmers. Under apartheid, he read Biko for tactical reasons. Then he continued to do so for heartfelt reasons. But the more time passed, the more he felt drawn back to his original conviction that learning about his black countrymen was solely tactical. That he was still, at the heart of it, a white man in Africa who had to call on dirty tricks to survive.

On his farm, he said, a group of poor black people had set up camp in an unused field. They'd been occupying more land every day. The legal eviction process was terribly slow. Then "one night there was a terrible storm. I had just found a dead baboon on the farm."

He decided to take matters into his own hands. He cut off the baboon's head, impaled it on a stick, and glued feathers and impala horns around its face to resemble a traditional demon. "I planted it among the shacks," he said.

It was a nasty deception. Yet his eyes were twinkling as he recounted it. "In the morning, most of them were gone."

That degrading backward pull—the necessity and ease of playing old, familiar roles—felt like it was everywhere. A black writer I knew told me about a trip he took to Germany for a conference. The organizers gave him a food and drink stipend. Being a relatively poor nonprofit, they asked he return whatever money he hadn't spent before he left the country.

He pocketed his excess cash. "I told myself, 'Being European, these white people can never pay me enough to make up for what they did to African people,'" he said—and then winked.

Objectively, he wasn't terribly poor. He didn't believe the conference's specific organizers owed him money. But at the time it seemed like a good—even provocatively funny—rationale for something he just wanted to do out of self-interest. He did feel a little guilty, and because the guilt lingered, he thought years later about the way he'd rationalized it. And the more he thought about that, the more he persuaded himself his behavior *had* been appropriate and just.

One day, the writer sent me a text message to ask if I would come to look for a preschool for his three-year-old daughter. I demurred. I didn't have kids, and I reckoned I wasn't a very good judge of preschools.

But he insisted. So I met him at the first place he'd researched. It was an expensive school in a formerly white neighborhood. We marveled at its gleaming Swedish playsets, then sat down in the headmistress's office.

"I'm her father," he said, gesturing at his daughter, who was sitting between us. Then he looked at me.

The headmistress, a white woman, turned toward me and smiled politely. "So you are the mother?"

I wanted to laugh. It seemed improbable: the child's complexion was darker than her father's. But South Africa's superficial post-apartheid etiquette required the headmistress to pretend she didn't see color and there was nothing illogical about the idea I was the child's biological mother. The writer's steady, level gaze dared me to disagree.

And then I realized he'd invited *me* to come look at preschools with him, and not his wife, because he believed his daughter would be taken more seriously if she had a white mother—or at least if a white woman appeared to be seriously involved in her life. If a white woman vouched for her. Sitting between us, the girl fiddled with her dress. The expression on her face was neutral and unsurprised, and I wondered if she had experienced something like this before—a lie told by her father about the family's intimacy with a white person. I didn't want to let her down, so I just smiled back at the headmistress.

Another school where he performed the same routine agreed

to admit his daughter. And then he basically never talked to me again.

For several years, we'd met regularly in cafés to talk about politics and art. He wrote about Black Consciousness—about the urgent need for black South Africans to shrug off the burden of white expectations. Who wants to be the man who sacrifices his own daughter, though, to an ideal which hasn't yet been realized? But once he had to reveal the compromises he was willing to make as a black man in the real world—as opposed to the ideal one—it was as if he had to eradicate the witness.

Without a reckoning, Malaika said, "there's going to come a time when black people are tired of being nice. I wish that time never comes. But what else must black people do to make you"—white people—"recognize our pain? There is nothing left to say. So perhaps we must show you. We've been bending over backwards, pleading, begging, crying. White South Africans are so resistant to change. There's frustration in the country right now. And impatience. And built-up anger and hatred. By the time white people decide, 'Okay, it's time to talk,' black people may have turned to a point where they are no longer able to talk. They will want to kill. Or to destroy. That is my greatest fear. I fear that the most."

I told her about a conversation I had with an Englishman whose family was from South Africa. He asked me about the tensions between black South Africans and African immigrants. "It's refreshing," he reflected—a startling word, until I realized he meant it felt refreshing to hear something about South Africa that didn't have to do with the tensions between black and white people.

Malaika acerbically noted that it no doubt felt "refreshing" to a white South African because such stories let his people off the hook from playing the villains. And yet it frustrated *her*, too, how often it felt there was never any truth for her to hold on to that wasn't fastened to an immense but still drifting and untrustworthy history. To the way South Africans understood and related to each other in the past. Reflecting on the fastidious cleanliness of many Sowetans' homes, at first she sounded proud. "At a psychological level, black people felt that they were trapped in concentration camps" under apartheid, she said. Keeping your house clean "was almost like a resistance. 'You can put us here,' our people said. 'But you're not going to take away our humanity. We are not going to live like rats in a nest.'"

At the same time, she envied the disorder in my cottage—the unwashed coffee cups, the unmade bed. If her house looked like that, she reckoned, a visitor would think she was dirty or careless, like the inhabitants of the chaotic black neighborhoods she traveled through on her way home from Melpark Primary. For a white woman, disorder could come off as "bohemian." But for her, disorder within her own house's four walls was a psychological freedom she still wasn't permitted, or she couldn't permit herself.

She felt furious about white people's apocalyptic criticisms of the black-led government. But sometimes she wondered if criticisms couldn't be right. It was unsettling how liberating it could feel to agree with them. When we went to a fast-food drive-thru in Soweto, a panhandler repeatedly knocked on my car window. Malaika made a contemptuous hissing noise. "People always game you in the townships, hey? He does not even bother to talk to me. He went straight to you. His thinking is: 'Number one, she is white, so she probably has money. And, number two: even if she doesn't have money, *because* she is white she probably feels guilty and is going to give whatever she has.'"

In my experience, people all over the world, in any kind of neighborhood, try to wring money out of other people. But it was a relief for Malaika occasionally to admit to some universal South African realities, some unassailable truths—like that black men in townships are unscrupulous hustlers.

Because otherwise it could feel like her entire life, everything she did and said, constituted a twenty-four-hours-a-day debate against white people's arguments. Often these arguments were no longer even expressed *by* white people. On social media, she argued with black friends about the "black tax," the term used for the obligation on upwardly mobile black South Africans to share their wealth with their extended families. This "black tax" could be financially hobbling. But since it was a black tradition, friends of hers attacked any critique on it. One said, "If you want to live by dog-eat-dog Western values, go for it."

Conversely, when Malaika complained that black men didn't seem to appreciate black women's natural hair—"they say [Black] Consciousness turns them on, but then they go and cheat on us with women in weaves"—another friend retorted that *she* wore a silky-straight weave because that was what Steve Biko would have wanted. "I'm tired of people making us feel bad for rocking weaves," she said. Now "we have choices in life." To be free to wear your hair like a white woman did, she declared, was one of the things Biko "died for."

Malaika often joked Biko might be horrified by a variety of episodes in her life. Like the time she spent a full month's paycheck buying her little brother Lumumba PlayStation games. But it was only half a joke. She thought in those terms all the time. The first time she stood in a voting booth, the sentence that ran through her head was, "Biko died for this country, and I have to ensure that it was not in vain."

But what did that mean? "Sometimes I find myself defending the ANC," Malaika told me, "just because whites hate it." That made her feel weak. Once, at university, she fled a student meeting in which a black woman raised the question, "Why do so many of our [black] men rape?"

Malaika agreed rape in black South African communities was a terrible problem. Yet the question felt "violent in ways that I can't explain. . . . We have kept quiet [about rape] for many reasons, the greatest one being shame. Shame to speak because others would vilify us [and] accuse us of wanting to destroy [black men]. . . . Someday, we will find the courage to point at our abusers and say: 'This is the man who gave me this scar!'"

But that day did not easily come. After graduating college, Malaika moved briefly back to Soweto while she looked for work. There, she began to suffer from debilitating sinus headaches. Some days her face felt like a rigid mask of pain. Google turned up a report that large trees humidify and cool neighborhoods by 2 degrees Celsius and their roots bind fine-particle pollution from flying around. Parceling out money for over-the-counter decongestants, Malaika had the acid thought that white people—who, earlier, had kept the big trees for themselves—owed her a refund for her pharmacy bills.

But she wasn't sure she wanted to pursue this refund. Black leaders had disappointed her so much, too. Might she be obscuring that disappointment with an easier resentment—resenting white people? The ANC had twenty-five years. Couldn't they have planted more trees? "I get so angry sometimes," she said. "I feel, just—fuck it. Black people will never be liberated."

But she went on, "I have to believe. I have to believe that things will get better."

"What gives you hope?" I asked.

"I don't get hope from anything I see," she said. "I only get hope from what I believe."

Malaika believes she will give birth to a son. She sometimes talks about Mwalimu, her future son, on social media. "Mama [of] Mwalimu," she captions selfies. "In [his] eyes I see the possibility of [a South Africa] unoccupied."

It was poignant to me that, while barely older than a child,

Malaika already had to imagine having a child of her own in order to imagine a South Africa proceeding reliably toward justice. Twenty-five years living in the real South Africa suggested there was no clear road there for her.

The name she chose was meaningful. In Swahili, *mwalimu* means teacher. To imagine a son on whom the name Mwalimu sits comfortably is to envision a world in which black people are no longer the ones waiting for instructions or admission. It's to envision a world in which they are the gatekeepers—the wise men, the consultants flown around to tutor the others.

It could feel, though, like Malaika's country was less dedicated to giving its children a future than to refurbishing its adults' pasts. "Sometimes, in the midst of heated debates and serious problems in the country, I will be found wrapped in Chiratidzo's arms, laughing and talking about sweet nothings," Malaika confessed on Facebook. Pleasure, so often, still felt like a betrayal. "But the truth is," she went on, "I'm tired. Being black is an exhausting existence. We spend our entire lives fighting. We fight to keep our natural hair. We fight to get into universities, and when we do we fight financial exclusions and institutional racism. . . . And as if this is not debilitating and exhausting enough, we fight a black government that is committed to protecting and maintaining a system that oppresses us. Sometimes I just want to be with the man I love. I just want to be happy. I am so tired. I have been tired for years."

One evening, washing dishes after dinner, Malaika shattered a glass. It hadn't been a bad day otherwise, but something snapped and she started to weep. Then she cried harder to realize how trivial an event this was compared to the suffering of her jobless friends back in Soweto. And then her mother's voice came into her head, as clear as if she were standing right next to her. "Lesego," Dipuo said firmly. "Take an axe and break everything."

34

Dipuo

DIPUO CAME TO MY COTTAGE often after her cancer diagnosis. She was continuing to lose weight, and during breaks in our conversations, she'd twirl in front of the mirror, twisting her torso to check out her reflection. Sometimes we'd turn off the tape recorder and just talk about our hair, our bodies, our mixed heritage. My mother is Jewish and my father is of British descent. Dipuo liked pointing out that I seemed to have inherited my father's narrow shoulders and my mother's ample rear end. "You're white on top and black on the bottom!" she'd howl.

Dipuo had always loved style. She was never seen without a beautiful scarf. It was embarrassing to say so—there was nothing good about cancer—but she did enjoy the new way her skirts hung on her slender hips and swirled free of her thighs.

She'd never been a fan of smoking marijuana. But, in her illness, she became a strong advocate for its medical use. Organic cannabis-oil capsules were expensive, but when she found a source online, she ordered them and made hours-long minibus taxi trips to Pretoria to deliver it to a friend in her organic-eating community. Dipuo said she was confident the treatment would work. Brashly, she described the plans she had for when the "cannabis kicks my cancer cells' asses."

She believed in cannabis, she said, because it was not Western medicine. There *had to* be something for her beyond Western understanding—something African; black people cultivated cannabis prior to white people's arrival in southern Africa. I wondered whether it wasn't also an approach that made her feel better about the fact that she couldn't afford fancy oncologists. This way, she wasn't getting sicker because of the history that had dogged her entire life. She'd made a free choice.

On her Facebook page, Malaika posted about how her mother was called "Stalin" and how much she wanted to live up to that legacy. Malaika liked to regale her friends with stories of how radical and terrifying Dipuo could be. "Three years ago," she once wrote, "when internet money-making schemes were at their peak, my mother received an SMS from 'Nokia' informing her that she'd won the equivalent of fifteen thousand dollars." But when Dipuo called the number provided, she discovered it was a scam. "Stalin was *angry*! So angry that she called that number every day to insult the poor [scammer]."

But Dipuo seemed to want me to record a gentler character, one with frailties and ambiguities. In a sense, she was contemplating another choice—choosing to find the irresolvable complexity of what had happened in her life and who she had become intriguing, even lively and open-ended. Malaika told me several times that Dipuo "hated white people." But before I dropped her off at a gas station to get a minibus taxi to Soweto one afternoon, Dipuo pointed at a white woman with a punk haircut standing near a pump.

She struck up a conversation with the woman the other day while waiting for the minibus taxis, she whispered conspiratorially. The woman mentioned she was a lesbian. That was "interesting," Dipuo said, a little smile spreading on her face. She added that the woman "seemed great" and that she intended to get her phone number.

Dipuo had always told herself love was less important than

justice. And maybe, when she first articulated this to herself, it was true. But when she beat her cancer, she said, one of the first things she wanted to do was to fall in love. She wanted to re-open the Danielle Steel books she had closed when she was four-teen. After pointing out the woman at the gas station, she checked her phone, which had pinged with a message from a man in her organic-eating movement.

She joked with a mixture of pride and shyness that it seemed like he might have a crush on her. "Would I even know how to tell?" she said out loud. And then—resolutely—"It doesn't mat-ter." She was going to follow leads now no matter where they led. It was her time to be loved in a way that recognized the divides in her, the gutters full of trash and the pristine, high ridges where ten-foot reeds guarded miniature but still bright, still emerald-colored meadows of hope.

When she was in too much pain to come to Kathy's, Dipuo would send me long text messages. She admitted taking the canna-bis capsules was hard. They gave her weird dreams. In one, she pi-loted a helicopter to the Eiffel Tower. In another, she took part in a race at the track where her friend Gadifele had worked. She rode a chimeric animal with the back end of a horse but the head of a cow. When she won, Adolf Hitler draped a gold medal over her head.

It was a crazy dream, we agreed. But it also seemed symbolic. For so long she'd been asking herself whether she was somehow guilty, though she was one of the people history books would de-pict as blameless. Whether she was, in fact, someone to whom Hitler might give a medal. And her whole life, she had struggled to ride terribly cross-bred dreams and expectations—the desire to re-sist whiteness and the pressure to show she could enter white cul-ture and prevail. I was struck that, in her dream, she still crossed a finish line.

Dipuo told me she was enduring the cannabis treatments be-cause she wanted "to see Malaika walk down the aisle." But in

May 2017, at age forty-four, Dipuo collapsed at home. She was brought to the emergency room at Leratong, a public hospital on the edge of Soweto.

Her sister Tshepiso got ahold of her phone and sent me a message. I drove out to the hospital. Even the underresourced Leratong attempted to play by globalized emergency room culture's stylistic rules. Its waiting room was fluorescently lit and painted brilliantly white, like the Paradise the Book of Revelations describes: *There will be no more night. . . . On no day will its gates ever be shut.* Over its entry, a cheerful placard read "Leratong! Practice a Healthy Lifestyle!" But in the women's bathroom, there was no toilet paper or soap. Some three dozen confused, sobbing relatives massed around a set of double doors that led into the wards.

Tshepiso said she asked me to go to the hospital in part because when *she* went, the guards didn't allow her to see her sister. She hoped I might have more success. The subtext—which nobody had to say out loud—was that I'd get past the double doors because I was white. Tshepiso was right. A security guard caught my eye and beckoned me through.

Dipuo was lying in a coma, shrouded in a knitwork of tubes and monitors: ventilator pipes, a heart rate monitor on her index finger, and a dozen electrodes attached to her head. The doctor who'd talked to Tshepiso had painted an upbeat picture for the family, telling her that Dipuo would be taken to the theater for an operation to remove the tumors that had spread to her brain. But her fixed pupils suggested she would not return.

And I suddenly felt how much would be lost by a single death: how many dreams met and unmet, how many longings revealed and unrevealed, how many insights and fantasies that now would never knit themselves into the labile, mysterious fabric of our world. When my grandfather died, my father recounted going through his desk and feeling that the man had been reduced to a pile of things, dust to dust: receipts, keys, clues to secrets his son now could never know. His father might never have chosen to reveal them. But while he was alive, he still could. Perhaps, in the end, we imagine heaven as infinite as a consolation. We know it is ourselves, our spirits, that are infinite while we still live.

At 6:30 the next morning Dipuo was pronounced dead. On Facebook, thousands of tributes flooded in to a "fighter," to "Stalin." Dipuo had more friends than she'd let on. Or perhaps she knew that some of them were not so much friends as admirers. And perhaps one of the pieces of wisdom she'd acquired in her life was to know that the two are not the same thing.

When I last saw Dipuo, her heart monitor was registering a particular shape: a ragged outline that mimicked a range of mountains. Intellectually, scientifically, I knew this pattern indicates distress, and I felt afraid for her. But my imagination also got the better of me, and I briefly fantasized that what it registered was a journey. In her life—the life we measure on résumés—Dipuo never quite made it over Rand Mine, not in the way that she'd wanted. But now, I thought, she was going over. She was going toward the lights of a different city, a city we do not know.

Acknowledgments

The Institute of Current World Affairs, the Fulbright U.S. Student Program, the Daniel Pearl Investigative Journalism Initiative, and the Ucross Foundation provided this book immeasurable support. Tariq Ali and Natalie Vlachakis, Bob Bland, Jim Burke, and Pippa and Alex Hetherington lovingly put me up in their homes while I wrote portions of the manuscript. Louise Ferreira, Gabriel Mavhuve, Lebohang Mathibela, Timothy Mokoena, and Ansie de Swardt helped with translations. Alessandra Bastagli, Jon Cox, Sarah Knight, and Katherine Marsh provided conceptual editing. Jane Ackermann, Ben Kalin, Liana Raguso, Anim van Wyk, and Paul Wise contributed crucial fact-checking. A number of fantastic readers pored over the manuscript and offered critical advice: Garnette Cadogan, Charles H. Fairbanks Jr., Jack Howard, Nkosikhona Kumalo, Dave Martin, Moses Masitha, Eusebius McKaiser, Chloe Safier, and Brian Umana.

I'm profoundly grateful to my agents, Gail Ross and Howard Yoon, who had faith in this book when it was barely more than a few lines. My brilliant editor, Megan Hogan, had an uncommon constancy and vision; I doubt there's a better editor and counselor in New York. And I can't ever repay the teachers, editors, and role models without whom I wouldn't have had the guts to write: Liza Baggott, Tristan Beach, Joshua Bendor, Jacob Brogan, David

Bromwich, Ryan Brown, Sarah Chang, Pierre Coetzer, Mark Cordover, Ronald Costell, Prince Decker, George Fayen, Franklin Foer, Glenn Frankel, Dan Grimm, Mary Hadar, Heidi Holland, Caroline Hopkins, Ruth Hopkins, Chris Howell, John B. Judis, Caroline Wanjiku Kihato, Doug Lawson, Bongani Madondo, Raj Malhotra, Nancy Manter, Heather Mason, Rachel Morris, Derek Ng, Jonathan Rauch, Mordechai Rodal, James Rohrbach, Philip van Ryneveld, Nadi Saleh, Melanie Samson, Michael Schwirtz, Jonathan Shainin, Lara Shainis, Mardy Shualy, Greta Shuler, Cynthia Skye, Steven B. Smith, Greg Veis, and Karsten Weyer. Thank you especially to Abraham Aviva Avnisan, Steven Butler, Garnette Cadogan, Adam B. Kushner, Fred Strebeigh, Anjan Sundaram, and—most of all—Wycliffe Muga.

Thank you, so deeply, to all the South Africans who guided me, far more than could ever be named. Four warm and courageous people shared especially large amounts of their time: Christo, Dipuo, Elliot, and Malaika. They have reflected deeply on their country, and I can never thank them enough for their surpassing insight.

Thank you to Vera Gogokhia, David Fairbanks, and Elizabeth Fairbanks. Thank you to my father, Charles H. Fairbanks Jr.—your frankness and daring spur me on—and to my mother, Joan Fairbanks. Your steadfast care makes a place for me to rest. And to Andreas Vlachakis. Your love was the womb in which this book was made.

Selected Bibliography

BOOKS AND TRANSCRIPTS

Ajala, A. *Pan-Africanism: Evolution, Progress and Prospects.* New York: St. Martin's Press, 1973.

Appiah, K. A. *Cosmopolitanism: Ethics in a World of Strangers.* New York: W. W. Norton, 2006.

Barnard, R., and G. Farred. *After the Thrill Is Gone: A Decade of Post-apartheid South Africa.* Durham, NC: Duke University Press, 2004.

Bernal, M., P. D. Gqola, X. Mangcu, N. Masilela, and F. van Zyl Slabbert. *Becoming Worthy Ancestors: Archive, Public Deliberation and Identity in South Africa.* Johannesburg: Wits University Press, 2011.

Blake, C. *Troepie: From Call-Up to Camps.* Johannesburg: Struik, 2009.

Booysen, S., ed. *Fees Must Fall: Student Revolt, Decolonisation and Governance in South Africa.* Johannesburg: Wits University Press, 2016.

Breytenbach, J. *The Buffalo Soldiers: The Story of South Africa's 32 Battalion.* Johannesburg: Galago, 2002.

Bundy, C. *African Peasants and Economic Change in South Africa, 1870–1913.* Oxford, UK: Oxford University Press, 1976.

Chalmers, J. A., and F. A. Hatch. *The Gold Mines of the Rand: Being a Description of the Mining Industry of Witwatersrand South African Republic.* London: MacMillan, 1895.

Chigumadzi, P. "Why I Call Myself a Coconut." Johannesburg: Ruth First Memorial Lecture, 2015.

Cohen, D. L., and J. Daniel. *Political Economy of Africa: Selected Readings.* Essex, UK: Longman Group Unlimited, 1982.

Cowling, R., and D. Richardson. *Fynbos*. London: Royal Botanic Gardens, 1995.

De Klerk, W. *Afrikaners: Kroes, Kras, Kordaat*. Cape Town: Human & Rousseau, 1999.

Delius, P. *The Land Belongs to Us*. Los Angeles: University of California Press, 1984.

De Wet, C. *Three Years' War*. New York: Scribner, 1903.

Dixon, G., R. Richards, A. Soule, and W. du Toit. *The Wynand du Toit Story*. Johannesburg: H. Strydom, 1987.

Dlamini, J. *Native Nostalgia*. Johannesburg: Jacana, 2009.

———. *Askari*. Johannesburg: Jacana, 2014.

Dlamini, J., A. Kirsten, M. Langa, N. Mogapi, S. Molapo, K. Ngubeni, and K. von Holdt. *The Smoke That Calls: Insurgent Citizenship, Collective Violence and the Struggle for a Place in the New South Africa*. Johannesburg: Center for the Study of Violence and Reconciliation, 2011.

Dlamini, N., G. Khunou, and A. Mbembe. *Soweto Now* (transcript). Johannesburg: University of the Witwatersrand, 2004.

Dolnick, E. *Isaac Newton, the Royal Society, and the Birth of the Modern World*. New York: HarperCollins, 2011.

Dubow, S. *Apartheid: 1948–1994*. Oxford, UK: Oxford University Press, 2014.

Ellenberger, D. F. and J. C. MacGregor. *History of the Basuto*. London: Caton Publishing Company, 1912.

Elphick, R. *Kraal and Castle: Khoikhoi and the Founding of White South Africa*. New Haven, CT: Yale University Press, 1977.

Elphick, R., and H. Giliomee. *The Shaping of South African Society, 1652–1840*. Middletown, CT: Wesleyan University Press, 1982.

Epstein, H. *The Invisible Cure: Africa, the West, and the Fight Against AIDS*. New York: Farrar, Straus & Giroux, 2007.

Etherington, N. *The Great Treks: The Transformation of Southern Africa, 1815–1854*. Harlow, UK: Pearson, 2001.

Fikeni, L., L. Naidoo, and T. Tusini. "On Revolution and the Rainbow Nation." Johannesburg: Ruth First Memorial Lecture, 2016.

Gevisser, M. *Thabo Mbeki: The Dream Deferred*. Johannesburg: Jonathan Ball, 2007.

Giliomee, H. *The Afrikaners: Biography of a People*. London: Hurst, 2003.

Glaser, C. *Bo-Tsotsi: The Youth Gangs of Soweto, 1935–1976*. Portsmouth, NH: Heinemann, 2000.

Gumede, W. *Thabo Mbeki and the Battle for the Soul of the ANC*. London: Zed Books, 2007.

Haffajee, F. *What If There Were No Whites in South Africa*. Johannesburg: Pan Macmillan, 2015.

Huxtable, M., M. Kalkwarf, and P. Matthyssen. *Recce: A Collector's Guide to the History of the South African Special Forces*. Durban, SA: 30 Degrees South, 2010.

Hall, R., and L. Ntsebeza. *The Land Question in South Africa*. Pretoria: HRSC Press, 2007.

Jansen, J. *Knowledge in the Blood: Confronting Race and the Apartheid Past*. Palo Alto, CA: Stanford University Press, 2009.

Kamongo, S., with L. Bezuidenhout. *Shadows in the Sand*. Durban, SA: 30 Degrees South, 2011.

Kane-Berman, J. S. *Soweto: Black Revolt, White Reaction*. Johannesburg: Ravan Press, 1978.

Keegan, T. *Facing the Storm: Portraits of Black Lives in Rural South Africa*. London: Zed Books, 1988.

Kriegler, A., and M. Shaw. *A Citizen's Guide to Crime Trends in South Africa*. Johannesburg: Jonathan Ball, 2016.

Langa, M., and M. Mandela. *Dare Not Linger: The Presidential Years*. Johannesburg: Pan Macmillan, 2018.

Langenhoven, C. J. *Donkerspore*. Cape Town: Tafelberg, 1973.

Litwack, L. *Been in the Storm So Long: The Aftermath of Slavery*. New York: Random House, 1979.

Louw, C. *Boetman en die Swanesang van die Verligtes*. Cape Town: Human & Rousseau, 2000.

Luthuli, L. *Let My People Go*. New York: McGraw Hill, 1962.

Madondo, B. *Sigh, the Beloved Country*. Johannesburg: Pan Macmillan, 2016.

Maisela, L. *The Empowered Native*. Johannesburg: Sizwe Publishing, 2004.

Malala, J. *We Have Now Begun Our Descent: How to Stop South Africa Losing Its Way*. Johannesburg: Jonathan Ball, 2015.

Mandela, M. *Long Walk to Freedom*. New York: Little, Brown, 1994.

Mangcu, X. *The Democratic Moment*. Johannesburg: Jacana, 2009.

———. *Biko: A Life*. Cape Town: Tafelberg, 2012.

Marais, E. *Soul of a White Ant*. Cape Town: Tafelberg, 1970.

Matlwa, K. *Coconut*. Johannesburg: Jacana, 2007.

Mattera, D. *Memory Is the Weapon*. Johannesburg: Ravan Press, 1987.

Mbeki, G. *The Peasants' Revolt*. Harmondsworth, UK: Penguin African Library, 1964.

Mbeki, M. *Architects of Poverty: Why African Capitalism Needs Changing*. Johannesburg: Pan Macmillan, 2009.

Mbeki, T. *Africa: The Time Has Come—Selected Speeches*. Cape Town: Tafelberg, 1998.

_____. *Africa, Define Yourself*. Cape Town: Tafelberg, 2002.

_____. "Youth Day Speech." Cape Town, 2008.

Mbembe, A. *On the Postcolony*. Oakland, CA: University of California Press, 2001.

Mbembe, A., and S. Nuttall. *Johannesburg: The Elusive Metropolis*. Durham, NC: Duke University Press, 2008.

McGregor, L. *Khabzela: The Life and Times of a South African*, Johannesburg: Jacana, 2005.

McGregor, L., and S. Nuttall, eds. *Loadshedding: Writing On and Over the Edge of South Africa*. Johannesburg: Jonathan Ball, 2008.

McKaiser, E. *A Bantu in My Bathroom*. Johannesburg: Bookstorm, 2012.

McKenzie, G. "Kill Zuma . . . By Any Means Necessary." Unpublished manuscript, 2017.

Meredith, M. *Diamonds, Gold, and War: The British, the Boers, and the Making of South Africa*. London: Simon & Schuster, 2007.

Mphalele, E. *Down Second Avenue*. London: Faber & Faber, 1959.

Mpofu-Walsh, S. *The New Apartheid*. Cape Town: Tafelberg, 2021.

Mpulwana, M., N. Pityana, M. Ramphele, and L. Wilson. *Bounds of Possibility: The Legacy of Steve Biko and Black Consciousness*. Cape Town: David Phillip, 1991.

Murray, C. *Families Divided*. Johannesburg: Ravan Press, 1982.

Nash, A. *The Dialectical Tradition in South Africa*. New York: Routledge, 2009.

Ngcukaitobi, T. *Land Matters: South Africa's Failed Land Reforms and the Road Ahead*. Johannesburg: Penguin Random House, 2020.

Nortje, P. *32 Battalion*. Cape Town: Zebra Press, 2004.

Nuttall, S. *Entanglement: Literary and Cultural Reflections on Post-Apartheid*. Johannesburg: Wits University Press, 2009.

Padayachee, V. *Shadow of Liberation: Contestation and Compromise in the Economic and Social Policy of the African National Congress*. Johannesburg: Wits University Press, 2019.

Patterson, O. *Slavery and Social Death*. Cambridge, MA: Harvard University Press, 1982.

Pelser, A. *Askoppies: Late Iron Age Sotho-Tswana Settlement on the Vredefort Dome*. Johannesburg: Wits University Press, 2003.

Penn, N. *The Forgotten Frontier: Colonist and Khoisan on the Cape's Northern Province in the 18th Century*. Athens, OH: Ohio University Press, 2006.

Reitz, D. *Commando*. London: Faber & Faber, 1924.

Sanders, M. *Complicities: The Intellectual and Apartheid*. Durham, NC: Duke University Press, 2002.

Schama, S. *The Embarrassment of Riches: An Interpretation of Dutch Culture in the Golden Age*. Oakland, CA: University of California Press, 1988.

———. *Landscape and Memory*. New York: Alfred A. Knopf, 1995.

Serote, M. W. *Third World Express*. Cape Town: New Africa Books, 1992.

Shell, R. *Children of Bondage: A Social History of the Slave Society at the Cape of Good Hope*. Middletown, CT: Wesleyan University Press, 1994.

Simpson, T., ed. *The ANC and the Liberation Struggle in South Africa: Essential Writings*. New York: Routledge, 2017.

Southall, R. *Democracy in Africa: Moving Beyond a Difficult Legacy*. Pretoria: HRSC Press, 2003.

Sparks, A. *Tomorrow Is Another Country*. Chicago: University of Chicago Press, 1995.

———. *The Mind of South Africa*. Johannesburg: Jonathan Ball, 2003.

Stakesby, L. *Evidence Submitted to the Native Affairs Commission Regarding the Success or Otherwise of Municipal Kaffir Beer Halls and Also to the Committee Appointed to Enquire into the Economic, Health and Social Conditions of Natives in Urban Areas*. Johannesburg: P. C. Westwood, 1941.

Steinberg, J. *Sizwe's Test*. New York: Simon & Schuster, 2008.

Tabata, I. B. *Education for Barbarism: Bantu (Apartheid) Education in South Africa*. Johannesburg: Prometheus, 1959.

Terreblanche, S. *A History of Inequality in South Africa, 1652–2002*. Pietermaritzburg, SA: University of KZN Press, 2002.

Thompson, L. M. *A History of South Africa*. New Haven, CT: Yale University Press, 2001.

Tutu, D. "Real Leadership." Harold Wolpe Memorial Lecture, Cape Town, 2006.

Uys, P. *The Essential Eva Bezuidenhout*. Johannesburg: New Africa Books, 1997.

Van Onselen, C. *The Seed Is Mine: The Life of Kas Maine, a South African Sharecropper.* Johannesburg: Jonathan Ball, 1996.

_____. *New Babylon, New Nineveh: Everyday Life on the Witwatersrand, 1886–1914.* Johannesburg: Jonathan Ball, 2001.

Van Vuuren, H. *Apartheid, Guns, and Money.* Johannesburg: Jacana, 2017.

Wilderson III, F. B. *Incognegro: Memoirs of Exile and Apartheid.* Boston: South End Press, 2008.

Wilson, F. *Diamonds, Dinosaurs, and Democracy: A Short, Short History of South Africa.* Johannesburg: Umuzi, 2009.

_____. *Labour in the South African Gold Mines, 1911–1969.* Cambridge, MA: Cambridge University Press, 2011.

Woods, D. *Biko.* New York: Henry Holt, 1978.

Wylie, D. *Starving on a Full Stomach: Hunger and the Triumph of Cultural Racism in Modern South Africa.* Charlottesville, VA: University Press of Virginia, 2001.

FICTION, POETRY, AND MEMOIRS

Abrahams, L., and P. Cullinan. *Lionel Abrahams: A Reader.* Johannesburg: Ad Donker, 1988.

Biko, S. *I Write What I Like.* New York: Harper & Row, 1978.

Bloom, K. *Ways of Staying.* Johannesburg: Pan Macmillan, 2009.

Breytenbach, B. *The True Confessions of an Albino Terrorist.* New York: Farrar, Straus & Giroux, 1985.

Bosman, H. *Mafeking Road.* Johannesburg: Central News Agency, 1947.

Busani-Dube, D. *Hlomu the Wife.* Cape Town: Protea, 2020.

_____. *Naledi: His Love.* Cape Town: Protea, 2020.

Coetzee, J. M. *Disgrace.* New York: Viking, 1999.

Dangarembga, T. *Nervous Conditions.* London: The Women's Press Limited, 1988.

_____. *This Mournable Body.* Minneapolis, MN: Graywolf Press, 2018.

Duiker, K. S. *The Quiet Violence of Dreams.* Cape Town: Kwela Books, 2002.

Gaelesiwe, A. *Remembering.* Cape Town: Tafelberg, 2016.

Krog, A. *Country of My Skull.* New York: Random House, 1998.

_____. *A Change of Tongue.* Cape Town: Random House South Africa, 2003.

Jennings, K. *An Island.* Newbury, UK: Holland House Books, 2020.

Jonker, I. *Black Butterflies: Selected Poems*. Trans. by A. Brink and A. Krog. Cape Town: Human & Rousseau, 2018.

Khumalo, S. *You Have to Be Gay to Know God*. Cape Town: Kwela Books, 2018.

Malan, R. *My Traitor's Heart*. Boston: Atlantic Monthly Press, 1990.

Mgqolozana, T. *Unimportance*. Johannesburg: Jacana, 2014.

Mhlongo, N. *After Tears*. Athens, OH: Ohio University Press, 2011.

Modisane, B. *Blame Me on History*. New York: Touchstone, 1990.

Msimang, S. *Always Another Country*. London: World Editions, 2018.

Omotoso, K. *Just Before Dawn*. East Lansing, MI: Michigan State University Press, 1998.

Paton, A. *Cry, the Beloved Country*. New York: Scribner, 1948.

Steel, D. *Summer's End*. New York: Dell, 1979.

——. *Palomino*. New York: Dell, 1985.

Themba, C. *World of Can Themba: Selected Writings of the Late Can Themba*. Johannesburg: Ravan Press, 2010.

Tlhabi, R. *Endings and Beginnings: A Story of Healing*. Johannesburg: Jacana, 2012.

Van Niekerk, M. *Agaat*. Trans. by M. Heyns. Portland, OR: Tin House Books, 2010.

Vladislavic, I. *The Restless Supermarket*. Cape Town: New Africa Books, 2001.

Wa Azania, M. *Memoirs of a Born Free*. Johannesburg: Jacana, 2014.

FILMS, TELEVISION, AND PLAYS

Blomkamp, N., director. *District 9*. Tristar Pictures, 2009. 112 minutes.

Dumisa, N., creator. *Blood & Water*. Netflix, 2020—.

Clegg, J., director. *A Country Imagined*. Curious Pictures, South African Broadcasting Corporation, 2010.

Eastwood, C., director. *Invictus*. Warner Bros., 2009. 134 minutes.

Enright, D., director. *Devilsdorp*. Showmax, 2021.

Fugard, A., J. Kani, and W. Ntshona. *Statements: Three Plays*. Oxford, UK: Oxford Paperbacks, 1974.

Hermanus, O., director. *Skoonheid*. Equation, Moonlighting Films, 2011. 99 minutes.

Hood, G., director. *Tsotsi*. The UK Film & TV Production Company, Industrial

Development Corporation of South Africa, the National Film and Video Foundation of South Africa, 2005. 94 minutes.

Lediga, K., director. *Late Nite News with Loyiso Gola.* Diprente, eNCA, 2010–2015.

Lindner, T., and Supastrapong, S., directors. *Orania.* Beuth Hochschule für Technik Berlin, 2012. 94 minutes.

Moleya, T., director. *Happiness Is a Four-Letter Word.* Ster-Kinekor Pictures, 2016. 88 minutes.

Mqolozana, T., director. *Inxeba (The Wound).* Urucu Media, Riva Filmproduktion, Das Kleine Fernsehspiel, 2017. 88 minutes.

Noyce, P., director. *Catch a Fire.* Focus Features, 2006. 101 minutes.

Odendaal, D., creator. *7de Laan.* Danie Odendaal Productions, 2000–.

Opperman, D. *Tree Aan! A Border War Musical*, first performed in Pretoria, 2011.

Silver, S., director. *Bang-Bang Club.* Foundry Films, 2011. 106 minutes.

Vundla, M., producer. *Generations.* Morula Pictures, 1993–2014.

Ziman, R., director. *Gangster's Paradise: Jerusalema.* Muti Films, 2008. 120 minutes.

ARTICLES AND PAPERS

Adam, H. "Corruption, Race Relations and the Future of South Africa." *Canadian Journal of African Studies*, 52 (2), 2018.

African National Congress. "Armed Struggle and Morogoro." Press release, London, 1987.

Ajam, K. "Energy Sector on the Brink of Collapse." *Pretoria News*, 2009.

Akinola, A. "Farm Attacks or 'White Genocide'? Interrogating the Unresolved Land Question in South Africa." Durban *Accord*, March 18, 2020.

Andreasson, S. "The African National Congress and Its Critics: 'Predatory Liberalism,' Black Empowerment and Intra-Alliance Tensions in Post-Apartheid South Africa." *Democratization*, 13 (2), 2006.

Anonymous. "Castro Hlongwane, Caravans, Cats, Geese, Foot & Mouth and Statistics: H.I.V./AIDS and the Struggle for the Humanisation of the African." Unpublished paper, 2002.

Ball, J. "The Ritual of the Necklace." Johannesburg: Centre for the Study of Violence and Reconciliation, 1994.

Barac, M. J. W. "From Township to Town: Urban Change in Victoria Mxenge

Informal Settlement, Cape Town, South Africa." Doctoral dissertation, University of Cambridge, 2007.

Beavon, K. "Nearer My Mall to Thee: The Decline of the Johannesburg Central Business District and the Emergence of the Neo-Apartheid City." Seminar paper, University of the Witwatersrand, 1998.

Beresford, D. "Sweeping SA Vote for Reform: Even Afrikaners Support de Klerk." *Guardian*, March 18, 1992.

Bhana, S. "Book Review: Bo-Tsotsi: The Youth Gangs of Soweto, 1935–1976." *African Studies Review*, 44 (3), 2001.

Bikitsha, N. "How Tight Is Your 'Strangulator'?" Johannesburg *Mail & Guardian*, January 29, 2010.

———. "When Big Bucks Maketh the Man." Johannesburg *Mail & Guardian*, August 23, 2010.

———. "I Love You, but I Love Your Bank Balance More." Johannesburg *Mail & Guardian*, January 24, 2011.

———. "Who Will Mend Our Broken Windows?" Johannesburg *Mail & Guardian*, March 9, 2011.

Bogdanich, W., and M. Forsythe. "How McKinsey Lost Its Way in South Africa." *New York Times*, June 26, 2018.

Bogopa, D. "African Cultural Systems and the Language in African Transition: The Case of Urban Youth in Tsakane Township, South Africa." *African Anthropology*, 6 (2), 1999.

Cantor-Graae, E., B. Rutten, J. Selten, and E. van der Ven. "The Social Defeat Hypothesis of Schizophrenia: An Update." *Schizophrenia Bulletin*, 39 (6), 2013.

Cauvin, E. "Privatization Snag in South Africa." *New York Times*, November 2, 2001.

Chatterjee, A. "Measuring Wealth and Inequality in South Africa." Working paper, Johannesburg: Southern Africa—Towards Inclusive Economic Development (SA-TIED), 2019.

Chikane, F. "Children in Turmoil: The Effects of the Unrest on Township Children." In S. Burman and P. Reynolds (eds.), *Growing Up in a Divided Society*. Johannesburg: Ravan Press, 1986.

Chipkin, I. "Whither the State? Corruption, Institutions and State-Building in South Africa." *Politikon*, 40 (2), 2013.

———. "Sovereignty and Government in Africa After Independence." *Social Imaginaries*, 4 (1), 2018.

Chipkin, I., and S. Meny-Gilbert. "Why the Past Matters: Studying Public Administration in South Africa." *Journal of Public Administration*, 47 (1), 2012.

Clymer, A. "Poll in South Africa Shows a Rise in Whites' Distaste for Apartheid." *New York Times*, August 3, 1986.

Conway-Smith, E. "Zuma's Nkandla Defense: No, No, That's Not a Swimming Pool. It's a Fire Pool! For Security!" *GlobalPost*, December 20, 2013.

Currie, W., and R. Horwitz. "Another Instance Where Privatization Trumped Liberalization: The Politics of Telecomunications Reform in South Africa." *Telecommunications Policy*, 31, 2007.

Daley, S. "As Crime Soars, South African Whites Leave." *New York Times*, December 12, 1995.

Davies, J. "The State and the South African University System Under Apartheid." *Comparative Education*, 32 (3), 2010.

Davies, R. J. "The Spatial Formation of the South African City." *GeoJournal*, 2, 1981.

"Did 34% of Households Have Access to Electricity in 1994?" Johannesburg *Mail & Guardian*, May 14, 2015.

Dlamini, J. "Apartheid Confessions." *Interventions: International Journal of Postcolonial Studies*, 2016.

Dludla, M. "Hustle and Flow! An Analysis of Naspers's Operationalization as Reported By Prominent South African Newspaper Publications Over a Three-Year Period." Master's thesis, University of Kwa-Zulu Natal, 2017.

Dugard, J. "From Low Intensity War to Mafia War: Taxi Violence in South Africa (1987–2000)." Centre for the Study of Violence and Reconciliation. Violence and Transition Series, 4, 2001.

Dugmore, C., and J. Stadler. "Honey, Milk, and Bile: A Social History of Hillbrow." *BMC Public Health Journal*, 17 (444), 2017.

Ekman, P., and R. Harrison. "TV's Last Frontier: South Africa." *Annenberg Journal of Communication*, 26 (1), 1976.

Ellis, S. "The Historical Significance of South Africa's Third Force." *Journal of Southern African Studies*, 24 (22), 1998.

"Employment, Unemployment, Skills, and Economic Growth." Statistics South Africa, 2016.

"Facebook Post on the 'Trauma of Poverty' Resonates with Many South Africans," Cape Town *Weekend Argus*, December 23, 2020.

Filatova, I. "The ANC and the Soviets." *PoliticsWeb*, August 10, 2011.

Gallo, M. "Bantu Education, and Its Living Educational and Socioeconomic Legacy in Apartheid and Post-Apartheid South Africa." Doctoral thesis, Fordham University, 2020.

Garwood, A. "The Holocaust and the Power of Powerlessness." *British Journal of Psychotherapy*, 13 (2), 1996.

Gastrow, P., and M. Shaw. "Stealing the Show? Crime and Its Impact in Post-Apartheid South Africa." *Daedalus*, 130 (1), 2001.

Gauger, C. "Reds and Patriots: The Alliance of the African National Congress and the South African Communist Party." *Oshkosh Scholar*, 2017.

Gelderblom, O., A. de Jong, and J. Jonker. "The Formative Years of the Modern Corporation: The Dutch East India Company VOC, 1602–1623." *Journal of Economic History*, 73 (4), 2013.

Giliomee, H. "Ethnic Business and Economic Empowerment: The Afrikaner Case, 1915–1970." *South African Journal of Economics*, 76 (4), 2008.

———. "A Note on Bantu Education, 1953 to 1970." *South African Journal of Economics*, 77 (1), 2009.

———. "Bantu Education: Destructive Intervention or Part Reform?" *New Contree: A Journal of Historical and Human Sciences for Southern Africa*, 65, 2012.

Githaiga, J., P. Gobodo-Madikizela, and W. P. Wahl. "'They Dug Up Wounds': University of the Free State Students' Experiences of Transformation and Integration in Campus Residences." *Race, Ethnicity, and Education*, 21 (6), 2017.

Glaser, C. "Violent Crime in South Africa: Historical Perspectives." *South African Historical Journal*, 60 (3), 2008.

Gobodo-Madikizela, P. "A Wounded Nation." Johannesburg *Mail & Guardian*, December 23, 2009.

Graybill, L. "Pursuit of Truth and Reconciliation in South Africa." *Africa Today*, 45 (1), 1998.

Grundlingh, A., and I. van der Waag. "In Different Times: The War for Southern Africa, 1966-1989." *African Military Studies*, 2, 2019.

Hirsch, A. "The Origins and Implications of South Africa's Continuing Financial Crisis." *Transformation*, 9, 1989.

Horwitz, R. "The Uneasy Relation Between Political and Economic Reform in South Africa: The Case of Telecommunications." *African Affairs*, 93 (372), 1994.

Hurst-Harosh, E. "Tsotsitaal and Decoloniality." *African Studies*, 78 (1), 2018.

Hyslop, J. "Political Corruption: Before and After Apartheid." *Journal of Southern African Studies*, 31 (4), 2005.

Karim, Q. A., and S. A. Karim. "The Evolving H.I.V. Epidemic in South Africa." *International Journal of Epidemiology*, 31 (1), 2002.

Khoabane, P. "Bok Coach Exemplifies the Cross All Blacks Have to Bear." Johannesburg *Sunday Times*, 2009.

Klopper, N. "Reviving Pre-1994 Historic Address Maps for Soweto." *PositionIt*, 2014.

Krige, D. "The Changing Dynamics of Social Class, Mobility, and Housing in Black Johannesburg." *Alternation*, 19 (1), 2012.

Krog, A. "A New Ancestor for Alienated Afrikaner Youth." Johannesburg *Mail & Guardian*, November 7–14, 2009.

Lane, C. "South Africa's Violent Road to Real Democracy." *New Republic*, May 2, 1994.

Legassick, M. "Capitalist Roots of Apartheid." *Journal of African History*, 25 (3), 1984.

———. "South Africa in Crisis: What Route to Democracy?" *African Affairs*, 84 (337), 1985.

———. "The Great Treks: The Evidence." *South African Historical Journal*, 46 (1), 2009.

Lehohla, P., ed. *Poverty Trends in South Africa, 2005–2016*. Statistics South Africa, 2017.

Levy, A. "Who Owns South Africa?" *New Yorker*, May 6, 2019.

Levy, P. "Sanctions on South Africa: What Did They Do?" Working paper, Economic Growth Center, Yale University, 1999.

"Living Conditions of Households in South Africa." *Living Conditions Survey*, Statistics South Africa, 2017.

Lotshwao, K. "The Lack of Internal Party Democracy in the African National Congress: A Threat to the Consolidation of Democracy in South Africa." *Journal of Southern African Studies*, 35 (4), 2009.

Louw, A. "Surviving the Transition: Trends and Perceptions of Crime in South Africa." *Social Indicators Research*, 41 (1), 1997.

Louw, C. "Alles stil en onrustig op De Wildt." Pretoria *Beeld*, August 29, 2009.

———. "Today We're Going to Arrest a Boer." Pretoria *Beeld*, November 17, 2009.

———. "Wanneer die polisie is nie daar vir jou nie." Pretoria *Beeld*, September 25, 2009.

———. "Ek het De Klerk onnodig gekwets." Pretoria *Beeld*, August 9, 2009.

———. "De Wildt-bloeding vir eers gestop." Pretoria *Beeld*, March 24, 2010.

Mabuza, B. "Old Flag Is Offensive, but It's Not Hate Speech, Argues Afri-Forum." *Sowetan*, December 3, 2019.

Madondo, B. "Jub Jub: The Life and Trial of a South African Child Star." Johannesburg *Mail & Guardian*, December 21, 2012.

Mafeje, A. "Soweto and Its Aftermath." *Review of African Political Economy*, 11, 1978.

Makhanya, M. "Zuma Must Reinvent Himself." Johannesburg *Sunday Times*, May 2, 2010.

Malan, R. "Confession of a White South African." London *Sunday Times*, March 27, 1994.

———. "I'm in Love and It Hurts." *Guardian*, May 5, 1994.

"Malema: This Land Belongs to Foreigners." Cape Town *Independent*, April 27, 2010.

Manby, B. "South Africa: The Impact of Sanctions." *Journal of International Affairs*, 46 (1), 1992.

"Man Imprisoned for 18 Months for Slogan on Teacup." Associated Press, December 5, 1983.

Mangcu, X. "If Dignity Prevails, So Will Tokyo." Johannesburg *Sunday Times*, May 27, 2007.

———. "From Mandela to Malema in Three Simple Steps." Pretoria *Business Day*, July 17, 2008.

———. "Ripping the Veil Off UCT's Whiter Shades of Pale." Johannesburg *Sunday Times*, July 6, 2014.

———. "Shattering the Myth of a Post-Racial Consensus in South African Higher Education: Rhodes Must Fall and the Struggle for Transformation at the University of Cape Town." *Critical Philosophy of Race*, 5 (2), 2017.

Mangona, S. "South Africa's Curse." *New York Times*, August 4, 1998.

Masondo, S., B. Mthethwa, and C. Prince. "SA in Dire Need of Surgeons." Johannesburg *Sunday Times*, 2009.

Mbeki, M. "Elite, Masses Clash in New Battle Over SA." *PoliticsWeb*, 2010.

Mbuqe, S. "Political Violence in South Africa: A Case Study of 'Necklacing' in Colesberg." Doctoral thesis, Duquesne University, 2010.

McDougall, D. "Racist YouTube Video That Shamed South Africa." London *Sunday Times*, October 11, 2009.

McGregor, R. "State in Party Service." Letter, *Cape Times*, 2009.

Mchunu, K. "Izikhothane Youth Phenomenon: The Janus Face of Contemporary Culture in South Africa." *African Identities*, 15 (2), 2016.

McKinley, D. "Umkhonto We Sizwe: A Critical Analysis of the Armed Struggle of the African National Congress." *South African Historical Journal*, 70 (1), 2017.

Meintjies, S., ed. "The Future of Penge: Prospects for the People and the Environment." Asbestos Relief Trust, 2008.

Mendes, B. C. "32 Battalion: Ex-Combatants' Reconstruction of Livelihoods Since 1993." Doctoral thesis, University of Pretoria, 2020.

Mfundisi, S. "Bophuthatswana Was Better." *PoliticsWeb*, February 18, 2010.

Mkhize, T., and S. Pather. "My Ordeal at the Hands of Racists." Johannesburg *Sunday Times*, February 28, 2008.

Mngxitama, A. "Words Don't Come Easy." Johannesburg *Mail & Guardian*, September 24, 2009.

———. "From Mbeki to Zuma: What Is the Difference?" *New Frank Talk*, 2, 2009.

———. "Blacks Can't Be Racist." *New Frank Talk*, 3, 2010.

———. "Blacks are Kwerekweres, Whites are Tourists." *New Frank Talk*, 7, 2009.

Molobi, V. "The Marginalisation of Women in the African Initiated Churches in South Africa, 1882–2006." *Studia Historiae Ecclesiasticaie*, 24 (1), 2008.

Mostert, C. "Reflections on South Africa's Restructuring of State-Owned Enterprises." Friedrich Ebert Stiftung, 2002.

Mswela, A. "Cultural Practices and H.I.V. in South Africa: A Legal Perspective." *Potchefstroom Electric Law Journal*, 12 (4), 2009.

Myburgh, J. "The Virodene Affair." *PoliticsWeb*, September 21, 2007.

Naidoo, N. "The Trust Feed Massacre: 25 Years On." Durban *Witness*, 2013.

Nana, N. "Defence Facilities Pose Risk." *Cape Times*, 2009.

Nattrass, N. "AIDS and the Scientific Governance of Medicine in Post-Apartheid South Africa." *African Affairs*, 107 (427), 2008.

Ndebele, N. "Of Pretence and Protest." Johannesburg *Mail & Guardian*, September 23, 2006.

Nkomo, M., and C. Soudien. "Racism Is Our Social Legacy." Johannesburg *Star*, 2009.

Nokwe, D. "Bantu Education in Action." *Liberation*, 13, 1955.

Ntletyana, M. "African National Congress: From an Emancipatory to a Rent-Seeking Instrument." *Transformation: Critical Perspectives on Southern Africa*, 87, 2015.

Nyamjoh, A. "The Phenomenology of Rhodes Must Fall: Student Activism and the Experience of Alienation at the University of Cape Town." *Strategic Review for Southern Africa*, 39 (1), 2017.

Nzongola-Ntalaja, G. "Patrice Lumumba: The Most Important Assassination of the 20th Century," *Guardian*, January 17, 2011.

Ofcansky, T. "South African Security Issues: Pretoria's Response." *Journal of Third World Studies*, 3 (2), 1986.

Ottaway, D. "Senior South African Police Officer Sentenced to Death." *Washington Post*, May 1, 1992.

"Painful Privatisation of South Africa." *Economist*, September 9, 1999.

Paton, A. "Why I'm Fleeing South Africa." London *Sunday Times*, September 1, 1998.

Phaahlamohlaka, L. A. "The Impact of Privatisation on the Electricity Industry." Master's thesis, University of Johannesburg, 2006.

Phillipson, D. "Bounded by the Zambezi." *Journal of African History*, 30 (2), 2009.

Philp, R. "Extreme Makeover of UFS." Johannesburg *Sunday Times*, November 27, 2010.

Pitcher, A. "Was Privatisation Necessary and Did It Work? The Case of South Africa." *Review of African Political Economy*, 39 (122), 2012.

"Private Sector Not Achieving Race Proportionality." Johannesburg: South African Press Association, 2009.

Ramahlele, B. "Account of the Transformation Process at the University of the Free State." Broad Transformation Forum, 1999.

Rapiti, R. "Anger of Black South Africans Stems from Lack of Real Change." Letter, *Cape Times,* 2009.

"Rise Up for Freedom." *Sowetan*, 2009.

Rothman, L. "See Photos from South Africa's Monumental Rugby World Cup Victory." *Time*, June 24, 2015.

Sachs, S. B. "The Meadowlands Method." *South African Medical Journal*, 33 (38), 1959.

"Shocking Pay Difference Between Black and White Professionals in South Africa." *BusinessTech*, July 13, 2016.

Shubin, V. "The Soviet Union/Russian Federation's Relations with South Africa, with Special Reference to the Period Since 1980." *African Affairs*, 95 (378), 1996.

Sibuyi, S. "Malema Wants to Reverse Apartheid." Letter, *Sowetan*, June 8, 2009.

Siyabonga, S. B. "Time for a Black Person to Be Pick n Pay Chief." Letter, Johannesburg *Mail & Guardian*, 2010.

Somdaka, S. "Evil Philosophy of Inferiority Persists." Johannesburg *Mail & Guardian*, 2010.

Sosibo, K. "The Burial of Lungani Mabutyana." Johannesburg *Mail & Guardian*, August 3, 2013.

Sparks, A. "A Miracle in South Africa." *Washington Post*, March 22, 1992.

Spinks, C. "A New Apartheid? Urban Spatiality, (Fear of) Crime, and Segregation in Cape Town, South Africa." Working paper, Development Studies Institute, London School of Economics, 2001.

Steadman, J. "Eve's Dream and the Convention of Witchcraft." *Journal of the History of Ideas*, 26 (4), 1965.

Stemmet, J. "Troops, Townships and Tribulations: Deployment of the South African Defence Force (SADF) in the Township Unrest of the 1980s." *Southern Journal for Contemporary History*, 31 (2), 2006.

Stewart, L. "Black South African Urban Music Styles." Doctoral thesis, University of Pretoria, 2000.

Suttner, R. "Culture(s) of the African National Congress of South Africa: Imprints of Exile Experiences." *Journal of Contemporary African Studies*, 21 (2), 2003.

Swart, S. "A Boer and His Gun and His Wife Are Three Things Always Together: Republican Masculinity and the 1914 Rebellion." *Journal of Southern African Studies*, 24, 1998.

Tabane, P. "Goodbye, Faded Rainbow." Johannesburg *Mail & Guardian*, December 23, 2009–January 1, 2010.

"This Is the Average Salary in South Africa by Race and Industry." *BusinessTech*, July 26, 2016.

"UV, Suid-Afrika: dis om van naar te word." Bloemfontein *Volksblad*, 2008.

Van der Merwe, D. M. "Taal op Tuks: A Reappraisal of the Change in Language Policy at the University of Pretoria, 1932." *Historia*, 53 (2), 2008.

Van Heerden, O. "Once We Were Bankrupt—The Uncomfortable Truths of History." *Daily Maverick*, September 18, 2018.

Van Slambrouck, P. "S. Africa's Black TV: On Air to Manipulate . . . or Educate?" *Christian Science Monitor*, December 24, 1981.

Vergnani, L. "Racial Segregation Is Revived in South Africa's Dormitories." *Chronicle of Higher Education*, 46, 2000.

Verschoor, Teuns. "The Mapping of Reitz." Working paper, University of the Free State, 2014.

Wessels, A. "Forged in Battle: The Birth and Growth of the 32 Battalion." *African Historical Review*, 47 (1), 2015.

"What We Inherited Corrupted Us: Mantashe." Johannesburg: South African Press Association, 2010.

Wren, S. "A Mandate for Change; For South Africa, Pace Is Now Issue." *New York Times*, March 20, 1992.

Zinkel, B. "Apartheid and Jim Crow: Lessons from South Africa's Reconciliation." *Journal of Dispute Resolution*, 229, 2019.

Zuger, A. "AIDS in Africa: Rising Above the Partisan Babble," *New York Times*, July 3, 2007.

Zvomuya, P. "Questions of Connection." Johannesburg *Mail & Guardian*, November 20, 2009.

ARCHIVES

Africa Check Fact Checks Archive
Bailey's African History Archive, University of Kwa-Zulu Natal
Frank Talk Journal Archive, Steve Biko Foundation
Global Nonviolent Action Database, Swarthmore College
Helen Suzman Foundation Archive
Historical Papers, University of the Witwatersrand
News Archive, University of the Free State
Padraig O'Malley Archive, Nelson Mandela Foundation
Republic of South Africa, Department of Defence Archives: 32 Battalion Group and Witwatersrand Command Group
Republic of South Africa, Department of International Relations and Cooperation, speeches
Republic of South Africa, Statistics South Africa, publications
South African History Online
Struggles for Freedom: Southern Africa, JSTOR
Truth and Reconciliation Commission Archive
Western Cape Government, Public Information

SELECTED BIBLIOGRAPHY

PERSONAL CONVERSATIONS

Thomas Acho
Adekeye Adebajo
Simon Aiken
Michael Aliber
Ward Anseeuw
Michael Antwi
Doreen Atkinson
Wim van Averbeke
Alana Bailey
Sipho Baloyi
Simon Barber
Henrico Barnard
John Battersby
Keith Beavon
Peter Beinart
Arnold Bender
Vernita Beukes
Haroon Bhorat
Vivian Bickford-Smith
Ishmael Biyoko
Dinky Bogatsu
Selby Bokaba
Carel Boshoff III
Carel Boshoff IV
Wynand Boshoff
Isak Bosman
Tammy Breedt
Karima Brown
Imraan Buccus
Loodt Buchner
Hanan Bushkin
Flip Buys
Michael Buys
Rudi Buys
Benedict Carton

Paul Cassar
S'thembile Cele
Panashe Chigumadzi
Kgotsi Chikane
Jose Chimupi
Ivor Chipkin
Sharai Chizivano
Madimetja Chuene
Philippe Clinckemaillie
Stefaans Coetzee
Pierre Coetzer
Toast Coetzer
Imraan Coovadia
Ben Cousins
George Curtis
Thandi Davids
Godfrey Dederen
Theo de Jager
Willem de Klerk
Chrisna de Kok
Peter Delius
Philani Dladla
Godknows Dlamini
Kuseni Dlamini
Bongiwe Dludlu
Christo Doherty
Zachary Donnenfeld
Richard Dowden
Mduduze Dube
Jacques du Plessis
Theo du Plessis
Anri "YoLandi"
    du Toit
Frances du Toit
Wynand du Toit

Mandisa Dyanti
Ntoni Edjabe
Tony Ehrenreich
Theuns Eloff
Emma-Lancia Faro
Yedit Fessehaie
Frederick Fourie
Steven Friedman
Sandile Fuku
Steve Galane
Manelisi Genge
Hermann Giliomee
Clive Glaser
Philip Atiba Goff
David Goldblatt
Peter Goldsmid
Danie Goosen
Peter Gray
Stephen Greenberg
Lance Greyling
Danie Grobler
Jaco Grobler
Albert Grundlingh
Nonzuzo Gxekwa
Adam Habib
Ruth Hall
Cois Harman
Salik Harris
Tim Hart
Peet van Heerden
Dirk Hermann
Geoff Hill
Andrea Hinckemann
Jay Hipps
Mukelwa Hlatshwayo

394

Sipho Hlongwane
Abel Hlungwane
Carel Hoffmann
Heidi Holland
Geoffrey Hosking
Marie Huchzermeyer
Daniel Hugo
Brannon Ingram
Peter Jablin
Wicus Jacobs
Jonathan Jansen
Naomi Jansen
Claude Jones
Watkin Tudor "Ninja"
 Jones
Abel Jordaan
Hilton Judin
Pie-Pacifique
 Kabalira-Uwase
Katlego Kekana
Shose Kessi
Mpho Khambule
Richard Khanyile
Benito Khotseng
Bertus Kirstein
Karabo Kgoleng
Susanne Klausen
Julius Kleynhans
Jaco Kotze
Rustum Kozain
Siphesihle
 Kubheka
Lucky Kunene
Loren Landau
Mampho Langa
Doug Lawson
Portia Lehasa

Thabo Leshilo
Thabiso Letsoale
Matshidiso Madia
Mhlanganisi
 Madlongolwana
Bongani Madondo
Itumeleng Mahabane
Ramabina Mahapa
Veronica Mahlakola
Brian Mahlangu
Vimla Maistry
Choice Makhetha
Itumeleng Makhoba
Khekhethi Makhudu
Rethabile
 Makoanyana
Mothakge Phillip
 Makwela
Rian Malan
Julius Malema
Tom Maliti
Lucy Maliwichi
Tshililo Manenzhe
Lefono Mangaka
Xolela Mangcu
Sebabatso Manoeli-
 Lesame
Kefiloe Manthata
Danie Marais
Mbali Marais
Sabine Marschall
Sifiso Maseko
Bongani Masemola
Peter Mashala
Yolisa Mashiloane
Mahlatse Mashua
Nonhlanhla Masina

Moses Masitha
Phiwe Mathe
Lebohang Mathibela
Walter Mathidi
Elias Matshubeng
Mamodupi
 Matshubeng
Surprise Matshubeng
Chumani Maxwele
Fawzia Mazanderani
Thandiswa Mazwai
Norma Mbambani
Thabiso Mbatha
Achille Mbembe
Wally Mbhele
Angela McIntyre
Sidwell Medupe
Thabo Meeko
Mothibi Melaceko
Sandile Memela
Philip Minnaar
Cindy Mkaza
Khanyisile
 Mkhetsane
Vusi Mlambo
Andile Mngxitama
Moss Moeng
Lesley Mofokeng
Tefo Mofokeng
Thapelo Mofokeng
Steven Mohale
Shaheed Mohammed
Hlonipha Mokoena
Steve Kwena
 Mokwena
T. O. Molefe
Ace Moloi

Tshepo Moloi

Victor Molopi

Inga Molzen

Derrick Montshwe

Gill Moodie

Riaad Moosa

Ezekiel Moraka

Palesa Morudu

Ernest Motsi

Palesa Segomotso
  Motsumi

Sisonke Msimang

Andile Mthembu

Jackson Mthembu

Justice Mukheli

Pieter Mulder

Riaan Muller

Samson Mulugeta

Doctor Mulutsi

Tinashe
  Mushakavanhu

Meriame Nainda

John Nankin

Charl de Villiers
  Naude

Mthuli Ncube

Siphawanda
  Ndawonde

Bele Ndivhuwo

Phumudzo
  Nemadzivhanani

Calvin Netshithuthuni

Elias Ngoma

Dineo Nhlengethwa

Noor Nieftagodien

Armstrong Nombaba

Ephraim Nong

Tomsen Nore

Piet Nortje

Chris Nthatkheni

Bonisile Ntlemeza

Sphiwe Ntuli

Sibusiso Nxumalo

Zinhle Nxumalo

Leslie Nyagah

Desmond Ogubi

Anwar Omar

Deon Opperman

Vishnu Padayachee

Nigel Penn

Arthur Peters

Gilbert Phalafala

Edgar Pieterse

john a. powell

Max du Preez

Max Price

Pumla Boipelo Radebe

Billyboy Ramahlele

Mase Ramaru

Mohau Rammile

Kopano Ratele

Solly Ratjomane

Riyaz Rawoot

David Rawson

Tony Rebelo

Francois Retief

Bradley Rink

Steven Robins

Ernst Roets

Dawie Roodt

Charles Rose

Greg Rosenberg

Mandy Rossouw

Melanie Samson

Sanza Sandile

Pieter Schuurman

Yonah Seleti

Jean-Paul Selten

Musa Senda

Thabo Sepedi

Thabiso Seshoka

Tshegofatso Setilo

Robert Shell

Kyle Shepherd

Daniel Shipenda

Shirhami Shirinda

Floyd Shivambu

Mardy Shualy

Moses Shuping

Busi Sibusiwe

Rob Siebörger

James Thapelo
  Silowa

Lesego Singo

Siyabonga Sishi

Zicco Sithole

Xola Skosana

Frank Slack

Deon Smit

Charles Smith

Edwin T. Smith

Kevin Smith

Marleen Smith

Nosana Sondiyazi

Kwanele Sosibo

Annalet Steenkamp

Johnny Steinberg

Marion Stevens

Vena Strauss

Francois Strydom

John Strydom

SELECTED BIBLIOGRAPHY

Mpho Tabane
Phillemon Talane
Sampie Terreblanche
Motsoahae Thabane
Niren Tolsi
Henry Trotter
Melusi Tshabalala
Sibusiso Tshabalala
Moses Tshuma
Keorapetse Tumagole
J. C. van der Merwe
Christo van der
  Rheede

Deon van der Ross
Paul van Deventer
Peet van Heerden
Braam van Niekerk
Charles van Onselen
Philip van Ryneveld
Teuns Verschoor
Anver Versi
Willem Viljoen
Adriaan Vlok
Saadique Waggi
Marc Wegerif
Graeme Williams

Vincent Williams
Francis Wilson
James Workman
Godfrey Zakhe
Lungile Zakwe
Rui Zhang
Xzavier Zulu
Bennie van Zyl

About the Author

EVE FAIRBANKS writes about change: in cities, countries, landscapes, morals, values, and our ideas of ourselves. A former congressional correspondent for *The New Republic*, her essays and long-form journalism have been published in *The New York Times*, *The Washington Post*, and *The Guardian*, among other publications. Her reporting has been funded by grants from the Fulbright Program, the Institute of Current World Affairs, the Daniel Pearl Investigative Journalism Initiative, the Pulitzer Center on Crisis Reporting, and the Writing Invisibility project at the Max Planck Institute. Raised in Virginia, she now lives in Johannesburg, South Africa.